THE HOOVER-WILSON WARTIME CORRESPONDENCE
September 24, 1914, to November 11, 1918

President Woodrow Wilson and his 1918 War Council (often called the "war cabinet"). *Seated, left to right: Benedict Crowell, William G. McAdoo, President Wilson, Josephus Daniels, and Bernard Baruch. Standing, left to right: Herbert Hoover, Edward N. Hurley, Vance McCormick and Harry Garfield.* (Photo 49–15258, courtesy National Archives.)

THE

HOOVER-WILSON
WARTIME CORRESPONDENCE

September 24, 1914, to November 11, 1918

EDITED AND WITH COMMENTARIES BY

FRANCIS WILLIAM O'BRIEN

THE IOWA STATE UNIVERSITY PRESS / AMES, IOWA

1 9 7 4

WILLIAM FRANCIS O'BRIEN is Director of Academic Programs for the Hoover Presidential Library Association, West Branch, Iowa. He holds the M.A. degree in history and political science from Boston College and the Ph.D. from Georgetown University. He has served as chairman of the political science department at Rockford College and is the author of numerous legal articles and a text on American constitutional law.

HOOVER PRESIDENTIAL LIBRARY ASSOCIATION SERIES

© 1974 THE IOWA STATE UNIVERSITY PRESS, AMES, IOWA 50010

ALL RIGHTS RESERVED

COMPOSED AND PRINTED BY

THE IOWA STATE UNIVERSITY PRESS

FIRST EDITION, 1974

Library of Congress Cataloguing in Publication Data

Hoover, Herbert Clark, Pres. U.S., 1874–1964.
    The Hoover-Wilson wartime correspondence,
September 24, 1914, to November 11, 1918.

    Bibliography: p.
    1. Hoover, Herbert Clark, Pres. U.S., 1874–1964. 2. Wilson, Woodrow, Pres. U.S., 1856–1924. 3. European War, 1914–1918—United States. I. Wilson, Woodrow, Pres. U.S., 1856–1924. II. O'Brien, Francis William, 1917–   ed. III. Title.

E802.H693   973.91'3   74-7094
ISBN 0-8138-0725-5

Woodrow Wilson

"With his courage and eloquence, he carried a message of hope for the independence of nations, the freedom of men and lasting peace."

HERBERT HOOVER

Herbert Hoover

"Mr. Hoover was one of the most eminent American public figures of his time, and his life was marked by broad interests and many constructive contributions."

Ambassador to the United Nations,
ADLAI E. STEVENSON

C O N T E N T S

PREFACE   ix

SOURCES   xiii

ACKNOWLEDGMENTS   xvii

LIST OF LETTERS   xix

LETTERS WITH INTRODUCTORY COMMENTARIES

      1 9 1 4   3

      1 9 1 5   5

      1 9 1 7   17

      1 9 1 8   127

FACSIMILE SECTION   ff. 134

EPILOGUE   293

INDEX   295

PREFACE

This volume presents the correspondence between President Woodrow Wilson and Food Administrator Herbert Hoover during World War I from September 24, 1914, to November 11, 1918. The general subject of most of the letters is, of course, food. In 1917 and 1918 the slogan blazoned everywhere was "Food Will Win the War." This suggests the great importance of the correspondence between the chief executive and the man most responsible for overseeing the acquisition of food for America, the Allies, and the neutral nations of Europe. The contrasts between these two men, so closely associated in America's first participation in an armed conflict of global proportions, were striking. It is probable that seldom in history have two Americans from such widely divergent ancestral and economic backgrounds been required to exercise such strong world leadership and to cooperate so closely in their world service.

Both Wilson's grandfathers were men of academic distinction and came from families remarkable for scholarly attainments. His father was a college professor and pastor in a Congregational church; his mother was from the Scottish Woodrow family that had produced recognized academicians for many generations. She was educated more than most southern women of the day and was thus well equipped to assist her husband in educating young Thomas Woodrow at home in their stately three-story manse with its white Doric columns and graceful sheltering trees.

Herbert Hoover, on the other hand, was born in a simple two-room frame house, eighteen by twenty feet, in the tiny village of West Branch, Iowa. Within its walls were no bookshelves filled with heavy tomes and exciting novels. Hoover's father was a blacksmith.

His mother, a Canadian-born Quaker, did have more schooling than most West Branch women of the time. She even attended classes at the University of Iowa. However, she died before Herbert was ten, four years after her husband had passed away. Thereafter, the future president of the United States was reared by relatives who were unable to provide him an early education to match that of Woodrow Wilson. Thus he entered Stanford University in 1891 only after he had prepared himself for the entrance examination by arduous study and application. At the university Hoover's interests were largely in the physical sciences as requirements for a degree in geology. Soon after graduation he entered the mining industry where his practical skills as an astute organizer soon brought him remarkable success.

In the meantime, Wilson, the southern intellectual aristocrat, was winning acclaim in the sheltered cloisters of academe. Then in 1908 politics intervened. Shortly thereafter, in November 1912, he was chosen for the highest office in the land. Two years later President Wilson wrote his first letter to Herbert Hoover, a private American citizen then living in London. This was the beginning of a highly important association, one which was weak at first but greatly strengthened in early 1917 when the ever-widening world conflict involved America.

This book portrays the association insofar as correspondence can reveal the relationships and nuances of feeling that existed between the two men—one a president, the other a president-to-be. But this is by no means a "Life and Letters" type of book, nor does it purport to be a history of World War I as seen through the eyes of Wilson and Hoover. Rather, the book presents, with introductory notes and connecting narratives, the letters of two highly important officials as they wrote to each other on a multitude of wartime problems affecting America and the world at large.

The letters for the period prior to America's active entrance into the war were very limited in number, but from early 1917 to late 1919 a steady stream of written messages passed between the two men. (The reader may find it curious that no letters are included for 1916, but none appear to be in existence.) Every effort has been made to include in this book all the letters from 1914 to 1918, exactly as they were written, in the hope that the collection may render a service to students and writers of history. This of course has meant the inclusion of many messages on routine, even boring, matters. Such letters, however, may lead to a better appreciation of the true nature of much of the daily wartime activity of Wilson and Hoover—highly important yet void of any surface drama. The letters will also show methods employed by each man in handling the minute details of administrative work and dealing with the many fractious personalities involved. Finally the correspondence will illustrate the great ordeal that was Hoover's because of his many so-called routine chores as Food Administrator. At the same time, it will reveal the compassion which Wilson displayed in his sincere efforts to cooperate with Hoover and assuage the stresses and strains of his position.

Wilson was the first Democratic president elected since 1893. Hoover was not a member of that party; yet he served his apprenticeship under this Democratic leader and thus prepared himself to take over that high office as a Republican in 1929. It is hoped these letters will attest to the influence of one man upon the other and the measure of confidence and respect that existed between them.

EDITORIAL PRACTICE

The correspondence is presented in chronological order; and the date, salutation, body, and complimentary close appear here just as in the original form in regard to usage, style, and punctuation. The following devices have been used as an aid to the reader:

1. Misspellings and typographical errors that appear in the original letters are marked [*sic*].
2. Handwritten insertions apparently added after the letter was typed appear in brackets with an explanatory footnote to the letter.

3. Deletions are printed between | | with an explanatory foot-
note; when an insertion is made as well, it is indicated as
above.

4. In the very few instances when the typescript was emended
by overwriting, these changes have been silently incorporated as clearly the intent of the writer.

S O U R C E S

The Letters

As far as can be ascertained, all the original Wilson-Hoover or Hoover-Wilson letters still extant are now housed in one of four documentary depositories: The Hoover Presidential Library at West Branch, Iowa; the Hoover Institution on War, Revolution and Peace at Stanford University; the Firestone Library at Princeton University; and the Library of Congress. I visited all four libraries during the course of this research and in almost every instance saw the original of the letters included here. A copy, generally a duplication, of every letter that passed between the two men is now in the Hoover Presidential Library at West Branch. Symbols in the List of Letters indicate the present location of the originals.

Most of the letters printed in this book are preceded by commentaries. However, in some instances none has been provided, either because none seemed called for or because a simple reading of the letter itself provides sufficient background information. In other cases, the briefest letter or a note of only a few lines seemed so highly consequential that lengthy information is given. Generally, biographical information on people mentioned in the letters, as well as other background material, has been given only to make the correspondence intelligible or to underscore the importance of the matter under discussion. Since the book is not meant to be a history of the times, a full historical account of every event mentioned is not appropriate.

Virtually all the letters bear the signature of either Woodrow Wilson or Herbert Hoover and were presumably composed by them. However, a few letters to or from one of Wilson's secretaries are included because they were clearly intended to be communications between the President and Hoover.

Secondary Sources

In preparing commentaries for the letters, I have been helped by many excellent secondary sources; however, it would be difficult to mention all these references. The following list includes only those cited and gives the abbreviated form used.

Except for rare instances, all statements relative to Hoover's appointments rely on a copy of the *Hoover Calendar 1917–1918* in the Hoover Presidential Library; therefore, no specific references were documented.

SOURCE	BRIEF REFERENCE FORM
Baker, Ray Stannard. *Woodrow Wilson, Life and Letters,* 8 vols. Garden City, N.Y., Doubleday, 1927.	*Life and Letters*
Bane, Suda L., and Lutz, Ralph H., eds. *Organization of American Relief in Europe, 1918–1919.* Stanford Univ. Press, 1942.	*Organization*
Baruch, Bernard. *The Public Years,* 1st ed. New York, Holt, 1957.	*Public Years*
Bolling, John R., and Pennington, Mary V. *Chronology of Woodrow Wilson.* New York, Stokes Co., 1927.	*Chronology*
Cronon, E. David, ed. *The Cabinet Diaries of Josephus Daniels 1913–1921.* Lincoln, Univ. Nebraska Press, 1963.	*Daniels Diaries*
Hoover, Herbert. *An American Epic,* 4 vols. Chicago, Henry Regnery Co., 1959.	*Epic*
———. *The Memoirs of Herbert Hoover,* 3 vols. New York, Macmillan, 1951–52.	*Memoirs*
———. *The Ordeal of Woodrow Wilson.* New York, McGraw-Hill, 1958.	*Ordeal*
Hurley, E. N. *The Bridge to France.* Lippincott, 1927.	*Bridge to France*
Lane, Franklin K. *Letters of Franklin K. Lane.* Boston, Houghton Mifflin, 1922.	*Letters of Lane*

Link, Arthur S. *Wilson*, vols. 3–5. Princeton Univ. Press, 1960, 1964, 1965. — *Wilson*

———. *Wilson the Diplomat. A Look at His Major Foreign Policies.* Baltimore, Johns Hopkins Univ. Press, 1957. — *The Diplomat*

Lochner, Louis P. *Herbert Hoover and Germany.* New York, Macmillan, 1960. — *Hoover and Germany*

Livermore, Seward W. *Politics Is Adjourned. Woodrow Wilson and the War Congress 1916–1918.* Middletown, Conn. Wesleyan Univ. Press, 1966. — *Politics*

McAdoo, William G. *Crowded Years.* Houghton Mifflin, New York, 1931. — *Crowded Years*

Mullendore, William C. *History of the United States Food Administration, 1917–1918.* Stanford Univ. Press, 1941. — *Administration*

New York Times. Selected issues—Feb. 1, 1917, through Sept. 12, 1918. — *Times*

Papers Relating to the Foreign Relations of the United States. Washington, D.C., USGPO, 1932. — *Foreign Relations*

Paxon, Frederic L. *American Democracy and the World War, 1913–1917,* 3 vols. New York, Cooper Square, 1966. — *American Democracy*

Pre-Commerce Papers. Hoover-Wilson Correspondence, Hoover Presidential Library, West Branch, Iowa. — *Pre-Commerce Papers*

Proclamations and Executive Orders by the President and by Virtue of the Food Control Act of August 10, 1917. Washington, D.C., USGPO, 1917. — *Proclamations*

Shaw, Albert. *The Messages and Papers of Woodrow Wilson.* New York, Review of Reviews Corp., 1924. — *Messages*

Seymour, Charles. *The Intimate Papers of Colonel House,* 3 vols. Boston, Houghton Mifflin, 1926. — *Intimate Papers*

Strauss, Lewis L. *Men and Decisions.* Garden City, N.Y., Doubleday, 1962. — *Men*

Surface, Frank M. *American Pork Production in the World War.* Chicago, Shaw & Co., 1926. — *Pork*

———. *The Grain Trade During the World War.* New York, Macmillan, 1928. — *Grain Trade*

A C K N O W L E D G M E N T S

I am genuinely grateful for the help of certain institutions and individuals who assisted so generously in the gathering of the materials for this volume:

The Herbert Hoover Library Association, West Branch, Iowa, for the original grant that made the undertaking possible.

John T. McCarty, formerly executive director of the Hoover Presidential Library Association, now assistant to the Chancellor at Pepperdine University, who first interested me in the library's rich holdings and in their possibilities for rewarding research in the field of political science.

The members of the Executive Committee of the Library Association for their keen interest in the Hoover-Wilson letters and aid given toward publication.

The entire staff of the Hoover Presidential Library at West Branch, Iowa, whose contagious enthusiasm and cheer lightened the burden of research and writing.

Thomas T. Thalken, director of the Hoover Presidential Library, and Robert S. Wood, assistant director, for their constant encouragement, many valuable suggestions, and useful bits of information.

Mrs. Mildred Mather, a most indispensable, willing, and trusty ally in guiding me to relevant Hoover material.

Mrs. Ruth Dennis and Mrs. Dale Cooper, vigilant librarians and watchful custodians of research materials.

Mrs. Betty Gallagher and Dale Mayer for a variety of assistance.

JOHN HENRY, DWIGHT MILLER, PATRICK WILDENBERG, and MRS. MATHER for reading the manuscript and for making valuable suggestions.

JANET KEPHART for the myriad aids that highly competent secretaries give to writers of books.

DR. ARTHUR S. LINK, editor, and DR. DAVID W. HIRST, associate editor of the multivolume work, *The Papers of Woodrow Wilson,* for graciously supplying me with copies of several letters from Wilson to Hoover that are in the Wilson collection at Princeton University and for other assistance during and after my visit with them in Princeton.

FRANZ LASSNER, archivist, and assistants CHARLES PALM and MRS. CRONE C. KERNKE of the Hoover Institution on War, Revolution and Peace at Stanford for furnishing copies of several of the Hoover letters.

KATE STEWART of the Manuscript Division of the Library of Congress whose keen and practiced eye helped in a most substantial way in the gathering of a great volume of letters from Wilson to Hoover.

LEWIS STRAUSS, Hoover's secretary from February 1917 to the conclusion of the Peace Conference in 1919, for granting a personal interview during which much valuable information was gleaned.

MRS. HOWARD HALL of Cedar Rapids, Iowa, who kindly passed on to me many useful insights about Hoover gained from her close personal contacts with him.

MRS. HELENE FELDMAN of Rockville, Maryland, who made copies of a large number of letters from the collections of the Manuscript Division of the Library of Congress.

To these and many others I am deeply indebted.

FRANCIS WILLIAM O'BRIEN

LIST OF LETTERS

Date	Writer	Subject Matter	Source†	Page
September 24, 1914	WW	Aid for Stranded Americans	LC	3
February 26, 1915	HH	Report on Belgian Relief Work	LC	5
March 19, 1915	WW	Thanks for Documents	LC	6
March 23, 1915	WW	Thanks for Letter of March 11	LCc‡	6
May 13, 1915	HH	Responsibility for World Order	LC	7
May 26, 1915	WW	Response to Hoover's May 13 Letter	HPLc	12
September 3, 1915	HH	Negotiations with Germany	LC	13
September 20, 1915	WW	Reply to Hoover's September 3 Letter	LC	14
November 3, 1915	WW*	Enlistment of Philanthropists	LC	15
November 3, 1915	WW	Godspeed Note with Letter to Philanthropists	HPLc	16
February 5, 1917	HH	Consolidation of Relief Efforts	LCc	17
March 6, 1917	HH*	Request to See Wilson	LC	18
March 10, 1917	HH*	Regrets for Not Seeing Wilson	LC	19
April 4, 1917	HH	Congratulations on War Message	LCc	20
April 4, 1917	WW	Reply to Hoover's Message	LC	21
May 21, 1917	HH*	Request for an Appointment	LC	22
May 31, 1917	HH	Deletions in the Food Control Bill	LC	22
June 4, 1917	HH	Securing Quarters for the Food Administration	LC	25
June 6, 1917	HH*	Decision to Rent Quarters	LC	26
June 8, 1917	WW*	Wilson's Aid in Securing Quarters	LC	26
June 9, 1917	WW	Letter from an Unidentified Woman	LCc	27
June 11, 1917	HH	Davis Letter on Food Problems	LC	27
June 12, 1917	WW	Volunteers for Food Conservation	HPLc	28

* Indicates an indirect communication through a secretary or other third party.

† HPL—Hoover Presidential Library, West Branch, Iowa; HIS—Hoover Institution at Stanford; PL—Princeton University, Firestone Library; LC—Library of Congress, Manuscript Division.

‡ Indicates that the original letter has not been located and that the letter presented is a copy (c).

Date	Writer	Subject Matter	Source†	Page
June 12, 1917	HH	Memorandum on June 11 Discussion	HPLc	29
June 13, 1917	WW	Garfield's Appointment to the Food Administration	HPLc	30
June 15, 1917	HH	Food Administration Position for Garfield	LC	30
June 15, 1917	HH*	Bringing an Idea to Wilson	LC	31
June 15, 1917	HH	Senator Kenyon and the Food Bill	LC	31
June 18, 1917	WW*	President's Aid for the Food Bill	LC	32
June 20, 1917	WW	Authorizing Additional Food Administration Funds	HPLc	32
June 22, 1917	HH*	Executive Order on Embargo	LC	33
June 28, 1917	HH	Method for Selecting Food Administration Men	LC	34
June 29, 1917	HH	Attempts to Weaken the Food Bill	LC	35
June 30, 1917	HH	Changes to Strengthen the Food Bill	LC	37
July 5, 1917	HH	Coordinating the War Agencies	LC	38
July 7, 1917	HH	Inability of Mills to Buy Wheat	LC	41
July 10, 1917	HH	Wheat and Excess Profits	HPLc	42
July 11, 1917	WW	Adamson's Suggestions on the Food Bill	HPLc	46
July 12, 1917	HH	Reply to Adamson's Suggestions	LC	47
July 12, 1917	WW	Apology for Not Seeing Hoover	LCc	48
July 12, 1917	HH	Gore Substitute for the Food Bill	LC	49
July 14, 1917	HH	Embargo Message for Neutrals	LC	50
July 17, 1917	WW	Approval for Embargo Note	HPLc	51
July 18, 1917	HH	Hollis Substitute for the Food Bill	LC	51
July 18, 1917	HH*	Message for the President	LC	52
July 19, 1917	WW	Assurances of a Suitable Bill	LC	53
July 26, 1917	HH*	Letters of Lever and Gronna	LC	53
August 1, 1917	HH*	Attempts to Phone Wilson	LC	54
August 1, 1917	HH	Removal of Part of the Food Bill	LC	55
August 6, 1917	HH*	Pressure for Draft Exemptions	LC	56
August 7 (?), 1917	WW*	Authorization of Hoover's Suggestion	LC	56
August 9, 1917	HH*	Picture of Signing of the Food Bill	LC	56
August 9, 1917	WW*	Declining Request for Picture-Taking	LC	58
August 13, 1917	HH	Executive Orders on the Food Bill	LC	58
August 13, 1917	HH*	Documents and Nominations	LC	59
August 14, 1917	HH	Nominations to a Committee	LC	60
August ?, 1917	HH*	A Note to Forster	LC	62
August 14, 1917	HH	Hallowell's Food Administration Appointment	HPLc	62
August 15, 1917	WW	Agreement on Hallowell	HPLc	63
August 15, 1917	HH	Patriotism of Grain Men	LC	64
August 15, 1917	HH	Committee of New England Hotel Men	LC	65
August 17, 1917	WW	Advice on Certain Proposals	HPLc	65
August 21, 1917	HH	School Courses on Food Use	LC	66

Date	Writer	Subject Matter	Source†	Page
August 21, 1917	WW	Approval of Food Administration Nominees	PLc	67
August 23, 1917	WW	Trade Restraint and Food Administration Controls	HPLc	67
August 23, 1917	HH	Reed's Anti-Hoover Activity	HPLc	68
August 24, 1917	WW	Reaction to Reed's Activity	HPLc	69
August 24, 1917	WW*	Thach of Alabama Polytechnic Institute	PLc	69
August 27, 1917	HH	Military and Key Farm Men	LC	70
August 28, 1917	HH	Distilled Spirits and the Food Control Act	LC	71
August 30, 1917	HH	Enforcement of Distilled Spirits Ban	LC	72
August 31, 1917	HH	Recommendations for Fat Shortages	LC	73
August 31, 1917	HH	Carter Harrison and the Brewing Trade	LC	75
August 31, 1917	HH	Auditing Methods for the Food Administration	LC	75
September 1, 1917	WW	Praise for Auditing Methods	LC	76
September 4, 1917	WW	Harrison and the Brewing Board	LC	76
September 4, 1917	HH	Stimulation of Hog Production	LC	77
September 6, 1917	HH	Draft of a Proclamation	LC	79
September 7, 1917	WW	Suggestion for Meeting Houston	LC	80
September 12, 1917	HH*	Wheat Price Demands	LC	80
September 17, 1917	WW*	Advice on Answering Bilbo	LC	81
September 18, 1917	HH*	Answer to Wheat Protesters	LC	82
September 18, 1917	HH	Money for Food Administration Building	LC	83
September 18, 1917	WW	Stearns's Appointment to the Food Administration	LC	84
September 20, 1917	WW	Protests against Stearns	LCc	84
September 22, 1917	HH	Approval of Sugar Controls	LC	85
September 25, 1917	HH	Defense of Stearns's Appointment	LC	85
October 1, 1917	HH	Sugar Rules and Regulations	LC	86
October 6, 1917	HH	Food Administration Contracts and the Sherman Act	LC	86
October ?, 1917	WW*	Permission to Use Opinion	LC	87
October 9, 1917	WW	Deferring Food Conservation Pledge Week	LCc	87
October 10, 1917	HH*	Chagrin over Deferral	LCc	88
October 10, 1917	WW	Second Deferral Request	LC	89
October 11, 1917	HH	Agreeing to the Deferral	LC	89
October 12, 1917	HH	White and the War Trade Board	HPLc	90
October 13, 1917	HH*	Thanksgiving Proclamation	LC	90
October 22, 1917	HH	Suggested Food Administration Nominees	HISc	91
October 24, 1917	HH	King Albert and Whitlock	LC	92
October 25, 1917	HH*	Louisiana Sugar Producer	LC	93
October 25, 1917	HH*	Thanksgiving Proclamation Reminder	LC	93
October 27, 1917	HH	Humanitarianism in Message	LC	94
October 27 (?), 1917	HH	Hoover's Proclamation	LC	94

Date	Writer	Subject Matter	Source†	Page
October 31, 1917	HH	Food Rules and Regulations	LC	95
November 1, 1917	WW	Approval of Food Regulations	LCc	96
November 5, 1917	HH	The Food Administration and the Civil Service	LC	96
November 6, 1917	HH	Food Savings by Bakers	LC	97
November 12, 1917	HH	Arsenic Proclamation	LC	98
November 15, 1917	HH	Data on the Crop Situation	LC	98
November 16, 1917	HH	Rules and Regulations for Bakers	LC	101
November 17, 1917	HH	Food Administration Conflict with New York State	LC	101
November 19, 1917	WW	Food Administration Arrangement for New York	LC	102
November 19, 1917	WW	Memorandum on the Crop Situation	LC	102
November 19, 1917	HH	Trouble with Pinchot and Lasater	LCc	103
November 20, 1917	WW	Comment on Gifford Pinchot	LC	104
November 20, 1917	WW	Three Percent Beer	LC	104
November 23, 1917	HH	Food Control Act Investigator	LC	105
November 23, 1917	HH	Continued New York Problem	LC	105
November 23, 1917	HH	Commissions to Control Milk Prices	LC	107
November 23, 1917	HH	Executive Order on Brewing	LC	108
November 24, 1917	HH	Requisitioning Feed for Cattle	LC	109
November 24, 1917	HH	Cuban Demand for High Sugar Prices	HLPc	109
November 26, 1917	WW	Approval of Action on Milk Prices	HLPc	110
November 26, 1917	WW	Comment on Conflict with New York	LC	111
November 26, 1917	WW	Food Administration Use of State Defense Councils	LC	111
November 26, 1917	HH	Limiting Excess Profits	LC	112
November 27, 1917	WW	Executive Order on Excess Profits	LC	113
November 27, 1917	HH	Problems in New York and Cuba	LC	114
November 28, 1917	HH	State Councils of Defense	LC	114
November 28, 1917	WW	Suggestions for New Legislation	LC	115
November 30, 1917	WW	Response to Solution of Problems in New York and Cuba	LC	115
December 1, 1917	HH	Gonzales and Cuban Sugar	LC	116
December 1, 1917	HH	Packers and Profit Limitation	LC	116
December 1, 1917	HH	Hoover's Suggested Legislation	LC	117
December 5, 1917	HH	Innes for Food Administrator	LC	120
December 10, 1917	WW	Avoiding Use of Word "Allies"	LC	121
December 23, 1917	HH	Statement on Senate Inquiry	LC	122
December 23, 1917	HH	Statement for Next Inquiry	LC	123
December 22, 1917	HH	Elliott for Food Administrator	LC	124
December 26, 1917	WW	Approval of Elliott	LCc	125
December 26, 1917	HH	Resignation of Legal Counsel	LC	125

Date	Writer	Subject Matter	Source†	Page
December 26, 1917	WW	Untermyer for Legal Counsel	LC	125
January 1, 1918	HH	Objections to Untermyer	HPLc	127
January 2, 1918	HH*	Glasgow for Legal Counsel	LC	128
January 3, 1918	WW	An Opinion by the Attorney General	LCc	128
January 5, 1918	HH	Mitchell for Food Administrator	LC	130
January 5, 1918	HH	Letter to Wheat Export Company	HPL	130
January 7, 1918	HH	Request for Additional Funds	LC	131
January 7, 1918	HH	Inter-Allied Food Committee	LC	131
January 9, 1918	WW	Approval of Lusk and Chittenden	LC	133
January 9, 1918	HH	Proclamation on Food Licenses	LC	134
January 10, 1918	HH	Report on the Food Administration for Congress	LC	135
January 17, 1918	HH	Proclamation on Food Conservation	LC	135
January 23, 1918	WW	Complaint from McAdoo	LC	136
January 24, 1918	WW	Advice on Answering a Letter	LC	137
January 26, 1918	HH*	Rules on Food Conservation	LC	137
January 28, 1918	HH	Answer to McAdoo Complaint	LC	138
January 28, 1918	HH	McAdoo and Transportation of Food	LC	140
January 28, 1918	HH	Proclamation Licensing Bakers	LC	141
January 29, 1918	HH	Bush's Complaint of Food Shortages	LC	142
February 1, 1918	HH	Discouraging Certain Industries	LC	143
February 4, 1918	WW	Approval of the Discouragement	LC	144
February 9, 1918	HH	United States Cereal Food Position	LC	145
February 14, 1918	HH	Bills to Raise Wheat Price	LC	150
February 18, 1918	WW	Opposition to Higher Wheat Price	LC	152
February 19, 1918	WW	Cattlemen's Complaint of Packers	LC	152
February 19, 1918	WW	Reprimand for Packers	LC	153
February 19, 1918	HH	Insufficient Boxcars in the West	LC	153
February 20, 1918	HH	Taussig and the Food Administration Investigation	LC	154
February 21, 1918	WW	Approval of Investigation	LC	155
February 21, 1918	HH	Packers, Prices, and Profits	LC	156
February 26, 1918	HH	Answer to Lord Reading on Food	LC	157
March 1, 1918	HH	Spreckels's Lack of Cooperation	LC	158
March 2, 1918	HH	Tyler for Food Administrator	LC	159
March 4, 1918	WW	Cooperation with Baruch	LC	160
March 5, 1918	HH	Congratulations for Baruch Appointment	LC	160
March 5, 1918	WW	Action against Spreckels	LC	161
March 6, 1918	HH	Lemon for Food Administrator	LC	162
March 7, 1918	HH	Reading and U.S. Sacrifice	LC	162
March 8, 1918	WW	Sacrifice of Food by Americans	LC	163
March 16, 1918	WW	Meeting of the War Cabinet	LC	164

Date	Writer	Subject Matter	Source†	Page
March 20, 1918	WW*	Return of the President's Letters	LC	165
March 21, 1918	WW	Suggestions on a Telegram	LC	166
March 22, 1918	HH	Suggested Reply to Hudson	LC	166
March 22, 1918	HH	Cereal Supplies and Lord Reading	LC	168
March 25, 1918	WW	Comments on a March 22 Letter	LC	170
March 26, 1918	HH	Commission for the Meat Problem	LC	170
March 27, 1918	WW	Barnes and Higher Wheat Prices	HPLc	176
March 27, 1918	WW	Western Grain Exchanges	LC	176
March 27, 1918	HH	Skinner for the Inter-Allied Council	LC	177
March 28, 1918	WW	Approval of Skinner for the Council	HPLc	178
March 29, 1918	WW	Approval of a Meat Commission	HPLc	178
April 1, 1918	HH	Additional Remarks on the Commission	LC	178
April 2, 1918	WW	Replacing Taussig in Grain Division Inquiry	LC	179
April 2, 1918	WW	Advice on Answering a Telegram	LC	180
April 4, 1918	HH	Suggested Treatment of Telegram	LC	181
April 4, 1918	WW	Report from the Federal Trade Commission	HPLc	181
April 4, 1918	HH	Ames for Food Administrator	LC	181
April 4, 1918	HH	Food Administration Nominees	LC	182
April 6, 1918	HH	Thanks for Report of the Federal Trade Commission	LC	182
April 8, 1918	HH	Ships for Belgian Relief	LC	183
April 12, 1918	WW	A Governor's Food Administration Nominations	LC	185
April 12, 1918	HH	Reply on Governor's Chagrin	LC	186
April 20, 1918	HH	Regulation of Fishermen	LC	186
April 23, 1918	HH	Sproul for Food Administrator	LC	187
May 3, 1918	HH	Proclamation for Food Licensing	LC	187
May 6, 1918	HH	Brooks for Food Administrator	LC	188
May 8, 1918	WW	Transfer of Workers	LC	188
May 13, 1918	HH	Report on Packing Industry	LC	189
May 17, 1918	HH	Cuban Sugar Ships for Belgium	LC	191
May 20, 1918	HH	Lloyd George and Ships for Belgium	LC	193
May 20, 1918	WW	Colver's Plan for Packers	LC	195
May 21, 1918	HH	Objections to the Colver Plan	LC	195
May 25, 1918	HH	Williams-Kennington Plan	LC	198
May 25, 1918	HH	Rejection of Kennington Proposal	LC	199
May 27, 1918	HH*	Closing Down of Breweries	LC	199
May 27, 1918	WW*	Caution on Brewery Suggestions	LC	201
May 27, 1918	HH	War Industries Price Board	LC	201
May 28, 1918	WW	Approval of Report	LC	202
June 5, 1918	HH	Sheppard and Prohibition	LC	202

Date	Writer	Subject Matter	Source†	Page
June 5, 1918	WW	Publishing of the Letter to Sheppard	LC	203
June 13, 1918	HH	Reason for Trip to Europe	LC	203
June 14, 1918	WW	Approval of Hoover's Trip	LC	205
June 14, 1918	HH	Report from States on Food Administration Work	LC	206
June 15, 1918	HH	Wheat Purchase by the Grain Corporation	LC	206
June 17, 1918	WW	Approval of Wheat Purchase Plan	LCc	207
June 18, 1918	WW	Regulation of Malt Products	LC	207
June 20, 1918	HH	New Executive Order on Wheat	LC	208
June 26, 1918	HH	Brauer Complaint on Beef	LC	208
June 29, 1918	HH	Bradley for Alaska Food Administrator	LC	209
June 29, 1918	HH	Plans for European Trip	LC	210
July 2, 1918	HH	Curtailing Nonwar Industries	LC	213
July 5, 1918	HH*	Request to See Wilson	LC	215
July 8, 1918	HH	Federal Trade Commission on Packers' Profiteering	LC	215
July 8, 1918	HH	Refutation of Federal Trade Commission Report	LC	216
July 8, 1918	HH	Reply to Simmons on Profiteering	LC	222
July 8, 1918	HH	Effect of $2.40 Wheat Guarantee	LC	222
July 8, 1918	HH	Glasgow and the War Cabinet	LC	224
July 8, 1918	HH	Committee in Hoover's Absence	LC	225
July 8, 1918	HH	Need for More Office Space	LC	226
July 8, 1918	HH	Sugar Equalization Board	LC	227
July 10, 1918	HH	Rise in Price of Wheat	LC	227
July 11, 1918	HH	Food Shipments to Allies	LC	228
July 20, 1918	HH*	Urgent Need to Support the President	LC	231
August 24, 1918	HH*	A Meeting with the President	LC	233
August 26, 1918	HH	Guaranteed Price for 1919 Wheat	LC	233
August 26, 1918	HH	Expansion of Views on Wheat Supports	LC	235
August 27, 1918	WW	Approval of Hoover's Wheat Views	LC	236
August 27, 1918	HH	Coordinating the Economic War Effort	LC	236
August 28, 1918	WW	Appreciation for August 27 Letter	LC	238
August 29, 1918	WW	Book Sent by A. G. Patterson	LC	238
August 29, 1918	HH	Cuban Sugar and Price Controls	LC	238
August 30, 1918	HH	Order and Statement on Wheat	LC	241
August 31, 1918	HH	Thanks for Patterson Book	LC	243
September 2, 1918	WW	Approval of Hoover's Sugar Views	LC	243
September 3, 1918	WW	Commandeering and the War Industries Board	LC	243
September 4, 1918	HH	Power of the Grain Corporation	LC	244
September 5, 1918	WW	Reply on the Grain Corporation	LC	245

Date	Writer	Subject Matter	Source†	Page
September 6, 1918	HH	Interpreting the Commandeering Rule	LC	245
September 6, 1918	WW	Approval of Interpretation	LC	246
September 6, 1918	HH	Cotton Telegram on U.S. Imports	LC	246
September 6, 1918	HH	Consulting Independent Packers	LC	249
September 7, 1918	HH	Taft's Food Administration Report	LC	250
September 9, 1918	HH	Armour Company and Profits	LC	250
September 9, 1918	HH	Draft Exemptions for Food Administration Men	LC	251
September 10, 1918	WW	Interpreting Draft Exemptions	LC	252
September 10, 1918	WW	Distrust of Packers	LC	252
September 10, 1918	WW	Daniels's Letter on the Beef Trade	LC	253
September 11, 1918	HH	Report on the Packers	HPLc	254
September 13, 1918	HH	Proclamation on Beer and Malt	LC	259
September 16, 1918	HH	Release of Report on Packers	LC	260
September 18, 1918	HH	Kellogg and "Rampant Business"	LC	261
September 18, 1918	HH	Appointment of Cotton to the Inter-Allied Council	LC	261
September 18, 1918	HH	Nominees for European Food Administration Staff	LC	262
September 19, 1918	WW	Approval of Cotton's Appointment	LC	262
September 20, 1918	WW	Approval of Men for Europe	LC	262
September 20, 1918	WW	Reply to Kellogg's Proposal	LC	263
September 20, 1918	WW	Publication of Report on Packers	LC	263
September 21, 1918	HH	Food Exports for 1919	LC	264
September 23, 1918	WW	Farmers' Complaint of Markets	LC	265
September 25, 1918	HH	Reply to Carr Letter	LC	265
September 26, 1918	HH	Stabilizing Price of Hogs	LC	266
September 30, 1918	HH	Regulations on Malt	LC	267
October 4, 1918	HH	Loss of Administrator to the Army	LC	268
October 7, 1918	HH	Maltbie for Food Administrator	LC	269
October 17, 1918	HH*	Appointment with President	LC	270
October 17, 1918	HH	Food Price Indices 1917–1918	LC	270
October 19, 1918	HH	Disapproval of Washington, D.C., Conventions	LC	271
October 21, 1918	HH	Restoring Belgium after the War	LC	272
October 24, 1918	HH	The United States and the Food Pool	LC	275
October 26, 1918	HH	Control of Belgian Restoration	LC	277
November 2, 1918	HH	Reported Destruction in Belgium	LC	279
November 4, 1918	HH	Available Food Supplies	LC	280
November 4, 1918	WW	Thanks for Election Support	LC	282
November 4, 1918	HH	International Control of Supplies	LC	284
November 7, 1918	WW	Authority for Belgian Work	LC	284
November 7, 1918	HH	Reply to October 30 Cables	LC	286
November 9, 1918	HH	Strengthening the Committee for Relief in Belgium	LC	287
November 9, 1918	HH	Feeding the Liberated People	LC	289
November 11, 1918	HH	Cotton's Cables on the Food Pool	LC	291

LETTERS

WITH INTRODUCTORY COMMENTARIES

1 9 1 4

Aid for Stranded Americans

When World War I came to Europe on August 3, 1914, Hoover had been living in London for several years. Although long before the beginning of hostilities he and Mrs. Hoover had booked passage on the *Lusitania* for America, the war made sailing impossible. Since all British sailings to the States were cancelled, like several hundred other Americans they were stranded in England. The closing of the banks brought additional distress since many could not obtain sufficient funds to live. Hoover was moved by their plight and organized a committee which in the ensuing six weeks aided 120,000 Americans who poured into London from all parts of Europe, and eventually he arranged for their passage home. On September 24, 1914, President Wilson recognized this charitable enterprise by sending Hoover and his wife a personal letter of congratulations. This appears to be the first contact of any kind between the two men.

When soon thereafter Hoover undertook relief work for Belgium, the President made additional inquiries. According to Ray Stannard Baker, in November 1914 Wilson asked Secretary of the Interior Franklin K. Lane to give him information about "the extraordinary American engineer who had stepped forward with such initiative and ability. The report . . . was 'most interesting and satisfactory.' " (*Life and Letters,* vol. 6, p. 336.)

However, some people in official Washington were somewhat concerned about the little-known American citizen whose initiative entangled him in war-torn Europe. On November 17, 1914, Lane addressed a letter to Secretary of State William Jennings Bryan that began thus: "If it is true that the State Department is not informed regarding Mr. Hoover and his entire responsibility, I can send to you today his attorney. . . . I know of Mr. Hoover very well. He is probably the greatest mining engineer that the world holds today, and is yet a very young man." (*Letters of Lane,* p. 163).

September 24, 1914.

My dear Mr. and Mrs. Hoover:

The American Ambassador at London has brought to my attention the excellent work which you have been doing for the relief of the many Americans in that city, and it affords me much gratification to say that the loyal support and hearty cooperation which have been so generously extended have impressed me deeply and have lightened the burdens of these troublous times.

I extend to you, my dear Mr. and Mrs. Hoover, sincere thanks in my own name and in the names of the many Americans who profited by your untiring labors in England.

Cordially yours,

WOODROW WILSON

1 9 1 5

Report on Belgian Relief Work

Hoover had no sooner completed securing passage home for thousands of Americans stranded in Europe than reports reached him of the food situation in overrun Belgium. Yielding to the importunities of a number of deeply concerned people, he agreed in late September 1914 to organize the Commission for Relief in Belgium (CRB). With Hoover as chairman operating mainly out of London and Brussels, the CRB grew into a giant enterprise and, within the next four years, was able to raise a billion dollars to transport five million tons of food to Belgium and northwestern France. The funds came partly from private charities and partly from the American, Belgian, British, and French governments. On February 26 Hoover sent President Wilson a letter and a copy of the commission's fortnightly report. Only the letter is given here. The colonel mentioned in the letter is Edward M. House, adviser on peace and war to Wilson. (For valuable general information on relations between House and Wilson see *Intimate Papers.)*

26th February, 1915

Dear Mr. President,

Learning from Colonel House of your interest in the work of this Commission, I take the liberty of sending you herewith a copy of our last fortnightly report, together with some small brochures bearing upon the work of the Commission.

You will appreciate that the American Ambassadors concerned and the Members of the Commission have realised that the survival of the 7,000,000 of people is, aside from the administrative work of this Commission, dependent either upon the support of the charitable world or upon some basis of arrangement amongst the belligerent powers, by which the financial problem of this Commission could be solved. This problem amounts practically to the finding of $7,500,000 per month and, although the flow of charity has been generous and of a volume hitherto unknown in relief work, it is entirely inadequate and we are, therefore, brought to the point of finding some solution in the way of financial assistance from the belligerent Powers themselves. This is not a matter on which we expect to trouble you in any way, except merely by way of an explanation of the activities of this Commission in negotiations with the various Governments concerned.

Yours faithfully,
HERBERT HOOVER

Thanks for Documents

It is difficult to determine exactly what "documents" Wilson referred to in this letter. Possibly the President was writing about the report on Belgium sent to him on February 26, but this seems to have come directly from Hoover's hand. More than likely he was speaking of material on the war situation in general, which Hoover frequently communicated to Colonel House from his coign of vantage in London. (*Epic,* vol. 1, p. 42; *Ordeal,* p. 3, n. 1.)

March 19, 1915

My dear Mr. Hoover:

Mr. House has kindly sent me the documents you were kind enough to place in his hands for my inspection.

May I not take this occasion in thanking you for the documents to express my sincere appreciation of the work that you have been doing? It has commanded the admiration and confidence of every one who has had a chance to know of it and I am sure that every American who has had any part in the work of relieving suffering in Belgium will feel, when the whole story is told, that the part you have played is one of distinguished service.

Cordially and sincerely yours,
WOODROW WILSON

Thanks for Letter of March 11

In the 1917–18 period Hoover frequently wrote letters to Wilson's secretary, Joseph P. Tumulty, that were clearly intended for the eyes of the President. It is difficult to say whether or not Hoover's March 11 letter, referred to in Wilson's brief note of March 23, took this indirect route.

March 23, 1915.

My dear Mr. Hoover:

Mr. Tumulty has handed me your letter of March 11th, and I thank you very warmly for having written. I have read it with genuine interest and appreciation.

Cordially and sincerely yours,
WOODROW WILSON

Responsibility for World Order

This long letter and extensive telegram seem to be an exhortation to the President on the absolute necessity for the United States to exercise firm leadership in order to guarantee world order. At the time, Hoover was still a private citizen, and his only prior contact with Wilson was through an exchange of letters on Belgian relief. However, there were a number of indirect contacts through Walter Hines Page, the American ambassador in London, and several through Colonel Edward M. House, one of the President's chief advisers. For instance, whenever House came to Europe to look into the advisability of the President's intervention in order to end the war, he would visit Hoover who was considered "a sort of outpost adviser for him on the political and emotional forces moving in the war." (*Ordeal*, p. 3; *Memoirs*, vol. 1, pp. 212–31.) Only seven weeks before Hoover sent the following telegram, he had received a letter of thanks from Wilson for certain documents transmitted personally to him by House. In view of all this, Hoover's May 13 advice on world leadership loses some of its boldness.

Hoover was undoubtedly prompted to dispatch the message by Wilson's Philadelphia address on May 10, 1915, in which he made these remarks: "There is such a thing as a man being too proud to fight. There is such a thing as a nation being so right it does not need to convince others that it is right." (*Messages*, p. 117.) These words were deeply disappointing to many at home and abroad for they were spoken just three days after the sinking of the *Lusitania*, an event that produced wide indignation. Hoover's telegram reflects the sentiment of Americans in England who were "filled with humiliation" at the "construction . . . universally assessed to it: that we are prepared to submit to the continued cold-blooded murder of our women and children and not fight."

Hoover's telegraphed message was sent on May 13 and most probably was received by the White House the same day. Also on May 13 Wilson dispatched the first of a series of protest notes over the sinking of the *Lusitania*. A slight possibility then exists that the President was influenced by Hoover's message, which due to time differences could have reached Washington late on May 12. But this seems improbable, for the note was composed in its final form on May 12 and underwent only one minor change before being telegraphed to Berlin on May 13. (*Wilson*, vol. 3, p. 386.) However, there is some similarity between the note and Hoover's telegram. In one passage Wilson wrote: "Expressions of regret and offers of reparation in case of neutral ships sunk by mistake . . . cannot justify or excuse a practice the natural and necessary effect of which is to subject neutral nations and neutral persons to new and immeasurable risks." (*Chronology*, p. 45.) Hoover's message carried these words: "We strongly protest that any demand for compensation in money . . . and the assurances of the German press that Americans can be satisfied in this manner are degrading to American ideals."

As for Hoover's four-page letter, two additional questions arise. First, what accounts for the heavy and awkward phrases that so obscure the idea in some passages? True, Hoover was not gifted with an elegant or limpid style, but he generally wrote with a clarity and a directness that communicated his message without ambiguity. The obscurity here may have resulted from hasty composition. A second question concerns the signature "H. C. Hoover." No other letter bears this form; almost invariably he concluded simply with "Herbert Hoover." It is possible that another person composed the letter from Hoover's ideas and signed for him.

The date of Hoover's dispatch makes it evident that in his *Memoirs* (vol. 1, p. 200) and in *Ordeal* (p. 2) Hoover erred when he wrote of a May 7 trip to America. This telegram could not have been sent from London on May 13 if that were true. Moreover, several events recorded as taking place in America on that trip do not fit in with a May date. In his *Epic* (vol. 1, p. 162) he recounts the same events during an October trip to America, leaving Europe October 16, 1915. This is undoubtedly the trip Hoover referred to in his *Memoirs* and *Ordeal*.

13th May 1915

Dear Mr. President,

I have taken the liberty of sending you an extensive telegram on behalf of myself and the American Members of this Commission. Our reasons for doing this are:

1.   The fear on our part that some feeling of responsibility that America might jeopardise the feeding of these nine millions of people and thereby you might find in this fear some limitation to otherwise freedom of action. It is our belief we can carry on in any event.

2.   In adding thereto our views as to the present situation we have been moved entirely by a desire to be helpful. There can be no body of men in the world which has such a deep appreciation of the horrors of war as those of us who have had to deal hourly with the aftermath of battle during these last eight months. Our one desire is to help to find some solution which would prevent our own country from being joined in this holocaust, but the belief on our part is that only a strong line of constructive character could prevent this catastrophe, and at the same time contribute something towards the ultimate redemption of Europe from the barbarism into which it is slowly but surely drifting from all sides. We all of us count our country as being most fortunate in possessing at this critical time, in its President, a man of such lofty ideals and in whose wisdon [sic] we are prepared so implicitly to trust. We have no doubt whatever that the course which is taken will be the wisest course that could have been adopted.

We may not have contributed anything to the combined wisdom which is so essential at such a time but an intimate contact with the peoples with whom these dealings must lie, some knowledge of their temper and of the means which must be used to bring a successful issue, justify us in adding our mite to the host of suggestions which you will no doubt have received.

Association with German authorities and German methods during the last eight months convinces us beyond all question that there is a curious mixture of two factors which count with these people. One of them is the conviction that force will be applied; the other—and a superficially contradictory one—is the enunciation that a high ideal is at stake upon which this action will be taken. The leaders of Germany to-day are convinced that they are themselves acting in the name of civilisation and they are extraordinarily anxious to maintain the confidence of the people throughout Germany that they are guided by these motives. The enunciation of a high ideal, or in effect a correction of their ideals from an exalted source such as yourself is bound to penetrate the whole of Germany and through their own public opinion in itself act as a deterrent to future transgressions. More especially is this so if it be coupled with a stern assurance that we intend to see such ideals lived up to so far as their relations with us are concerned. It is our belief that such a course would save us from the necessity of further steps. On the other hand, it is our dread that this situation may be dealt with in such a manner that German attention is held only to incidents. We fear this will fail to bring the German people to a right appreciation of our cause, and by repetition of such incidents arouse a flood of feeling on the part of our countrymen such as manifested itself at the time of the Spanish war and which could not be controlled by the sane minds at the head of our Government.

You will forgive our directness of expression in the attached telegram because of our disinterestedness and our anxiety.

Yours faithfully,
H. C. Hoover

Telegram, *May 13, 1915*

This Commission being responsible for the relief work carried on in Belgium and France, upon which the lives of nine millions of people are dependent, has a great concern in the present crisis on behalf of the whole of these people and bearing in mind this deep responsibility we wish to state frankly our views to you in this emergency.

This Commission is international in character and embraces several other neutrals, principally Dutch and Spanish. American influence with Germany has sunk to such a low ebb that American members in Belgium and France no longer constitute any particular protection to the food-stuffs which we distribute, which in fact rests solely on German good faith. We think we should be able to withdraw the Americans and substitute other neutrals therefor and thus continue the work. We should if such circumstances arose, continue to ship foodstuffs into Belgium and France just so long as the Germans do not interfere with their destination, and such interference, in any event, would cause the Allied Powers to bring the whole enterprise to an end. We cannot say positively that a break in relations between America and Germany would not jeopardise the feeding of these people, [but]¹ if the Allied Governments continue their approval and if the Germans continued to respect the destination

---

1. Handwritten insertion.

of the supplies, the work could go on and it must be borne in mind that the Germans are anxious that the food supplies should be maintained. In any event, important as this work of humanity is in our minds, it pales, however, into insignificance in proportion to the other issues to the whole future of humanity. We also take this opportunity of expressing to you our views as to the whole situation, based upon some intimate knowledge of these countries and the issues at stake. We are certain that unless America to-day takes a strong lead in the vindication of the rights of neutrals and the upholding and enforcement of international agreements, the world will have slipped back two hundred years towards barbarism. Since this war began one agreement after another has been set aside by one belligerent after another, and as the sanctity of international undertakings and the proof of their ability to stand is fundamental to the world's ultimate peace, any deviation from the insistence by neutrals of these undertakings undermines irretrievably the whole future hope of civilisation. We believe that the hour has struck when America must stand on this issue. We do not believe that our country should go to war over the incidents which have occurred so far, but we believe that the American Government to-day must, while not condoning anything, enunciate a policy which will not necessarily lead to war but which in its vigor might bring to an end at least some phases of these violations of international law and humanity. It is our belief that you should sharply define the distinction between violations against property and violations against life. The former can be compensated for in money and the collection of this money can well be deferred if necessary until times are propitious to securing it without violence. Continued transgressions against life, however, can only be met by punishment, and if the American Government would announce that from to-day forward they would demand that the actual perpetrators and those responsible for such violence should be handed over to them or some independent tribunal, for trial and execution, and that the whole of our resources would be pledged to secure this, it is our belief that these acts would be brought to an end. It is not our belief that we should make war on a people for the crimes of individuals, and we should sharply make this distinction.

Every American to-day in England is filled with humuliation [sic] at the interpretation which has been placed here on your Philadelphia speech: that we are too proud to fight. We do not believe that you ever intended a construction to be placed upon this which has been universally assessed to it: that we are prepared to submit to the continued cold-blooded murder of our women and children and not fight. It is not upon this doctrine that the American Republic has been built up, maintained, and can endure.

The foreign trade of the United States is as important as any other function of the American Government. This foreign trade cannot be carried on without the presence of numbers of our citizens abroad and on the high seas. We disregard all extreme claims that we have a right to call upon our Government to go to war in support of our rights of property, but we do insist that the agreements carefully developed and entered upon over the whole history of our Republic, which gives us the right to escape with our lives, shall be maintained, and that, for instance, no ships shall be sunk where the safety of the lives of our citizens is not provided for. We strongly protest that any demand for compensation in money for the lives lost on the "Lusitania" and the assurances of the German Press that Americans can be satisfied in this manner are degrading to American ideals. We believe that all such diplomatic inventions as the withdrawal or dismissal of Ambassadors are puerile. We believe that if the American Government will take the strong line in support of the ideal that international agreements must from this day forward be upheld so far as they affect neutrals, with the above definitions, you will have the unqualified support of all the neutral powers and will have restored the prestige of America to the position we have a right to demand for it and we do not believe that there will be a repetition of these actions, but if so we shall have gone to war for an ideal which history will justify. We believe you could secure the adhesion of other neutrals to this course and thus strengthen your demands.

Response to Hoover's May 13 Letter

May 26, 1915

My dear Mr. Hoover:

I appreciate very sincerely your letter of the thirteenth of May and the telegraphic message which preceded it. You may be sure that I not only understand the motives which lay behind both your letter and the telegram, but also the patriotic desire on your part and on the part of those associated with you to contribute to the common counsel which is our only safe guide in times so troubled as these.

Cordially and sincerely yours,
WOODROW WILSON

Negotiations with Germany

On August 19, 1915, the Germans torpedoed the *Arabic,* the 15,801-ton pride of the White Star Line, as she sailed from Liverpool carrying 423 passengers in addition to crew. Among the forty-four casualties were two Americans. For nearly two weeks the nation was in high tension. Calm was restored only because of the determined but patient negotiations of Wilson and Secretary of State Robert Lansing. As a result, on September 1 the German government assured the United States that in the future no liners would be sunk without warning and without providing safety for noncombatants on condition that they offered no resistance and made no efforts to escape. Two days later, from his outpost in London, Hoover sent the President a long letter of congratulations for the success of his negotiations. (*Wilson,* vol. 3, pp. 551–81. See also *The Diplomat* for further information on Wilson and foreign policy.)

3rd September, 1915.

Dear Mr. President,

I should like to convey to you on behalf of myself and all my colleagues in this Commission the sincere gratitude which we feel to you over the success of the German negotiations. We are certain, from intimate contact in Germany, that this has only been accomplished with the extraordinary appeal which you formulated to justice and humanitarian sentiment in Germany as well as the firmness you displayed, and that in any less able hands the situation would have drifted us into the appalling result of war.

While the work of this Commission would undoubtedly have been continued by the help of other neutral Governments, even in that contingency it would have most certainly diminished in efficiency. More especially is this true now than some months ago as we are about to expand our operations greatly by the import of raw material and export of manufactures from Belgium, in the hope that we may stem the tide of destitution through productive labour.

This is, however, an infinitesimal matter compared to the infinite disaster to the American people which would have been involved in engaging in this conflict, and it is a condition which no good American could for one moment consider [except][1] as the last alternative to continued transgression.

---

1. Handwritten insertion.

Also we feel that the great success which you have had in this negotiation is of the widest possible import in the matter of the rehabilitation of a sense of the responsibility for international engagement. That
this rehabilitation has got to come before there can be any hope of successful peace negotiation is obvious. Incidentally we have the view that
no peace can be hoped for until the bitterness of hatred on all sides has
been somewhat diminished and it is our further view that the bitterness
at present existing is more the result of war directed against civilians
on all sides than it is from original causes or the losses by military operations, and that every step which tends to diminish the amount of impact
on civilans [sic] will contribute materially towards letting down public
feeling to a point where a peace proposal might be possible of execution.
At the present moment it is obvious that no European statesman could
carry peace with his own people on any terms which would be within
the range of possibility.

I take the liberty of sending you herewith a copy of our recent report, covering a period of eight months' work. I do not assume you will
have time to look it over but at least if you have such a leisure moment
we should feel honored if you would do so.

Your obedient servant,
HERBERT HOOVER

Reply to Hoover's September 3 Letter

September 20, 1915

My dear Mr. Hoover:

It was a real pleasure to receive your letter of September third. I
have for a long time wanted to express to you the great admiration with
which I have followed the extraordinary work that you have been doing
as chairman of the Commission for Relief in Belgium. It has been a work
wonderfully done and my thought has followed you very constantly in it.

I warmly appreciate your thought of me as expressed in your letter
and thank you for it from the bottom of my heart.

Cordially and sincerely yours,
WOODROW WILSON

P.S. Thank you also most sincerely for the report which you were thoughtful enough to send me.

Enlistment of Philanthropists

When the financial difficulties of the Commission for Relief in Belgium increased, Hoover left London on October 16, 1915, for a personal interview with President Wilson asking him to solicit the support of American businessmen and philanthropists. The interview took place on November 3. The President responded to Hoover's pleas and took positive and enthusiastic action, writing directly to several men of means and asking them to join a special committee through which they would be able to channel their assistance. In addition, he enclosed an encouraging letter to Hoover bidding him "Godspeed in the splendid work." A rough draft of Wilson's letter to the businessmen appears below with his handwritten changes included but not indicated. (See facsimile section.) The letter is included here because it is essential to the message in Wilson's "Godspeed" letter to Hoover. *(Life and Letters, vol. 6, p. 336; Memoirs, vol. 1, p. 200; Epic, vol. 1, p. 162.)*

November 3, 1915

Mr. Hoover, the Chairman of the Commission for Relief in Belgium, has approached me with regard to difficulties which have arisen in the conduct of that great humanitarian work, in which he feels he needs the support of an enlarged Committee of gentlemen of large experience to co-operate with him in settling and conducting the Administration of the Branch of the Commission in the United States.

I am so much impressed with the importance of this institution, on which the lives of so many people are dependent that I venture to say to you that I would personally be very much gratified if you could see your way to join such a Committee.

The other gentlemen with whom I am communicating in this particular are Messrs. Alexander Hemphill, Otto T. Bannard, S. Bertron, Oscar Strauss, Melville Stone, Herbert S. Eldridge and John Beaver White. Of course you may wish to add others to your number, either from the Officers of the Commission or otherwise.

Godspeed Note with Letter to Philanthropists

3 November 1915

My Dear Mr. Hoover

I am taking great pleasure in sending you the enclosed letters for the several gentlemen about whom you spoke today, and take this occasion again to bid you Godspeed in the splendid work you are doing.

Cordially and sincerely yours,

WOODROW WILSON

1 9 1 7

Consolidation of Relief Efforts

On January 31, 1917, Germany declared unlimited submarine warfare on the vessels of all nations approaching Allied ports. An exception was made for ships of the Commission for Relief in Belgium provided they sailed directly from a neutral port to Rotterdam. However, Britain required that all CRB ships call at a British port for inspection before unloading their cargo at Rotterdam. After some negotiation, Hoover succeeded in convincing the British to yield on the inspection calls. Nonetheless, on February 3, the CRB ship *Euphrates* was torpedoed by the Germans in a supposedly safe zone despite its illuminated "Belgian Relief" markings. Although Wilson had thus far resisted heavy pressures to join the war, he now felt compelled to register an emphatic protest against such German provocations. Thus on February 3, 1917, he broke off relations with Germany. This meant the recall of the American ambassadors from Germany and Belgium and presaged problems of immeasurable proportions for the CRB.

Hoover was already in the States, having reached New York from Europe on January 21. He saw the President on January 31, and sensing the clear drift into war, he began to mobilize various relief organizations to meet the enormous problems certain to ensue upon America's entrance into the conflict. His letter to Wilson on February 5 sketches his mobilization plans. The cosigner of the letter, Eliot Wadsworth, represented the American Red Cross. (*Epic*, vol. 1, pp. 284–91; *Memoirs*, vol. 1, p. 219.)

5th February, 1917.

Dear Mr. President,

At a recent informal meeting in New York, of Members of the principal relief organisations, called to discuss a better consolidation and furthering of relief efforts abroad, it was considered that it would be very desirable, as a matter of preparedness, to take early steps for the formation of a great national relief fund, to meet the present crisis at home, this fund to be raised primarily for the American Red Cross and secondarily for other relief measures at home and abroad.

Those present were Mr. Elliott [*sic*] Wadsworth of the American Red Cross, Mr. John R. Mott of the Y.M.C.A., Mr. Herbert Hoover and Mr. W. L. Honnold of the Belgian Relief Commission, Mr. Frederick Walcott of the Rockefeller Foundation, Mr. Cleveland H. Dodge of the Armenian Relief Commission, and Mr. C. A. Coffin of the American Relief Clearing House.

It appeared to us that in the period of emotion which must ensue if war is declared, thousands of disconnected and unorganised efforts will arise, much waste of money and effort will ensue, and the country would not as a whole give such a response as could be summoned by better organised effort.

This group therefore authorized us to lay before you the desirability of at once assembling a small committee comprising men representing the larger efforts throughout the country, which should act as preliminary committee for the organization of a large National Committee embracing every element of American life, which should take in hand, under the official authority of yourself, the collection and administration of a consolidated National Relief Fund.

We realise full well the burden and anxiety resting upon your shoulders, and it is the desire of all of these gentlemen to lighten it in any way and to place their services at your disposal if you should wish them to act as above, and they would of course be glad to embrace any gentlemen in such a preliminary Committee whose names might suggest themselves to your wisdom. Before any general committee were launched we should desire to submit the personnel for your approval and revision, and to have your authority for them to act.

Yours faithfully,
HERBERT HOOVER
ELIOT WADSWORTH

Request to See Wilson

TELEGRAM, *March 6, 1917*
J P Tumulty Esq
Sec'ty to President Washington DC

Could you possibly arrange for me to have a five minute interview with the President any time Wednesday.

HERBERT HOOVER

Regrets for Not Seeing Wilson

Hoover arrived in New York from London on January 13, 1917, for certain financial negotiations relative to Belgian relief work. For the next two months he divided his time between New York and Washington. Hoover's calendar for January 27 reveals that on that day he communicated with Tumulty about "arranging for a conference at 5:00 P.M. January 31st." He and Wilson discussed Belgian relief at the White House on that day. (*Times*, Feb. 1, p. 2.) The word "President" appears in pencil in the margin of the calendar for January 31 and also for February 17, indicating that he saw Wilson on both days. Hoover's *Epic* (vol. 1, p. 313) speaks of such a meeting sometime around February 15.

Neither the Hoover calendar nor Baker's several volumes report any other such meeting during March, but Hoover's *Memoirs* (vol. 1, p. 220) contains these words: "Early in March, I called upon the President at his request." This was a most critical time for the nation and for the world. On February 18 the German government had warned Washington that the arming of American merchantmen would be regarded as a war move. On March 1 the House passed such a bill by a 403 to 13 vote, but a small group of senators employed the filibuster to prevent the upper chamber from voting on the matter. A solemn and sober inaugural ceremony took place on March 4. The legislators had adjourned the previous day, thus ending the Sixty-fourth Congress. Late in the evening of his second inaugural, Wilson issued his "willful men" statement to the nation. The whole country was in an uproar and the feeling on both sides was bitter.

Such was the situation when Wilson and Hoover met "early in March." Hoover writes that the "President's mind was full of the anxieties and probabilities of our joining the war." (*Memoirs*, vol. 1, p. 220.) Both still clung to a vague hope that such involvement could yet be avoided. Nonetheless they felt compelled to discuss the food, general economic and military problems that would ensue if the country were actively drawn into the conflict. A few days later Hoover wired Tumulty for another meeting. We can only speculate as to Hoover's desire to return from New York for a "five minute interview" with Wilson on March 7. Actually the meeting did not take place, and

Hoover expressed his regrets in a letter on March 10, the day after Wilson announced that he himself would authorize the arming of American ships.

10th March, 1917.

Dear Mr. Tumulty,

I was very sorry not to be able to see the President, but I am leaving for Europe at once and shall probably be absent for two months.

Yours faithfully,
HERBERT HOOVER

Congratulations on War Message

On January 31 Germany announced resumption of unrestricted submarine warfare. Wilson responded by severing diplomatic relations and arming American merchantmen. On April 2, after the early-spring sinking of several unarmed American vessels, he appeared before a joint session of Congress to present a review of the pertinent international situation and to ask for a declaration of war, which followed on April 6. On April 4 Hoover sent a telegram to Wilson from London, congratulating him on his April 2 message. (For a general review of the American position during World War I, see American Democracy.)

Hoover reached London on April 2, having sailed from New York on March 13 aboard the Antonio López, a Spanish vessel of 4,100 tons. Hoover's Memoirs (vol. 1, pp. 219–22) suggests that at this time both he and Wilson had serious reservations about entering the war. However, during his two-week sea trip from New York to Cadiz, four American merchant ships were sunk by German submarines. In addition, a revolution had broken out in Russia and the Czar had abdicated. The wireless aboard the López brought this news to its passengers. Undoubtedly these two events greatly influenced Hoover's thinking on the war and accounts at least in part for the tone of his April 4 message to President Wilson, sent at 2:50 A.M.

April 4, 1917.

President Wilson
Washington.

The members of the American Commission for Relief in Belgium ask me to transmit to you the expression of our united devotion and of our admiration of the courage and wisdom of your leadership. We wish to tell you that there is no word in your historic statement to Congress but finds response in all our hearts. For two and a half years we have been obliged to remain silent witnesses of the character of the forces dominating this war, but we now are at liberty to say that although we break, with great regret, our association with many German individuals who have given sympathetic support to our work, yet, your message enunciates our conviction, born of our intimate experience and contact, that there is no hope for democracy or liberalism and consequently for real peace or the safety of our country unless the system which has brought the world into this unfathomable misery can be stamped out once and for all.

HERBERT HOOVER

Reply to Hoover's Message

This short reply from the President contains no mention of Hoover's appointment as Food Administrator. However, while Hoover was in Washington in January and February 1917, Secretary of the Interior Franklin K. Lane had informed him that Wilson would want him back in the country for food organization should the country be drawn actively into the European conflict. A few days after the declaration of war, the American ambassador at London, Walter Hines Page, informed Hoover that such was actually the President's wish. He agreed after being assured he would be allowed to continue to conduct his Belgian relief activity. Three weeks were required for urgent relief matters, then in late April he sailed for New York. (For a comprehensive review of the U.S. Food Administration see *Administration*.)

April 4, 1917

Message to be transmitted by the State Department through the Embassy to

Mr. Herbert C. Hoover,
London, England.

I thank you with my whole heart for the message you were generous enough to send.

WOODROW WILSON

Request for an Appointment

This memorandum is representative of the method frequently employed
to set up meetings between Hoover and Wilson. Hoover, probably by
telephone or private courier, would inform the President's secretary,
Joseph P. Tumulty, or a confidential clerk of his desire for a conference. The request would then be typed as a memorandum and sent
to the President, usually the same day. Wilson often jotted down his
answer in the shorthand he had taught himself many years before,
suggesting a time for the meeting, which frequently took place on the
same day that Hoover had sent in his request. On the following memorandum, Wilson wrote that he could not see Hoover on May 21 but
suggested May 24 at 3:15, at which time the meeting took place at
the White House. This was the third such conference since Hoover's
arrival in Washington on May 4.

May 21, 1917.

Memorandum for the President:
    Mr. Hoover wishes to see the President today.

J.P.T.

Deletions in the Food Control Bill

On April 6, the same day that America declared war on Germany,
Colonel Edward House contacted Hoover, who was then in London,
and communicated President Wilson's desire that he return home to
take charge of the nation's food organization. Hoover arrived in New
York on Thursday, May 3, aboard the *Philadelphia,* one of the first
merchant ships to come through the submarine zone armed with large
guns mounted on her deck. The next morning he reached Washington
and asked for an appointment with Wilson.
    The scheduled meeting took place on May 9 from 2:00 to 3:00
and the President personally requested that Hoover take over as the
country's food dictator. "I don't want to be a food dictator," was his
response. "The man who accepts such a position will die on the barbed
wire of the first line entrenchments." (*Life and Letters,* vol. 7, p. 61.)
This reported sentiment conflicts with that revealed in the cryptic diary
notes of Secretary of the Navy Josephus Daniels, whose telegraphic
memoir for Monday, May 7, 1917, reads: "Long talk with Hoover.
There must be, he said, a Food Dictator, and no wheat or barley should
go into intoxicants. As an ethical question he believed in it, but he advocated it purely as a war plan. He wished to be Food Dictator. Thinks

it should not be under Agriculture. People fear beaurocrocy [sic] and would wish dictatorship ended when war ends." (Daniels Diaries, p. 148.) Hoover did indeed insist on authority being concentrated in one man rather than divided in a committee, but he subsequently disavowed dictatorial ambitions on numerous occasions and time and again insisted on the need for voluntary cooperation rather than coercion.

A May 9 meeting of the National Council, a war agency that included six cabinet members, heard Hoover converse "about conditions abroad." He also "enlarged upon ideas stated in previous conversation with me [Daniels]." At the same meeting Secretary of Agriculture David Houston asserted that he "did not wish [a] Food Controller, but for the Department of Agriculture to control it." (Daniels Diaries, p. 149.) This notwithstanding, Houston and Food Administrator Hoover engaged in friendly cooperation and experienced only the most minimal friction.

The President saw Hoover at 6:30 on Sunday, May 13. Then on May 21 Hoover requested another conference with Wilson and the two men met at 3:15 on Thursday, May 24. Undoubtedly the subject of their conversations was the newly created post of Food Administrator. Actually, however, no congressional authority for this position yet existed. This was not to come until August 8 with passage of the Lever Act (Food Control Act) named after its sponsor, Representative A. S. Lever, Democrat of South Carolina.

Hoover and Wilson were anxious to secure the legislative support for the Food Administration provided by the Lever Bill (also called the Food Control Bill). As June approached both men grew somewhat impatient, for the bill had been under study by the House Agricultural Committee for five weeks. In his May 31 letter to Wilson, Hoover suggests certain deletions in the measure that might expedite its enactment.

Actually, at this particular juncture considerable uncertainty existed as to what Hoover himself really desired. On the evening of his May 4 arrival in Washington, he commented, "I have been called a food dictator, but that is incorrect. What I am here for is to give my services to the nation in any way I can be of use. Secretary Houston will control the country's food supply under bills pending in Congress, and I will assist him and the Council of Defense by supplying information gathered in relief work abroad." (Times, May 5, 1917, p. 6.)

On the other hand, Ray Stannard Baker reports that Colonel House, who had seen Hoover on the day of his arrival from London, stated in a letter to Wilson (undated, but presumably written on or close to May 4): "I trust Houston will give him full powers as to food control. He knows it better than anyone in the world and would inspire confidence both in Europe and here. Unless Houston does give him full control I am afraid he will be unwilling to undertake the job for he is the kind of man that has to have complete control in order to do the thing well." (*Life and Letters*, vol. 7, p. 51.) A week later, June 6, the President had conferences with eight senators to impress them with the urgency for early passage of the bill. (*Life and Letters*, vol. 7, pp. 101–2.)

On June 8 Hoover again requested a meeting with Wilson. That meeting took place on June 11 and the matter discussed is covered in the June 12 letter that is included for that date.

May 31, 1917.

Dear Mr. President:

I have had an opportunity, at the request of various Senators and Congressmen, of discussing with them the Lever bill and the proposed methods of giving administration to it. I find the general feeling that the whole matter can be expedited in Congress and a great deal of opposition overcome if certain provisions of the bill are deleted.

In particular, Section 5, which provides for the establishment of standards and grades in all sorts of foodstuffs. This is a reform which is of very minor importance from a war point of view and is a power which could not be executed by the Food Administration and would necessarily be put upon the Department of Agriculture. It would seem to me undesirable to establish the large administrative measures necessary to give it effect unless this administration is established for a longer period than the war, and if in your judgment it is desirable that such measures should be taken, they might be separated from the Lever bill,—a war measure.

Another clause which is arousing a great deal of opposition is Section 16, allowing mixtures of wheat flour with other cereals. It is my belief that we would probably not want to take advantage of this section because it will open the doors to adulteration which we could not control without a very large administrative staff embracing a representative in every milling plant in the United States. On the other hand we can accomplish the problem of securing consumption of other cereals in substitution for wheat by such voluntary methods as the establishment of cornbread days and other devices of this kind. If these voluntary methods should fail we could then come back for powers at a later stage.

Somewhat the same argument applies also to Section 15 which provides for the establishment of minimum percentages of wheat milling. Inquiry into the mechanical situation of milling in the country indicates that this could not be accomplished in the smaller mills without imposing a great deal of expense upon them and will arouse a great deal of opposition. The national saving to be made therefrom is of somewhat doubtful importance when we weigh all the various factors that enter into the question. Moreover, there are a great number of misguided faddists in the country who will bring constant pressure to bear upon us to take drastic action along these lines and whose antagonism we will certainly incur if we have the powers and do not make use of them. I am somewhat in doubt as to whether this clause should be deleted as it has its certain value in enabling us to force the millers to do certain other things we want by threatening the use of these powers, but if any very considerable fight is made over it, it is my view that it is not critical.

Another matter in connection with the bill seems to me of vital importance and that is that we should have an appropriation of at least $100,000,000 as working capital in purchase and sale of foodstuffs and to supplement the minimum guarantee provisions of the bill.

I am informed by various Congressmen with whom I have discussed the matter that there would be no difficulty in the inclusion of such an appropriation and I cannot conceive that it would result in any financial loss to the country. Probably we would never call upon the appropriation at all, but the fact that we had it would enable us to establish banking credits on a much more positive scale.

I do not wish to take any particular attitude with regard to the bill without your kindly counsel as to whether or not the above ideas should be put into action.

Yours faithfully,
HERBERT HOOVER

Securing Quarters for the Food Administration

Hoover here speaks of a building that is well suited as permanent quarters for his Food Administration and asks the President's cooperation in helping him secure the desired space.

June 4th, 1917.

Dear Mr. President:

We have canvassed the city thoroughly for permanent quarters and find only one available building that is well adapted to our requirements. This is the Homer Building, located at Thirteenth and F [NW]

Streets. We are anxious to lease one-half of the second, third and fourth floors of this building with a total floor area of approximate [sic] thirty thousand square feet.

The Interstate Commerce Commission is now occupying the second and third floors but expect to move to their new quarters between June 15th and July 1st. The fourth floor is occupied by the Bureau of Railway Economics. It is necessary for us to have that half of the fourth floor occupied by the Bureau of Railway Economics to make the second and third floors serviceable for us. This building is admirably adapted to our purpose because it is centrally located and well lighted and the floors are not cut up by partitions, all of which makes for economy and efficiency. If you will request the Bureau of Railway Economics to find other quarters, we will give them the benefit of our knowledge of the available buildings and use our best endeavor to satisfy them.

Our option on the second and third floors expires to-night. Would you be willing to authorize us to assume closing of the lease for the second and third floors on the assumption that we are to get within the next two or three weeks that half of the fourth floor now occupied by the Bureau of Railway Economics.

Very respectively [sic],
HERBERT HOOVER

Decision to Rent Quarters

June 6, 1917.

Memorandum for the President:

Mr. Hoover stated that they had on their own responsibility rented two floors of this building and that there was nothing further to be done in the matter just now. He will be glad to let the President know if, later on, they need assistance.

[unsigned]

Wilson's Aid in Securing Quarters

The following two memos involve Rudolph Forster, Wilson's executive clerk, and Charles L. Swem, his confidential stenographer, through whom he was sending messages to Hoover.

June 8, 1917

Dear Forster:

Please telephone Mr. Hoover that I was not well yesterday and did not get a chance to see this letter until the time had expired of which he speaks; that he did not mention in the letter what the rental would be, but if the building is still available, I should like to have an opportunity to assist him in the matter.

The President.
C.L.S.

Please say to Mr. Hoover that I shall be disappointed if I cannot help them.

The President.
C.L.S.

Letter from an Unidentified Woman

> Although the President gives no indication in this short letter who the woman of "high character" was, it is clear that he referred to a certain Mrs. Ellen Duane Davis of Philadephia.

9 June, 1917

My dear Mr. Hoover,

The writer of the enclosed letter is a woman of such high character and such genuine practical experience that I feel justified in sending the letter to you as an item in the case that you are trying to deal with.

Cordially and sincerely yours,
WOODROW WILSON

Davis Letter on Food Problems

> Mrs. Ellen Duane Davis had written Wilson about high food prices and other distressing conditions in Philadelphia. Her letter was sent to Hoover whose reply follows. The President and Hoover had a conference the same day. They had also met on June 9 at 3:30.

June 11, 1917.

My dear President Wilson:

May I thank you for referring to me a most interesting letter written you by Mrs. Ellen Duane Davis, of Philadelphia.

When Congress has acted it is probable that we can be of some service in such conditions as she mentions. In the meantime, I am writing her and attach hereto a copy of the letter.

Faithfully yours,

HERBERT HOOVER

Volunteers for Food Conservation

> The Food Control Bill would not become law until August 8, but in June food conditions were such that some kind of immediate action was imperative to conserve foodstuffs and to stimulate production. To these ends Hoover relied on the country's voluntary forces. In the following letter Wilson strongly supports him in this matter. Hoover was not slow to utilize the "full authority" conferred on him. Within days he appealed to women to register for the food-saving "army," asked cooperation from the clergy, and conferred personally with James Cardinal Gibbons. (*Times,* June 16, p. 6; June 18, pp. 1, 2.)

June 12, 1917.

My Dear Mr. Hoover:

It seems to me that the inauguration of that portion of the plan for food administration which contemplates a national mobilization of the great voluntary forces of the country which are ready to work toward saving food and eliminating waste admits of no further delay.

The approaching harvesting, the immediate necessity for wise use and saving not only in food, but in all other expenditures, the many undirected and overlapping efforts being made toward this end, all press for national direction and inspiration. While it would in many ways be desirable to wait complete legislation establishing the food administration, it appears to me that so far as voluntary effort can be assembled we should not wait any longer, and therefore I would be very glad if you would proceed in these directions at once.

The women of the nation are already earnestly seeking to do their part in this our greatest struggle for the maintenance of our national ideals, and in no direction can they so greatly assist as by enlisting in the service of the food administration and cheerfully accepting its direction and advice. By so doing they will increase the surplus of food available for our own army and for export to the Allies. To provide adequate supplies for the coming year is of absolutely vital importance to the conduct of the war, and without a very conscientious elimination of waste and very strict economy in our food consumption we cannot hope to fulfill this primary duty.

I trust, therefore, that the women of the country will not only respond to your appeal and accept the pledge to the food administration which you are proposing, but that all men also who are engaged in the personal distribution of foods will cooperate with the same earnestness and in the same spirit. I give you full authority to undertake any steps necessary for the proper organization and stimulation of their efforts.

Cordially and Sincerely yours,
WOODROW WILSON.

Memorandum on June 11 Discussion

> After discussing with Wilson a variety of questions dealing with food control, Hoover sent the President the following letter for purposes of reference. The discussion mentioned took place on Monday, June 11, at 3:30. In addition to his listing of the major points discussed, Hoover enclosed in his letter several pages of memorandums giving details of their conversation. These pages are omitted here.

June 12, 1917.

Dear Mr. President:

In case it may be of interest to you for reference purposes, I enclose herewith copies of the memorandums which we discussed yesterday:

First, one on the necessity of early legislation;

Second, on the question of the organization of commodity controls;

Third, on the organization of voluntary conservation;

Fourth, some preliminary lists of names of purely technical men to be assembled for the assistance of the conservation committees.

I also enclose copy of brief which has been presented to me by William C. Edgar, of Minneapolis, with the backing of the principal millers of the country, which is some indication of both the sentiment with regard to control and also the desire on the part of this trade to support the proposed Food Administration.

I beg to remain, Your obedient servant,

HERBERT HOOVER

Garfield's Appointment to the Food Administration

Dr. Harry Garfield was president of Williams College and son of the assassinated James Garfield, president of the United States. He early became a member of Hoover's Food Administration. Baker states that the meeting referred to in the following letter took place on June 11. (*Life and Letters*, vol. 7, p. 107n.)

13 June, 1917

My dear Mr. Hoover:

Thank you very warmly for your letter of yesterday with the accompanying memoranda.

After you left, I wondered why when you spoke of Doctor Hadley of Yale I had not thought of President Garfield of Williams, a man of fine capacity and of the finest principle and spirit.

In haste, Cordially and faithfully yours,

WOODROW WILSON

Food Administration Position for Garfield

Hoover immediately accepted Wilson's suggestion of Garfield for work with the Food Administration. Because Garfield and the President enjoyed an old friendship rooted in their common profession as academicians, the Williams College head immediately accepted Hoover's offer. In August 1917 Hoover suggested that Wilson make Garfield Fuel Administrator to help solve a disturbing coal and oil problem. The President gladly accepted this suggestion, thus displaying his usual wariness of delegating such measures of power to unknown businessmen. (*Memoirs*, vol. 1, p. 262.)

June 15, 1917.

Dear Mr. President:

I am greatly obliged for your note with regard to President Garfield and I have telegraphed him today asking him if he would be willing to accept the position suggested; that is, as chairman of the committee for determination of prices of food commodities.

I remain, Your obedient servant,

HERBERT HOOVER

Bringing an Idea to Wilson

This short handwritten note from Hoover to Tumulty most likely accompanied Hoover's letter to Wilson with an "idea" for speeding passage of the Food Control Bill. Someone in Tumulty's office jotted on the note that it was acknowledged on June 15, the same day Hoover sent it. (See facsimile section.) No written acknowledgment has been discovered, but on June 18 Wilson dispatched a brief note to Hoover that was probably an answer to his "idea."

June 15, 1917

Dear Tumulty

Could I impose on your good offices to bring this idea before the President at an early moment.

H.C.H.

Senator Kenyon and the Food Bill

William S. Kenyon, Republican from Iowa, believed that the Senate Agriculture Committee could be persuaded to allow the Food Control Bill to go immediately to the Senate chamber if the President would make a request that this be done. Hoover duly sent the word on to Wilson, but the Senate was not so amenable. On June 18 Wilson told his secretary to inform Hoover that "I have exerted my influence to the best of my ability in exactly the direction he suggests." Notwithstanding such pressure, the committee kept the bill locked up until August.

June 15, 1917.

Dear Mr. President:

Senator Kenyon informs me that he believes great expedition could be accomplished with the Food Bill in the Senate by the introduction of the Lever Bill at once from the Senate Agricultural Committee to the floor of the Senate as the Senate measure. I understand from him that the Committee, owing to its internal divisions, would only be likely to do this "by request" and that the request would need [to] come from yourself. If it were done it would place the Food Bill in front of the discussion on the Revenue Bill and would probably save a month or two in time.

I am, Your obedient servant,
HERBERT HOOVER

President's Aid for the Food Bill

At 8:00 on the day Wilson sent this message, Hoover and directors of the Commission for Relief in Belgium had dinner with the President. In the previous few days the President had seen several key senators in his office and spoken to them about the food bill. (*Life and Letters*, vol. 7, pp. 113, 117.) On the day Wilson wrote his note of June 18, he penned a message to Representative William P. Borland, Democrat from Missouri, who had requested a firm word of support to parry the strong attacks from people in the Midwest. Wilson replied that the bill was "one of the most important and imperatively necessary" of the war measures. He added that it was a "disservice" to call it a *control* bill because its purpose was "to release it from the control of speculators." Although he asserted that it should be passed by July 1, enactment did not come until August 8. (*Life and Letters*, vol. 7, pp. 119–20.) All this was part of the "influence" that Wilson tells Tumulty he had been exerting to aid Hoover in securing passage of the food bill.

June 18, 1917

Dear Tumulty:

Please let Mr. Hoover know that I have exerted my influence to the best of my ability in exactly the direction he here suggests.

The President.
C.L.S.

Authorizing Additional Food Administration Funds

The letter referred to in this note does not seem to be in existence, thus it is impossible to ascertain the purpose for which Hoover requested additional funds.

20 June, 1917

My dear Mr. Hoover:

I have your letter of yesterday and take pleasure in authorizing the additional sum of $20,000 to be placed at your disposal from the fund voted me by the Congress for National Security and Defense.

Cordially and sincerely yours,
WOODROW WILSON.

Executive Order on Embargo

The day after Hoover wrote the following letter to Joseph Tumulty, the Food Control Bill passed the House by a vote of 365 to 5. This was a source of great satisfaction for the head of the Food Administration. He was nonetheless much pained by the many attacks then being made upon him, one that very day by Senator Lawrence Y. Sherman, Republican from Illinois.

On Saturday, June 23, even in the midst of his many appointments, Hoover felt compelled to dispatch this message to Sherman: "My attention has been called to your statement, which appears on page 4438 of Friday's Congressional Record, that a sign faces visitors in my office bearing the legend 'To hell with yesterday,' etc.

"There is not nor has ever been such a sign or sentiment either inside or on the outside of my office.

"A canvass of the entire office reveals that the only possible color to such a statement that exists was in an anonymous post card received by one of the clerks to some such import and was immediately destroyed.

"It seems to me but fair that I should ask you to correct the statement, for I can not conceive that you wish to find ground for opposing the food bill by such methods as this."

June 22 1917

Dear Mr. Tumulty:

I understand that the Executive Order will come out today with regard to the embargo, and it seems to me very desirable that some sort of statement should be made from the White House to the Press in connection with its operations.

This should be made on the general lines that the embargo is not a prohibition to export foodstuffs or any other commodity, but simply a limitation of such exports to such people who have been granted licenses to so export. That the Government is anxious to determine what our available remaining supplies are as to wheat and corn and their products from out of the old harvest and that this survey will be taken in hand by the Agricultural Department as quickly as the food survey bill passes Congress. It should also be made known that the Government wants to know from each of the countries exporting [*sic*] these materials from this country, what their purchases are in the United States; where they are and what their needs are, in order that we may adjust these things as far as possible in connection with our own supplies. The statement should also include that it appears that so much wheat and corn had been purchased by foreign powers as to embarrass our local consumers—as witness the very high price of cash wheat and corn—and that this embarrassment is not only working great hardship on our own people, but is having a great many indirect evil effects. Cattle are being driven to the markets because of the cost of feed grains, and injury is being done to our dairy industry. The price of old wheat is so high that the price of flour is intolerable to a great mass of our people, and that before licenses will be granted for the export of these products, the Government will require a complete disclosure of all operations by foreign powers.

The Allies have already placed this information in the hands of the Government and that arrangements will be made for their continued supply temporarily, pending adjustment of the whole problem; that the high prices which have made themselves evident has caused a scarcity in supplies and we must safeguard the position of our own people while we make every endeavor to supply the whole world with foodstuffs. That the embargo is not designed to place anyone in difficulties but to get proper correlation on all sides.

Yours faithfully,
HERBERT HOOVER

Method for Selecting Food Administration Men

In this letter Hoover sketches the method employed for screening top personnel for the Food Administration. Vance McCormick was chairman of the War Trade Board.

June 28, 1917.

Dear Mr. President:–

In laying the groundwork for organization we have initiated a wide-spread series of inquiries from Governors, State Councils of De-

fense, citizens and institutions as to the men whom we should select
for the Federal Commissioners representing the Food Administration
in each state. In these inquiries we first asked for five names embracing
both political parties and subsequently initiated check inquiries in
person and otherwise as to the favorites developed.

We have now gone over part of the lists with Mr. Vance McCormick and have found ourselves in practical agreement in fifteen states
and the others are still under consideration and inquiry. If these fifteen gentlemen should meet with your approval we are anxious to approach them at an early date as their services are badly needed to
manage our state campaigns on conservation. They are, of course, to
be volunteers.

I remain, Your obedient servant,
HERBERT C. HOOVER

Attempts to Weaken the Food Bill

On May 4 President Wilson asked Hoover to become Food Administrator. However, it was not until August 8 that congressional authority
was sealed by passage of the Food Control Act. The measure was introduced in the House on June 11 and approved on June 23, but in
the Senate the bill met resolute opposition. Hoover's complaint, as
expressed in the following letter, underscores the crippling amendments added by several hostile solons. Hoover also mentions a list of
suggested revisions drawn up by him to nullify the adverse effects of
these changes. Actually the objectionable amendments were not ex-
punged from the bill until the conference committee took action on
August 3. The Democratic senator mentioned by Hoover was G. E.
Chamberlain of Oregon, who was favorably disposed to Hoover's views
on food control. Hoover saw Chamberlain on June 30 at 11:45.

On the day that Hoover wrote Wilson of efforts to weaken the
bill, the President sent a message to the Reverend James Cannon, Jr.,
chairman of the Legislative Committee of the Anti-Saloon League of
America, that "immediate passage of the bill" was "of vital consequence"; but he warned of indefinite delay if the beer and wine prohibition was "insisted upon." Accordingly the league ceased its demands
for adding a prohibition rider to the bill. (*Life and Letters,* vol. 7, p.
137, n. 2.)

In the cabinet meeting for Friday, June 29, the question came up
again, and Secretary of the Navy Daniels asked Wilson if he wanted
the "beer amendment" killed. The President said anything should be

removed that was delaying passage of the bill. Then on June 30 Wilson had a protracted conversation with Irving Fisher, a professor of political economy at Yale University. This prominent prohibitionist and chairman of a subcommittee on alcohol for the Council of National Defense criticized the President, asserting that his stand merely fortified the beer faction in their determination "to fight till hell freezes over." (*Daniels Diaries,* p. 170.)

June 29, 1917.

Dear Mr. President:

The Food Bill receives such radical alterations so often in Congress that it seems difficult to determine when intervention should be made in order to secure a proper formulation of its critical features. As the bill has so far been amended in the Senate there have been introduced into it some measures which render the bill nugatory for food administration.

The most pertinent of these is the practical reduction of the operations of the Food Administration to the interstate commerce. If this is to stand it would be impossible for us to control any commodity unless it had some time in its career passed a state line. It consequently introduces a myriad of difficulties that render the whole operation hopeless and worthless to undertake.

Another one of these amendments is in the matter of farmers' cooperative associations. These associations are very numerous, especially in the ownership of elevators and have large position in the handling of the grain crop. If they are to be excepted from the bill, it is hopeless for us to control the movement of grain and entirely unfair to private interests.

Another amendment to the bill practically throws open speculation to all persons who are not regular dealers in foodstuffs. The most vicious form of speculation is precisely of this nature.

The general changes made in the bill in various particulars and the inclusion of many other commodities of such widely different character, combined with the difficulties which we now see in necessarily adjusting commercial operations to Government practice, make it desirable to have some new amendments added to the bill. This is particularly true with regard to the handling of the $150,000,000 working capital provided in the bill for the purchase and sale of foodstuffs by the Government. It is impracticable to conduct the essential activities in this direction without conforming to the usages of the trade, and the delays which will arise in closing transactions by the necessity of passing through the Treasury channels under the general laws, will be fatal. This could be solved by the authorization to yourself to create one or more corporations to be used as agencies for the purpose of food administration and the working capital could be subscribed as [the whole][1] capital stock to such corporations. This arrangement is not without precedent, as witness the Emergency Shipping Corporation. By such arrangement the different commodities and the different circumstances can be competently handled. It has also the advantage that it would center the limelight on a definite organ of the Government for a definite purpose and would permit of its creation along normal commercial lines, understandable by the entire people with whom it has to deal.

I have had the advantage of advice from Judge Curtis Lindley of San Francisco, Mr. Edward F. Burling of Chicago and we have called into consultation Mr. Joseph Cotton of New York and Mr. Roublee. They have formulated the attached amendments embracing not only the above, but some other matters of less importance.

It may be possible that these amendments should be taken up in conference and I would like to have your advice as to whether they should be presented to Senator Chamberlain at once or whether we should wait until the conference.

I am, Your obedient servant,
HERBERT HOOVER

---

1. Handwritten insertion.

Changes to Strengthen the Food Bill

Having informed the President of the undesirable amendments being made to the Food Control Bill by certain senators, Hoover wrote him of an amendment "suggested by us," which, although desirable, might bestir opponents and promote bitter debate. Judge Curtis H. Lindley and Judge Edward Burling of Hoover's legal staff thought the bill as it stood allowed for a generous interpretation sufficient to permit the object sought. A secretary to Wilson wrote this message on Hoover's letter: "Telephoned Mr. Hoover that the President thought they were right and that the power was sufficient."

Hoover met with Wilson at 4:30 on July 2, the day after the meeting mentioned in this letter of June 30.

30 June 1917.

Dear Mr. President:

I have been asked to attend a meeting tomorrow morning at ten o'clock with those senators who are endeavoring to get the Food Bill through, to discuss the amendments with regard to which I addressed you yesterday. One of the amendments suggested [by us][1] embodies more specific power for the creation of corporations to handle the purchase and sale of commodities. The bill as it stands at the present moment authorizes the President to ["][1] create and employ any agencies["][1] desired.

Judge Lindley and Judge Burling, who are advising me, believe that this power is sufficient to cover the creation of corporations, if it should become absolutely necessary; and if you believe that this is the case, it would not be necessary for | you | [us][2] to inject a new and probably bitter discussion into the bill.

The other amendments proposed by us we find are more or less in accord with the views of the Senators concerned, and I think there will be little difficulty in securing their adoption in the Senate or in conference.

Sincerely yours,
HERBERT HOOVER

---

1. Handwritten insertions.
2. |you| changed by hand to "us."

Coordinating the War Agencies

> Hoover had been Food Administrator for only six weeks when he presented President Wilson with a plan to coordinate the various agencies involved in war administration so that overlapping might be prevented and efficiency increased in such areas as purchasing supplies and regulating production.

July 5, 1917.

Dear Mr. President:

I am taking the liberty of addressing you on a matter of somewhat wider import than my own department. My justification lies in the feeling of your own receptivity of suggestions, in the two years of opportunity which I have enjoyed in the observation of the growth of war governments in Europe, and in some two months study of the situation in Washington.

It appears to me that we have now reached the stage in war experience when we can safely enlarge into a series of broad positive steps in war administration. The mixture of administrative and advisory functions in the Council of National Defense and its collateral organizations and other departments, may now be clarified by the creation of a number of positive administrative organs out of the totality of their experience and personnel. It does seem to me that all of these extra war administrations require definite coordination in order to prevent overlap and loss of efficiency. Therefore, to take a broad view of the whole war functions in the purchase of supplies for both home and abroad and in the regulating of domestic production and trading, I should like to submit for your consideration the following suggestions:

1. FEDERAL TRADE COMMISION. The functions of the Federal Trade Commission to be extended to cover investigation and determination of cost in primary production and manufacture and the reasonable profits upon all of the ordinary commodities. It is not to be predicted that these costs can be determined within five or perhaps ten percent, but in any event a generalized figure must be obtained as the fundamental basis for administration by the other departments.

2. FOOD ADMINISTRATION. That its functions include not only the regulation of distribution to our civilian population, but that it should have considerable voice in the placing of Government contracts for food supplies. And furthermore, that it should absolutely control the purchase of supplies for export abroad.

3. RAW MATERIALS ADMINISTRATION. This body to be created to administer the regulation of price, stimulation of production, to secure economy and eliminate waste in the fuel, iron, steel, cotton and other great materials, both in the field of civilian and Government requirements.

4. MUNITIONS ADMINISTRATION. This administration to take over from the Army and Navy and from the Allied Governments, the purchase and administration of all munitions; to cooperate with the Food Administration in matters affecting our Government foodstuffs and with the Raw Materials Administration in that field.

5. PRIORITY ADMINISTRATION. This administration to cover the absolute decision between the various other administrative arms of the Government and between the demands of the different civilian institutions as to priority in the delivery and consumption of materials and supplies.

Under the above plan, the Food, Raw Materials and Munitions Administrations would rely upon one body—the Federal Trade Commission—for the determination broadly of price levels. It appears to me that this is fundamental, first, to obtain independent and thorough consideration and second, to secure coordination of the price levels between commodities, and third, adjustment in the general price levels will be necessary in the country from time to time in the face of inflation which will be our curse and burden during the war. These changes in price levels cannot be solved by haphazard or independent determination by the various departments. Furthermore, it is unjust to our people that the Government buy at specially reduced prices, for this is simply taxation in a wrong form.

The three administrations mentioned would also depend upon the Priority Administration for the practical coordination of the use of primary materials and their distribution.

It appears to me that these administrations should be set up under single-headed control, responsible to yourself, under men who must have no personal interest in any enterprise in this country which bears upon his department and that each should be staffed in such a manner as to secure entire independence of interest. In order, however, to take full advantage of the wide spirit of patriotism and service in the trades, all of the three administrations mentioned should make use of committees comprised of representatives of the great trades, thus securing not only technical advice but may be in position for general bargaining with the trades as a whole so that burdens may fall equally upon all. Under this plan a final shaping of policy and final decision would rest in the hands of the officials not connected with any interested trade organization, yet preserving their interest and cooperation.

I would also like to suggest that the precedent which has been set up in the Exports Council of combining various heads of departments for coordination of interest and elimination of overlap, can be extended in other directions, and if the above additional administrations were set up, by the creation of such coordinating committees.

As an instance of this I would like to suggest that we need strong coordination on the question of national saving. It is true that the current expenses of the war must be paid from, (a) savings before the war; (b) from savings during the war; (c) from inflation which will be a double burden on savings after the war. All that we can genuinely save in the reduction of consumption of commodities and the reduction of non-productive labor will be just that much reduction of the penalty of inflation. If the Food Administration can effect a saving in actual commodities of six cents per capita per day, it will have saved $2,000,000,000 annually available generally for investment in the war. It ought to be possible by propaganda to similarly save on fuel and mineral consumption, to reduce the amount of labor employed in nonproductive fields throughout the country, etc., etc., and therefore if this were accomplished in addition to the current savings of our people we would have met from day to day the cost of the war, except for loans to the Allies. It would therefore logically arise out of the above administrative scheme that a Savings Council could be formed from representatives of the Federal Reserve Board, the Food Administration, the Raw Materials Administration and from the Treasury and Department of Labor. Such a Council could coordinate the propaganda on savings efforts in all directions. I mention this only as an instance, but before such coordination can be undertaken it does appear to me that we need the erection of the fundamental branches of administration underneath.

I trust you will forgive my trespassing outside my own field for it arises solely from a desire to serve.

I remain, Your obedient servant,
HERBERT HOOVER

Inability of Mills to Buy Wheat

Here Hoover complains of the inability of mills to buy wheat in spite of an abundant supply in the country. He suggests that an embargo be imposed on wheat to European neutrals, an act that would remedy this anomalous situation, especially after passage of the Food Control Bill then under consideration by the Senate. At 12:30 on Saturday, July 7, Hoover and Secretary of Agriculture Houston met with the President and discussed with him the "very serious crisis . . . with respect to wheat and corn" and underscored the necessity of an immediate embargo and an early passage of the food bill. (*Life and Letters*, vol. 7, p. 151.) It is possible that Hoover wrote the letter to Wilson after their meeting as a kind of memorandum of the matter discussed. It is also possible that he wrote it earlier in the morning and posted it before being called for an unexpected Saturday noon conference with the President. In his *Epic* (vol. 2, pp. 136–52) Hoover includes much information on the embargo and on the many problems involved in providing food for the neutral nations.

July 7, 1917.

Dear Mr. President:

I am very anxious to bring to your attention a very serious crisis that is daily gathering with respect to wheat and corn owing to the very considerable drain by the neutrals and the apparent holding of grain in the country by someone, possibly their agents.

We are faced with an actual shortage in liquid supplies of such dimensions as to seriously imperil the situation until the new harvest arrives. The flour mills in Minneapolis are practically all closed down owing to their inability to buy wheat, although statistical information shows over 3,000,000 bushels available in that territory. The price of wheat is rising steadily again. Furthermore, the drain of fodder material from the country is going on at a very rapid rate; prices have risen very largely in the past thirty days and one of the many results from this is the forcing of dairymen to sell their cattle for meat as they can no longer, at the ruling prices of dairy products, afford to purchase fodder materials on the present terms. In fact, we are today shipping fodder to European neutrals to maintain the cattle which furnish dairy products to the Germans while our own cattle are being slaughtered because our dairymen can no longer maintain them.

Altogether, I feel greatly disturbed over the situation between now and the flow of the new harvest and there appears to me to be no remedy to our internal situation but immediate embargo. If this is followed by the passage of the Food Bill at an early date, we should be able to then procure liquidation of the held stocks. In any event, the embargo is the most critical portion of the operation.

I remain, Your obedient servant,
HERBERT HOOVER

Wheat and Excess Profits

Less than two months after America plunged into the war, President Wilson, whether orally or by letter is not certain, requested from Hoover information relative to the maintenance of a suitable price for wheat. Hoover replied on July 10, 1917. Shortly thereafter the Food Administration Grain Corporation was established with Hoover as its head. Then, following a determination by the wheat board that $2.20 at Chicago was a fair price for No. 1 northern wheat ($2.26 with freight rates), Hoover bid that price and the speculators went out of business. Several years later on April 24, 1929, when the Senate was debating a farm bill "to establish a Federal farm board to aid in the orderly marketing . . . of agricultural commodities," Senator Smith Brookhart, Republican of Iowa, read Hoover's letter and commented upon it at length to prove "the ability of Herbert Hoover to solve the farm problem." (*Cong. Rec.,* 71st Cong., 1st sess., 71, pt. 1:436–39.)

On July 11, 1917, probably only a few hours after receiving Hoover's letter, Wilson wrote to Representative W. C. Adamson, Democrat of Georgia, who had suggested that profit-limiting provisions be included in the food bill. The President said: "I am going to take the liberty of clarifying my own judgment a little further by consulting Mr. Hoover about the practicability of enforcing provisions such as you suggest, for I have learned to have great confidence in his practical judgment in these matters." (*Life and Letters,* vol. 7, p. 157.)

July 10, 1917

Dear Mr. President:

In response to your request I send you herewith the following notes compiled by myself and my associates upon the present situation with regard to wheat.

1. The 1917 harvest promises to yield 678,000,000 bushels. The normal internal consumption and seed requirement, (assuming a carry-over of same volume in 1918 as in 1917), amounts to about 600,000,000 bushels, thus leaving a theoretical export balance of 78,000,000 bushels. The conservation measures are already having a marked effect and it is not too much to hope that the national saving may be 80,000,000 to 100,000,000 bushels, and therefore the export balance increased to, say, 158,000,000 to 180,000,000 bushels.

2. The experience this year in the rampant speculation, extortionate profits and the prospect of even narrower supplies than 1916 harvest and carry-over, must cause the deepest anxiety. No better proof of the hardship worked upon our people during the past year needs be deduced than the recitation of the fact that the producer received an average of $1.51 per bushel for the 1916 wheat harvest, yet wheat has been as high as $3.25 at Chicago and the price of flour has been from time to time based upon this speculative price of wheat, so that through one evil cause or another, the consumer has suffered from 50 to 100 percent, and the producer gained nothing. After much study and investigation, it is evident that this unbearable increase in margin between producer and consumer is due not only to rank speculation, but

more largely than this to the wide margin of profit naturally demanded
by every link in the chain to insure them from the great hazards of
trade in the widely fluctuating and dangerous price situation during
the year when all normal stabilization has been lost through the interruption or [of?] world trade and war. All these factors render it
vitally necessary to initiate systematic measures which will absolutely
eliminate all possibility of speculation, cure extortionate profits, effect
proper distribution and restriction on exports to a point within our
own protection. These measures cannot be accomplished by punitive
prosecution of evil-doers, but only by proper and anticipatory organization and regulation all along the distribution chain.

　　3. During recent months the Allied Governments have consolidated their buying into one hand in order that they might relieve the
burden of speculation from their own consumers and | as to restricted
exports to neutrals are but a minor item, |[1] the export price, if not
controlled, is subject to the will of the Allied buyer and in a great
measure the American producer [is][2] left to his judgment and without
voice. Furthermore, in normal circumstances, United States and Canadian Wheat is moved to Europe largely in the fall months, such
shipments averaging about 40,000,000 bushels per month and relieving a corresponding flow from the farms into the interior terminals.
This year, owing to the shortage of shipping, the Allied supplies must
proceed over a large period of the year and will not, during the fall
months apparently average over 20,000,000 to 25,000,000 bushels per
month. We must, therefore, expect a glut in our interior terminals
during a considerable period. The financial resources of the grain
trade are probably insufficient to carry this extra load without the help
of speculators, and moreover, the consolidation of practically all foreign
buying in the hands of the Allied buyer has further tended to diminish
the capital resources available by placing a number of firms out of
business, and limits the financial capital available in export trade. The
net result of this situation is that unless some strong and efficient Government action is immediately settled and brought into play, the
American producer will face a slump in wheat. In any event, the
price of export wheat will be dictated by a single agency. The American consumer will be faced with a large part of the essential bread-
stuff having passed into the hands of speculators for someone must buy
and hold not only the normal flow from the farmer but this probable
glut.

---

　　1. Deleted by hand.
　　2. Handwritten insertion.

4. With great reduction in the consumption of wheat bread now fortunately in progress, the employment of our mills must be greatly diminished and with the reduction of domestic flour production, and our daily feed from wheat residues will be greatly curtailed. Therefore, we must induce foreign buyers to accept flour instead of wheat.

4 [5]. In order to do justice to the producers who have shown great patriotism in a special effort to increase production in 1917 | and to further stimulate the efforts of 1918, |[1] it is absolutely vital that we shall protect the farmer from slump in price this year due to glut as above or from the uncontrolled decisions of any one buyer. I am informed that most of the Allied countries have fixed the price of wheat to the farmer at $1.80 per bushel and many of | their producers | [them][3] believe that as Allies it is our duty to furnish wheat at a price which delivered to them will not exceed their domestic price, in other words, about $1.50 per bushel Chicago. Neither the responsible officials nor I hold this view, because I consider the stimulation to production, if [for] no other reason, is in the long run, in the interest of the Allies. There is, however, a limit to price which so trespasses upon the rights of the consumer as to defeat its own object through strikes, raises in wages, and social disturbances in the country. It is with the view to finding a solution to those problems, filled with the greatest dangers to both our producers and consumers, that legislation has been proposed, and pressed for speedy enactment.

6. The proposed Food Administration has conferred with many hundred patriotic men engaged in production and distribution and has investigated the condition of the consumers in many centers as well. Many plans have been tentatively put forward and abandoned and others have been developed, but in any case, none has nor can be settled until legislation has been completed. Three facts stand out plainly enough from our investigations: First, that in this situation, the farmer will need protection as to the price of wheat, and second, that large masses of people in the consuming centers are being actually undernourished today due to the exorbitant cost of living, and these conditions, unless some remedy be found, are likely to repeat themselves in even more vicious forms at this time next year: third, the speculator, legitimate or vicious, has taken a large part of the money now being paid by the consumer.

7. It seems to be overlooked in some quarters that the marketing of this year's wheat is surrounded with circumstances new to history

---

3. Words between | | deleted by hand, followed by handwritten insertion in [ ].

and that the old distributing safe-guards are torn away by isolation
from the reciprocal markets abroad and the extinction of a free export
market and free export transportation. The harvest has begun to move
and from these very causes the price of wheat has begun to drop and
if the farmer is to sell his wheat, either the speculator must return to
the market to buy and carry not only the normal flow from the farmer
in excess of domestic and foreign requirements but also the glut due to
the restriction upon the outlet to the latter and he must charge his toll
to the producer and the consumer and this latter upon a more extensive
scale than last year as his risk will be greater and the practically [*sic*]
export buyer must fix his own price for export wheat from the sole
outlook of his own clients and in execution of his duty he will in all
normal circumstance follow the market down by buying only his time
to time requirements as he cannot be expected to carry the load of our
domestic accumulation. Or the Government must buy the surplus
wheat at some reasonable minimum price, allowing the normal domestic trade of the country to proceed with proper safeguards against
speculation. Nor would the services of the speculator be necessary for
the Government should be able to stabilize the price of wheat without
his assistance and can control the price of export wheat.

I remain, Your obedient servant,
HERBERT HOOVER

Adamson's Suggestions on the Food Bill

> Wilson here asks Hoover for his views on the suggestions of Repre-
> sentative Adamson on the Food Control Bill, one of which was a pro-
> vision that limited the profit the first purchaser might realize and
> aimed at preventing the holding of commodities for speculative pur-
> poses. On July 16 Wilson wrote to Adamson that "it is safe to be
> bound by his [Hoover's] judgment if he thinks that the provisions of
> the pending food bill as they will probably come out of conference
> constitute a sufficient safeguard against the speculators." (*Life and
> Letters*, vol. 1, pp. 166–67.)

11 July, 1917

My dear Mr. Hoover:

I would be very much obliged for your judgment on the suggestions of Judge Adamson made in the enclosed letter. I have told him

that I would wait to hear from you before discussing the matter further with him.

Cordially and sincerely yours,
WOODROW WILSON.

Reply to Adamson's Suggestions

July 12, 1917
Dear Mr. President:

In response to your esteemed note of the 11th of July, so far as the Food Bill is concerned the whole machinery is designed to carry out precisely the points proposed by Mr. Adamson, the whole conception of food control being, (a) through prevention of hoarding and exchange speculation to make it impossible for any person to hold or deal in food beyond the immediate necessities of his business; (b) by the licensing clause to make it possible for yourself to lay down regulations and to enforce them by licenses which will require the licensee to "discontinue unjust, unreasonable, discriminatory and unfair storage charges, commission charges or practices." (c) At my request the Act was altered in the House to include the purchase and sale of commodities by the Government in substitution of all previous schemes of maximum and minimum prices, this to be applied probably on only two or three of the great commodities. (d) The provision in the House Bill, that we could in a final necessity requisition and operate for the Government, food manufacturing plants, etc., will, in my belief, never be necessary in actual practice but is a reserve club.

Also the Food Bill, subject to emasculation by the Senate, has running through it a theme of voluntary agreement and we have already made great progress in organizing several trades with the patriotic assistance of its members to limit the differentials and charges made in the trade and to limit wasteful practices and practices which lead to speculation, it being our firm conviction based on the evidence of now almost hundreds of meetings, that the leaders of the great trades are only too anxious to enter National service in this particular. If we apply the powers of the bill, it will be with the approval of most of the well-thinking men in the trade as against the selfish and avaricious members, but they could not be induced to enter into such agreements unless they were assured protection from unfair competition.

The net result of these various directions of attack on the problem should be to eliminate waste, speculation and extortion at each link in the distribution chain of each given commodity and to do this without any disruption of the normal flow of honest commerce. I see no reason why this same machinery should not apply to any of the great commodities of the country. There is, however, a distinction between control of food and control of other raw materials, especially those of a mineral character, in the fact that whereas the whole control of food commodities must be based upon a control of their distribution because the production arises from millions of centers, the control of minerals must include the production agencies as well as the manufacturing and distributing agencies. The introduction of other commodities than food into the Lever bill is wholly wrong and should have separate legislative treatment. However, it may be desirable to include them to secure any early action in this regard.

I remain, Your obedient servant,
HERBERT HOOVER

Apology for Not Seeing Hoover

> This warm letter of apology from Wilson for his inability to see Hoover on July 11 suggests that Hoover might well have requested a conference on the complicated food bill, at that time bogged down in the Senate. The bill was the subject of Hoover's long letter of July 10 and of Wilson's brief note of July 11. Moreover, two Democratic senators, T. S. Martin of Virginia and F. M. Simmons of North Carolina, had visited the President on July 12 and left him a substitute bill for the administration's proposal. This suggested measure produced in Wilson such disquietude that the next day he composed a long letter of complaint, saying in part that "in practically every particular it emasculates the original measure." (*Life and Letters,* vol. 7, pp. 158, 163–64.) Perhaps, then, the President had more than abundant reasons for his regret in not being able to see Hoover on July 12.

12 July, 1917

My dear Mr. Hoover:

I was really distressed yesterday that I could not see you in response to your request for a short interview. When the request reached me, I had already mortgaged every hour I had until bedtime. I watched for intervals in order than I might send word to you, but they did not come. I hope that you were not seriously embarrassed for the lack of what you sought.

Cordially and sincerely yours,

WOODROW WILSON.

Gore Substitute for the Food Bill

The House passed the Food Control Bill on June 23, 1917, but in the Senate it was greatly weakened by the addition of amendments, a sample of which provides the material for this letter. Drawing particular fire from Hoover was the proposal of Oklahoma's Democratic Senator T. P. Gore to substitute a board of three commissioners for a single food administrator. Hoover had for some time opposed such divided authorities in agencies that required energy and dispatch for their effective operation. He had seen the frictions, the delays, and the indecision that characterized the divided executives of European boards and commissions. By drawing upon his personal experience he was able to construct arguments that finally won Wilson's agreement to a single head for the Food Administration. The President still had "a troubled mind" on the matter (*Memoirs,* vol. 1, pp. 241–42); however, once convinced, Wilson was resolute in his opposition to any plan that provided for a board or a commission. (See letters of July 18 and 19 and August 1.)

July 12, 1917.

Dear Mr. President:

Considerable effort will be made in the Senate to secure the substitution of Mr. Gore's amended bill, though I am uncertain as to what the possibilities of success are in this effort. I enclose for your information some notes on Mr. Gore's substitute which have been furnished me by Judge Curtis Lindley who is assisting us on the legal side.

I would like to point out in this matter that Mr. Gore's substitute extracts absolutely the whole of the teeth from the bill and renders it impossible for us to control speculation, for it reduces the hoarding and board of trade provisions to a nullity and makes it impossible for us to control wasteful practices in distribution and manufacture and impossible to control extortion in profits and charges. If the bill should pass Congress in this form the whole objective of the Food Administration in the sense of securing for the consumer in this country foodstuffs at a reasonable ratio to the return to the producer, is entirely hopeless. I may also mention that the form of administration proposed by Mr. Gore also destroys the whole question of the imaginative side of leadership of yourself and sense of volunteer service in the interest of the Nation, which is absolutely critical in order to amass the devotion of the people. I simply cannot hope to secure this sort of administration if it is to be controlled by a meticulous "board" with its impossible mixture of irresponsible executive and advisory functions. Moreover, at your wish the Food Administration was launched upon this basis and it becomes merely a drive at yourself personally and to a lesser degree at me.

I remain, Your obedient servant,
HERBERT HOOVER

Embargo Message for Neutrals

In his letter of July 7 to the President, Hoover complained that America was shipping fodder to European neutrals to feed their cattle and that these neutrals then sold dairy products to Germany. To put a stop to this practice, and also to guarantee sufficient fodder for domestic cattle, Hoover suggested an immediate embargo. The same suggestion was urged upon Wilson by Secretary of Agriculture Houston and by Hoover when the two men called at the White House in the early afternoon of Saturday July 7. (See July 7 letter.) In the following letter Hoover writes of the memorandum that he intended to hand to the minister of Holland at their meeting to discuss the embargo. The draft of this memorandum is not now in the Hoover or Wilson papers. However, in his *Epic* (vol. 2, p. 142) Hoover includes the letter that he presented to the minister on July 31, 1917, as a confirmation of their conversation on that day. In all probability it was in substance the memorandum that he sent to Wilson on July 14 and that the President approved on July 17.

July 14, 1917.

Dear Mr. President:

Please find attached hereto a preliminary draft of an informal memorandum which I propose to hand to the Holland Minister when I take up with him negotiations in connection with embargo.

I have a strong feeling that it is extremely dangerous to have informal conversations without a written note expressing exactly the tenor of such conversations. Although this note is drawn entirely in an informal way and with no spirit of ultimatum, it is still of great importance that it should be first submitted for your approval.

The draft has been presented to the Export Council, who are in accord with the text, and it is at their request that I forward the same to you. A similar text will be presented to the representatives of Sweden and Denmark.

I remain, Your obedient servant,
HERBERT HOOVER

Approval for Embargo Note

17 July, 1917

My dear Mr. Hoover:

I am returning this with my approval. I have made only one change. I think you will see the reason for that.

In haste, Cordially and sincerely yours,
WOODROW WILSON.

Hollis Substitute for the Food Bill

Hoover complains here of an attempt by New Hampshire's Republican Senator Henry F. Hollis to offer his own food control bill and to represent it as incorporating the views of the President. Hoover reaffirmed his opinion that adherence to the Food Control Bill was the only means of getting effective action, and he asked Wilson to disavow the Hollis measure.

July 18, 1917.

Dear Mr. President:

You are probably aware that a new substitute food bill has been introduced to the Senate this morning by Senator Hollis and some of his friends. I hear from many quarters that this is being represented as the Administration bill and this impression is today being systematically given to the press.

The bill contains many vicious provisions and does not return to the text of the Lever Bill, which should be made the Administration measure. It contains a provision for putting the Food Administration under commission form and it seriously alters the provisions of the bill in many directions already attempted by the Gore substitute.

To my mind it is very important that the Senators who are desirous of getting legislation satisfactory to yourself, and workable from an Administration point of view, should be informed as quickly as possible that this bill does not conform with the desires of the Administration and that great damage is being done by these reports which have been spread that it does so fulfill the requirements.

I am having a memorandum prepared showing the deficiencies of this measure, practically all of which arise by departure from the original Lever bill. Among others, I may mention that practically the flour millers, the refiners, importers, exporters, commission men, and many other food distributors are immune from the action of the bill. The bill also contains a provision which guarantees the price of wheat at $1.75 per bushel without establishing any adequate basis or having given adequate consideration as to whether this is a right or justifiable price or not.

I remain, Your obedient servant,
HERBERT HOOVER

Message for the President

A handwritten note to Joseph Tumulty was a method frequently employed by Hoover for putting messages into Wilson's hands without delay. Such communiques were probably sent by private courier since they reached the President more directly and with greater dispatch than if entrusted to the ordinary mails. The "note" to the President mentioned here is not to be found in the Hoover or the Wilson papers, unless it was Hoover's letter about the Hollis proposal also written on July 18. Hoover may have enclosed it in his message to Tumulty.

July 18, 1917

Dear Tumulty

Herewith a note to the President which I would like very much if you could get to his attention.

Sincerely H.

Assurances of a Suitable Bill

The fears expressed by Hoover over the food bill were well founded; on July 21 the Senate passed the Lever proposal but with such amendments that the President himself felt compelled to register a vigorous protest. Section 23 provided for a "Joint Committee on Expenditures in the Conduct of the War." Wilson objected to the "constant supervision of executive action which it contemplates." This, he complained, would "render my task of conducting the war practically impossible." To justify his apprehension, he referred to the "very ominous precedent" of the committee that caused Lincoln "distressing harassment" during the Civil War. (*Life and Letters,* vol. 7, p. 185; *Times,* July 31, 1917, p. 1.) Hoover likewise had objected to this feature of the Senate's measure. Wilson assures him in his July 19 letter that a desirable bill will ultimately be forthcoming. On the subject of setting up a board the President wrote thus on July 24: "If I can help it, 'there ain't going to be a Food Control *Board.*'" This was in response to a request from a Princeton classmate recommending a cousin for a position on such a board. (*Life and Letters,* vol. 7, p. 191.)

19 July, 1917

My dear Mr. Hoover:

In reply to your letter of yesterday, may I not convey at least this degree of reassurance: I am keeping a very careful watch on the progress of the Food Bill in the Senate and believe that, although the measure will go into conference with many undesirable and perhaps impossible features in it, it will come out of conference with practically the provisions we have all along urged.

It is a tedious and vexatious process but necessary to be endured.

Cordially and sincerely yours,
WOODROW WILSON

Letters of Lever and Gronna

The Food Control Bill had been passed with certain features highly unacceptable to Hoover and Wilson. Moreover, the means employed by many opponents of the bill to cause its defeat greatly distressed them. One such opponent was Republican Senator A. J. Gronna of North Dakota who, among other things, had misquoted Hoover, attributing to him the statement that "wheat might be forced down to

75¢." On July 25, Hoover wrote Gronna asking him to correct "this repeated misstatement."

The other letter mentioned in the following message to Tumulty was addressed to Representative Lever whose bill had recently been amended by Senator Gronna in a manner unacceptable to Hoover. He states that "the Senate provisions as to the market base for wheat to be calculated, are wholly neubula [sic] . . . and the whole matter needs revision. . . ."

The final paragraph suggests that Hoover had reluctantly accepted Wilson's policy of patient suffering with the Senate's actions and that he really wanted Wilson "to say something rather loudly" right at this critical moment.

July 26, 1917

Dear Mr Tumulty:

Please find enclosed herewith copy of a confidential letter which I addressed yesterday to Congressman Lever and also copy of a letter which is the end, so far as I am concerned, to certain correspondence with Senator Gronna.

The letter to Congressman Lever is, I think, worth bringing to the attention of the President. This whole matter gives me some anxiety for fear the Administration may be blamed for a situation which has been created absolutely by the wholly unconsidered action of the Senate. I bow to the President's judgment that we shall say nothing at the present tine [sic], but I think he should reserve the right to say something rather loudly, later on, as we may have to face a perfect storm from the consumers of this country.

Yours faithfully,
HERBERT HOOVER

Attempts to Phone Wilson

It seems more than likely that Hoover's attempts to telephone Wilson were prompted by his deepening anxiety over the food bill, then in the conference committee, and by his eagerness to persuade the President to dispatch a special message to Senator Chamberlain who was shepherd of the measure in the upper chamber. He sent the following handwritten note to the President expressing his concern.

August 1, 1917

Dear Tumulty

I have been endeavoring to reach the President by telephone without result. Would you see that he receives this note as soon as possible as the Senator wants same indication from him at once.

Sincerely,
H. HOOVER

Removal of Part of the Food Bill

When the Food Control Bill was passed by the Senate, it still provided for a joint congressional committee to maintain a vigilant watch over the Food Administration. Hoover was adamantly opposed to this provision and wrote Wilson about a plan to have it removed in conference. On July 30 at 11:30 Wilson received Representative Lever who reported on the deadlock in the conference over the food bill. The President took the occasion to assert that he was unalterably opposed to any divided authority for the Food Administration. At 11:50 he saw Senator George Chamberlain who was chairman of the Senate Committee on Military Affairs. Senator T. S. Martin of Virginia, Democratic floor leader, called on him in the afternoon, and in the evening Senator F. E. Warren, Republican from Wyoming, was summoned for a discussion on the food measure. Having won Warren over to his views, Wilson telephoned Lever to stand pat, for he thought all would come out satisfactorily in a few days. (*Life and Letters*, vol. 7, p. 199.)

August 1, 1917.

Dear Mr. President:

Senator Chamberlain has asked me to convey to you the following message.

He states that he thinks the section in the food control bill providing for the joint Congressional Committee can be eliminated in conference, provided it is agreed that it shall be raised as a joint resolution. He further believes that the joint resolution can be defeated on the floor of the Senate, and that if this course has your approval, he feels that he could win over one or two more votes on the conference committee to this program. He would like to have some indication of your feelings in the matter.

I remain, Your obedient servant,
HERBERT HOOVER

Pressure for Draft Exemptions

> A suggestion made by Hoover (in a handwritten note) about draft
> exemptions was favorably received by Wilson, as revealed in his brief
> August 6 note to Tumulty. On August 7 Wilson himself was com-
> pelled to decline a request that he intervene with the Board of Ex-
> emption Appeals on behalf of a constituent of Senator Marcus A.
> Smith, Democrat from Arizona. (*Life and Letters,* vol. 7, pp. 207–8.)

August 6, 1917

My dear Tumulty—

We are under constant pressure—even from Senators—to intervene
with the war department in the matter of exemptions. Those that come
to us are "critically necessary" to maintain the food engine of the country. I dont [*sic*] like to be interfering in the business of other departments nor to be subject to such pressure. Could not a hint be given us—
in fact a direction to all departments that we should not do it? We could
escape a lot of trouble and while some meritorious cases may arise their
very merits should secure their settlement by exemption officials without
our intervention.

Sincerely,

H. HOOVER

Authorization of Hoover's Suggestion

August 7(?), 1917

Dear Tumulty:

I think Mr. Hoover's suggestion is entirely proper and I authorize
you to make the suggestion to him which he indicates.

The President.

C.L.S.

Picture of Signing of the Food Bill

> The two brief notes that follow are messages Wilson and Hoover sent
> to one another indirectly. The Food Control Bill, as it came from
> conference, was finally accepted by the Senate August 8 and was signed
> into law by Wilson August 10. Hoover was anxious to exploit the
> signing ceremony for publicity purposes. Hence his memorandum was

carried to the President by Arthur S. Friend of the Motion Picture Bureau of the Food Administration. Friend had "suggested an interesting program of activity," to borrow from Hoover's August 9 letter introducing him to Wilson's secretary Joseph Tumulty.

It is possible that Hoover intended to suggest the idea of a picture-taking ceremony personally to Wilson. On August 8 he asked for an August 9 meeting with the President who, however, jotted these words on the request: "In up to the neck to-day. Would be glad to see Mr. H. tomorrow at 5:00." The meeting actually took place at 4:30 on August 10. Two days later the two had another discussion which concerned the grain corporation.

Another reason that possibly could have prompted Hoover on August 8 to ask for a meeting with Wilson was the cascading attack being made on him and on the Food Control Bill. On the day he requested the meeting, Hoover wrote Tumulty that one recent statement about the measure was "just on a par with the other damn lies that have been perpetuated during the last ten days."

Then referring to one fierce foe, Democratic Senator James A. Reed of Missouri, Hoover wrote: "I have made no reply to anything said by Mr. Reed or the others. Scarcely a statement made contains an element of truth except in regard to some foolish stuff sent to the press as a result of a hurried volunteer organization and overzealousness on the part of some ladies who were anxious to get their stories in the papers. This was put under iron-clad restraint a fortnight ago, but in any event, it seems too trivial for words.

"Just as one illumination out of many that have come to hand, I enclose you copy of some correspondence between Senator Reed and a certain Miss Todd." (For more on this incident, see the letter of August 23 on Reed's anti-Hoover activity.)

August 9, 1917

Memorandum for the President:

Mr. Friend called this morning with the attached letter. He states that the Food Administration is anxious to make full use of the motion picture in furthering its work among the people, and to that end it is particularly desired to head a reel with a picture of the President signing the food bill. They also hope that Mrs. Wilson will consent to have her picture appear in the film, possibily [*sic*] receiving some of the ladies who are assisting Mr. Hoover while wearing the uniforms designed for the food conservers.

[unsigned]

Declining Request for Picture-Taking

This brief answer to Hoover's propaganda scheme is similar to the President's negative response of March 15, 1918, to a proposal from David Lawrence to do an article for *Collier's Weekly* on his executive work. On that day he wrote that "I am hopelessly useless for publicity purposes. I have long been convinced of that. . . ." On March 13, he had written Lawrence, "I can't for the life of me think it out in any way that would be striking or effective. That is my trouble. The day seldom seems impressive when summed up. . . . My interviews and consultations are chiefly with people who need not have taken my time, and lead to nothing except the gratification on the part of those who see me that they have had their say." (*Life and Letters*, vol. 8, pp. 25, 32.) Two weeks later a request came that Wilson permit a recording to be made of his Flag Day speech. He refused because he could never get "the 'emotional power' into my voice when speaking into a phonograph. As a matter of fact, I sound like a machine and I should hate to have the address so read given any perpetuity. . . ." (*Life and Letters*, vol. 7, p. 235.)

This note declining Hoover's suggestion was written to Rudolph Forster, Wilson's executive clerk.

August 9, 1917

Dear Forster:

Please explain to Mr. Hoover that both Mrs. Wilson and I are absolutely incapacitated by temperament from doing this sort of thing well and that any picture that might be attempted would be sure to be a failure.

The President.

C.L.S.

Executive Orders on the Food Bill

Wilson and Hoover had a conference on August 10 at 4:30. On that day the President signed the Food Control Act, which was made effective by certain executive orders and was one of the subjects of the conference. The men mentioned in the following letter are Gates W. McGarrah of New York City, one of four directors to be named by Wilson in his August 14 order, and William McAdoo, the President's son-in-law and Secretary of the Treasury. On August 13 Hoover wrote to Wilson on his forthcoming executive orders suggesting the wording of Curtis Lindley, general counsel of the Food Administration. On the same day Hoover and Wilson had a conference on the Grain Corporation.

August 13, 1917.

Dear Mr. President:

Please find enclosed herewith the two executive orders I discussed with you on Saturday.

In respect to the grain corporation, it is our idea, at the necessary moment, to simply explain it to the country as being an accounting and organization engine, manager [sic] entirely by the Food Administration.

I may mention that I have now discussed Mr. McGarrah with Mr. McAdoo and find that Mr. McAdoo joins with me in the confidence that he is the ideal man for the situation. We desire to find two more directors for the corporation, one of whom, at least, should represent the agricultural interests, but as yet we have not found the ideal men. In the meantime, we can save a good deal of time by proceeding with the organization.

The second executive order is in respect to licensing grain storage in the country, as I explained on Saturday.

I also enclose herewith two duplicates of the executive orders mentioned above, together with [a] letter from Judge Lindley explaining some minor alterations.

I remain, Your obedient servant,

HERBERT HOOVER

Documents and Nominations

This letter to Rudolph Forster appears to have been one in which Hoover enclosed the previous letter to Wilson and "the two executive orders," referred to here as "documents." (Note that Hoover consistently referred to Wilson's executive clerk as "Foster.") Hoover frequently dispatched letters for the President to Forster or Joseph Tumulty; undoubtedly, he hoped that they would put the communique directly into the President's hands and perhaps add a word about its urgency.

Hoover and Wilson had numerous personal interviews during the war years, but the President preferred a letter or a memorandum whenever it was possible. He also liked the sender to enclose drafts of documents ready to sign whenever written authority was necessary for some action. (*Ordeal*, p. 12.)

In this letter to Forster, Hoover states that he met with Wilson "on Saturday," which was August 11. This does not seem possible because in the late afternoon of the previous day Wilson left Washington aboard the *Mayflower* for a weekend trip (*Life and Letters*, vol. 7, pp. 210–11.) But Hoover did have a meeting with the chief executive at 4:30 on Friday, August 10. The *New York Times* (Aug. 11, 1917, p. 1) wrote of it as "a long conference at the White House tonight." Undoubtedly, in his letter Hoover was referring to this meeting with Wilson.

August 13, 1917.

Dear Mr. Foster [*sic*]:

Please find enclosed herewith letter addressed to the President which explains itself.

I went over these matters with the President on Saturday but we were unable to complete the execution of the documents then because of certain undetermined dates and names. They are now in final form, ready for signature, and I am extremely anxious to get them out today if possible.

Also I submitted to the President on Saturday a list of names of principals of staff and if the President has had time to look them over and give me his views thereupon, it would held [*sic*] enormously, because we can carry out but little machinery without having our men positively engaged, and a large number of the men for State Commissioners we have not approached, and we need their assistance before our machinery can be put into execution.

I would be greatly obliged if you could take these matters up with the President for me.

Yours Faithfully,
HERBERT HOOVER

Nominations to a Committee

August 14, 1917.

Dear Mr. President:

Dr. Garfield and I wish to present to you the following names of gentlemen to comprise the committee to determine a fair basic price for 1917 wheat. President Garfield will, of course, act as chairman:

Barrett, Charles J President, Farmers' Union	Union City	Georgia
Doak, Wm. N Vice-Prest., Brotherhood of Railroad Trainmen	Roanoke	Virginia
Funk, Eugene E Prest., National Corn Ass'n.	Bloomington	Illinois
Ladd, Edwin F Prest., North Dakota Agricultural College	Fargo	No. Dakota
Rhett, R Goodwyn Prest., Chamber of Commerce of the United States	Charleston	So. Carolina
Shorthill, J. W. Sec'y., National Council of Farmers' Cooperative Ass'ns.	York	Nebraska
Sullivan, Jas. W American Federation of Labor	Brooklyn	New York
Tabor, L. J. Master, Ohio State Grange	Barnesville	Ohio
Taussig, Frank W Chairman, Federal Tariff Comm.	Cambridge	Massachusetts
Vail, Theo. N Prest., American Telegraph and Telephone Company	New York City	New York
Waters, Henry J Prest., Kansas State Agricultural College	Manhattan	Kansas
Garfield, Harry A, Chairman President, Williams College	Williamstown	Massachusetts.

I would be glad to know if this selection meets with your approval
and if we may state that it is your wish that they serve.

I beg to remain, Your obedient servant,
HERBERT HOOVER

Approved
WOODROW WILSON [handwritten by Wilson]

A Note to Forster

These few scribbled words to Wilson's executive clerk help reveal the
feverish activity in which Hoover engaged immediately after passage
of the Food Control Act. This appears to have been the cover note
for Hoover's letter on the Hallowell appointment. Someone at the
White House wrote these words on the note: "Retd to Mr. Hoover
approved 8/14/17."

Dear Mr Foster [sic]—
Herewith a letter to the President—upon which we are very anxious
to get action today if possible—

Sincerely
HERBERT HOOVER

Hallowell's Food Administration Appointment

It is not unlikely that at their Friday meeting (not Saturday as in the
August 13 letter above) Hoover recommended John Hallowell to President Wilson for a position with the Food Administration. But on
August 14 the President informed Hoover through Forster that he
"would not like to see the firm of Stone and Webster of Boston represented in the Food Administration because of their very unsatisfactory
attitude in a good many matters concerning labor and their very extended monopoly of power enterprises in the West." Hoover's letter
of clarification about Hallowell's assignments is given below.

August 14, 1917.
Dear Mr. President:
In respect to Mr. Hallowell, one of the office men of Stone & Web-
ster, about whom I have received a note from Mr. Foster [sic], I am in

entire agreement as to the inadvisability of anyone representing this firm in the Food Administration. This is hardly the case and I am to blame for not explaining his relationship on the list I sent in. In justice to the young man I should have explained that he is a minor light in their establishment who was recommended to me for his public spirit and as one who had developed considerable genius for the correlation of branch businesses, from an office point of view. Of course, so long as he remains with us, he is entirely disassociated with that firm's business.

Mr. Hallowell's position with us is to correlate office correspondence work as between ourselves and State Commissioners. He therefore has no interest or influence in matters affecting food control and has proven himself so very capable and so anxious to give his career to national service, that I am loth to make a change without further presentation of his case. I can, of course, rearrange the work so that he is not one of the principals in the organization.

Mr. Vance McCormick has come into intimate contact with Mr. Hallowell and could, I think, re-assure you in the matter.

I remain, Your obedient servant,

HERBERT HOOVER

Agreement on Hallowell

Hoover's letter of August 14 supplied the President with information on Hallowell that dissipated doubts concerning his suitability for the Food Administration. Principally, Hoover assured Wilson that he would no longer be associated with the law firm of Stone and Webster with whose labor policies both disagreed. Thus satisfied, the President (in a handwritten note) approved Hoover's appointment of Hallowell to the post of chief of States Administration Division; he remained in this position throughout the war. In November 1918 when Hoover sailed for Europe to establish a program for reconstruction of that ravaged continent, Hallowell was one of six men accompanying him.

15 August, 1917

My dear Mr. Hoover,

This is all right. I did not understand.

W. W.

Patriotism of Grain Men

The Food Control Act became law just five days before the "exhibit of patriotism" on the part of grain dealers and elevator men that evoked this letter. A copy of the resolution these men had passed was enclosed in Hoover's letter.

August 15, 1917.

Dear Mr. President:

I would like you, if you could take a moment, to consider what I think is the finest exhibit of patriotism shown by the commercial men in this country, that has been seen in Washington.

After launching our plan for total control of the wheat and rye business of the country, we invited between one-hundred and one-hundred and twenty of the principal dealers and elevator men in the country concerned in the grain business, to come to Washington to meet us, realizing that it was desirable that we should secure their cooperation and that the action we had taken meant a greater sacrifice to them than any other action which may be taken by the Government in trade matters, because it marks the elimination of some of them absolutely from business until after the war, and minimizes the business of all of them. The attached resolution should not only give you confidence in the soundness of the program, but also encouragement as to the willingness of our people to sacrifice.

Some fifteen of these gentlemen are coming on the Food Administration as volunteers to carry out the work of the Grain Division in the purchase and sale of grain, and these particular men have divested themselves of all interest in the grain trade, and are, at their express wish, serving the government for the period of the war without compensation.

I feel that if you could at some appropriate occasion give some expression of appreciation of the fine action of this whole trade, it would be a great stimulous [sic] to others in undertaking the lesser burdens which we are asking of them.

I beg to remain, Your obedient servant,

HERBERT HOOVER

[ENCLOSED RESOLUTION]

Realizing that the operation of Government control in wheats and rye is essential under present war influences in order to adequately protect our home supply and furnish our Allies with the aid we owe, and

realizing that the establishment of an efficient Government plan of operation means to all of us curtailment of our business and to some of
us actual retirement from active business during such period, we do express our pride in the character of service tendered by the grain trade
in the sacrifice by these men of ability who are placing their experience
and energy at the service of their Government, and that we approve the
general plan of operation as explained to us today as being sound, workable, and necessary, and in its general lines it appears to us as being the
most efficient and just plan of operation which we can conceive.

Committee of New England Hotel Men

The telegram mentioned in the following letter was a message of congratulations to be conveyed to Wilson for his success in getting Congress to pass the Food Control Act that endowed Hoover with power
to conserve food and coal.

August 15, 1917.
Dear Mr. President:—
Mr. Henry B. Endicott, the Food Commissioner in Massachusetts,
recently appointed a Committee of New England Hotel Representatives
to assist in handling food conservation problems.
This morning I received a wire dated yesterday at Worcester, Mass.,
a copy of which I enclose for your information. I have merely replied to
Messrs. Averill, Hurlburt and Davis that I have transmitted a copy of
their wire to you.
I remain, Your obedient servant,
HERBERT HOOVER

Advice on Certain Proposals

This short letter refers to some unspecified matter about which Wilson
solicited Hoover's judgment. It is not unlikely that "the proposals"
mentioned were the peace proposals made by Pope Benedict XV
around August 13. On August 16 Wilson had written Colonel House
that "I do not know that I shall make any reply at all to the Pope's
proposals." On August 17 he met in the late afternoon with seven
senators to discuss the matter, and at 6:00 he met with Hoover. Later
in the evening the Secretary of State called at the White House. It is

possible that Wilson brought up the question of the Pope's peace proposals with Hoover on this occasion. However, the meeting was in all probability not arranged for this purpose in view of the fact that Hoover had requested an appointment in a short note dated August 16, the day before Wilson had requested Hoover's advice on the unspecified "proposals." On August 27 the President responded to the Pope's proposals underscoring the impossibility of negotiating with the German government then in power.

At 11:45 on Saturday, August 18, Wilson walked over to Hoover's office for another conference. It is possible that on this occasion the President may have spoken of the Pope's peace "proposals," for the subject continued to be very much on his mind. On the same day Secretary of State Lansing telegraphed the American diplomatic representatives in Allied countries requesting a prompt response on the views of the governments to which they were accredited. (*Life and Letters,* vol. 7, pp. 217–26.)

17 August, 1917

My dear Mr. Hoover:

I would very much appreciate a suggestion from you as to the reply I should make to this letter and the attitude I should assume towards its proposals.

Cordially and faithfully yours,
WOODROW WILSON

School Courses on Food Use

August 21, 1917.

Dear Mr. President:

We are engaged in organizing a definite course of instruction in all of the schools, primary as well as secondary, on nutrition and food economics generally. We are having the fine co-operation of the Bureau of Education in the preparation and distribution of a series of minor textbooks on this subject. We have secured Dr. Judd, of Chicago University, to take charge of the actual work of preparation.

We feel that, by taking advantage of the war emotion, we here have an opportunity of introducing intelligibly into the minds of the children, not only fundamental data on nutrition, but also of being able to probably secure its permanent inclusion in school curricula, and, therefore, feel that it is a matter of more than ordinary propaganda importance.

After, however, preparing the material and securing, through the

Bureau of Education, its introduction, we still need some strong incentive for the public schools to adopt it, and it is the feeling of all our co-workers that if you could see your way to address a letter somewhat after the enclosed text to Professor Thach, which letter we would circulate to the whole of the public school system, it would have an enormous influence in securing the adoption of this instruction.

I hesitate greatly to trouble you over such matters, but I believe it is of such character that it warrants some attention in the midst of your great multitude of labor.

I remain, Your obedient servant,
HERBERT HOOVER

Approval of Food Administration Nominees

21 August, 1917

My dear Mr. Hoover:

I take real pleasure in approving the enclosed list of appointments.

Cordially and faithfully yours,
WOODROW WILSON

Trade Restraint and Food Administration Controls

In order to prevent the collapse of farm prices and the total depletion of the country's flour supply, Hoover permitted intratrade agreements whereby the millers fixed maximum prices, regulated individual outputs, and allocated sales. On August 23, the Attorney General ruled that such agreements did not violate the Sherman Anti-Trust Law. Wilson expressed his personal opinion in the following letter to Hoover, prior to the issuance of the official opinion of the Attorney General. Eight weeks later, as the letter for October 6 reveals, Hoover requested a copy of this latter opinion to parry the thrusts of several attacking congressmen. (See pp. 86–87.)

23 August, 1917.

My dear Mr. Hoover,

Personally I entirely approve of a "combination" such as the one here proposed, for it is *not* in restraint of trade.

I have taken pleasure in approving your request for an opinion from the Attorney General.

Faithfully Yours,
WOODROW WILSON

Reed's Anti-Hoover Activity

Miss Helen Todd, a New York social and political activist, met Hoover in mid-July 1917, and her ensuing interview with reporters resulted in an embarrassing newspaper story. She was recorded as having stated that ghetto women were losing faith in Hoover. One story ascribed to him certain sharp remarks about laggard congressmen. Although Miss Todd repudiated the stories, she could not repair the damage done. They were seized upon by Missouri's Senator James A. Reed, an implacable Hoover foe, and became grist for his propaganda mill, particularly for the letter mentioned below.

As early as May 21 Reed had spoken against Hoover's appointment as Food Administrator, and on May 23 had blamed him for rising wheat prices. On June 15 he attacked the Food Control Bill, which was intended to provide the legal basis for Hoover's food conservation programs. On July 10 he assailed Hoover as a food gambler for the benefit of the Belgians. Six days later, he offered a bill to replace the Food Administrator with a board of three. On August 6 and 13 he renewed his verbal assaults from his Senate sanctuary and then circulated throughout the country a letter that urged noncompliance with directives of the Food Administration.

The long-suffering Hoover at length expressed his anguish to President Wilson, who readily expressed his sympathetic understanding. The two men's letters are given here. The letter of Senator Reed is omitted. Hoover's letter also mentions Senator Asle J. Gronna, Republican of North Dakota, who was a member of the House Agriculture Committee. He had been one of the "little group of willful men" who in March filibustered against Wilson's plan to arm merchant ships. On April 4, he voted "no" on the declaration of war with Germany. During the ensuing conflict, he continued to be an obstructionist on many war measures, especially those providing for controls of wheat. (*Times*, Aug. 19, 1917, sec. 6, p. 3; Sept. 20, 1917, p. 24; Sept. 24, 1917, p. 13.)

The third man referred to by Hoover was Representative George Young, Republican of North Dakota, with whom he met on August 24.

In the evening of August 23 Hoover dined with the President. Miss Todd had seen Wilson at the White House on August 20. (*Life and Letters*, vol. 7, p. 226.) One might speculate on whether or not the Hoover-Wilson table talk reached the subject of this feminine activist, her supply of ammunition to Senator Reed, and the anxious letter she had caused the Food Administrator to write the day before.

August 23, 1917.
Dear Mr. President:
I attach herewith copy of a letter which has been circulated in large numbers, and certainly to the whole of the agricultural press of the country, by Senator Reed. I may also mention that Senator Gronna and Congressman Young have both been telegraphing to their constituents in North Dakota making misrepresentations as to the objectives of the Food Administration and encouraging farmers to withhold their wheat from sale, despite the fact that North Dakota is fully represented on the Fair Price Committee under Dr. Garfield.

This attempt to stir up the agricultural sections of the country against our efforts to secure an equitable position between the producer and consumer will, if it is successful, absolutely break down the whole question of food administration and thereby seriously imperil the whole problem of feeding the Allies and protecting our own people over the coming winter.

I beg to remain, Your obedient servant,
HERBERT HOOVER

Reaction to Reed's Activity

24 August, 1917
My dear Mr. Hoover:
Thank you for letting me see Senator Reed's letter. Of course, it is perfectly outrageous, but I think that Senator Reed and those who are like him have already tarred themselves so distinctly with the same brush that their influence will be negligible if they will only be kind enough to attach their names always to what they write.

Cordially and faithfully yours,
WOODROW WILSON

Thach of Alabama Polytechnic Institute

This letter refers to one written by Hoover on August 21. In it he had asked the President to write a letter to Professor Thach on the subject of introducing into the public schools courses on "nutrition and food economics generally."

August 24, 1917.

My dear Mr. Hoover:

Referring to your letter of August 21st, the President has written to President Thach of the Alabama Polytechnic Institute in accordance with your suggestion. I am sending you the letter herewith.

Sincerely yours,
J.P.T. [?]
Secretary to the President.

Military and Key Farm Men

> The problem treated here concerns the manpower shortage in agriculture, aggravated both by the draft and by the patriotic enlistment of key men. This problem had its counterpart in the Food Administration and plagued Hoover into the final days of the war.

August 27, 1917.

Dear Mr. President:

Delegations from several parts of the country have been to see me in connection with the exemption of a certain class of agriculturalists under the draft, and I have, in addition, had the advantage of a conference in Chicago with two hundred odd editors of agricultural publications from all over the country on this and other subjects.

It does appear to me that a serious situation is arising from the operation of the draft law against men who may be styled "key men" in agriculture, that is, men of the foreman, manager and ownership type, the draft of whom will certainly diminish the food production.

From all quarters I have found no disposition of a desire to diminish the quotas of the states in question, but a desire that some definite form of exemption should be initiated towards men of this character, and a larger proportion of the draft thrown upon the purely laboring and town classes.

A difficulty also lies in that a great many of the "key men" in question have too much patriotism to themselves make application for exemption.

I regard the matter as one of extreme importance to our whole food supply, and that these men should receive even greater consideration than "key men" in industrial establishments.

It does not appear that any action can be taken without inspiration from you, and I sincerely hope you may be able to give it consideration.

If it seems desirable to you that this class should be exempted, it would be very desirable to have, in addition to instructions to this effect, some expression from you that such men are as much in the service of the nation as men at the front, in order that the patriotic scruples of many should be overcome.

I beg to remain, Your obedient servant,

HERBERT HOOVER

Distilled Spirits and the Food Control Act

> In this message to the President, Hoover revealed a loophole in the Food Control Act that could have led to a circumvention of the ban on the use of food materials in the production of distilled spirits for beverage purposes. A handwritten note on the letter says, "Approved and to Food Ad. 8/28/17."

August 28, 1917.

Dear Mr. President:

In respect to the regulations sent you on August 25th for approval, the following is the situation:

Section 15 of the Food Control Act prohibits the use of food materials in the production of distilled spirits for beverage purposes after September 9, 1917, but provides that such materials may be used in the production of distilled spirits exclusively for other than beverage purposes, or for the fortification of pure sweet wines after that date "under such rules, regulations and bonds as the President may prescribe." The counsel of the Food Administration have conferred with the Acting Commissioner of Internal Revenue, and have formulated the rules and regulations enclosed, for your approval, with his assistance. The Commissioner has prepared additional regulations, administrative in nature, for the guidance of the Internal Revenue officers in enforcing the Act. The Act, however, only makes criminal the production of distilled spirits for beverage purposes, and without additional regulations it would be quite possible for distillers to manufacture spirits in good faith for non-beverage purposes, and yet have those spirits used by subsequent purchasers for the manufacture of beverages, without infringing the terms of the law. I have therefore considered it necessary to issue regulations which will first identify all spirits manufactured after September 9, 1917

(Regulations II and IV), second, forbid the use of any such spirits in the manufacturing or preparing [of] beverages, and, third, prohibit the sale of any such spirits for beverage purposes (Regulation V). Regulation III is designed to provide a complete record of sales, so that violations of the law may be traced. As it may be necessary in the future to institute criminal proceedings under the Act, I am advised that the regulations under the terms of Section 15, require your approval.

I remain, Your obedient servant,

HERBERT HOOVER

Enforcement of Distilled Spirits Ban

A major problem of the distilled spirits section of the Food Control Act concerned its enforcement. Hoover was opposed to having the Food Administration assume this task and suggested the Internal Revenue Department as a suitable agency. The executive order for this purpose was signed by Wilson on September 2, 1917, and sent to the State Department on September 4.

Hoover met the President at 11:30 and sometime during the day Wilson issued a public statement on the price of wheat. (*Life and Letters,* vol. 7, p. 244.) He also wrote a letter to the Secretary of the Treasury on the same subject, observing: "I have just this moment come from an interview with Mr. Hoover about it." (*Life and Letters,* vol. 7, p. 245.)

August 30, 1917.

Mr. President:

A question has arisen in regard to the enforcement of Section 15 of the Food Control Act, prohibiting the use of foods in the production of distilled spirits, and with regard to Section 17, authorizing and directing the President to commandeer such spirits.

The Law Department of the Food Administration, acting in conjunction with the Commissioner of Internal Revenue, has formulated rules and regulations governing the production of distilled spirits for non-beverage purposes, but it is now necessary for some agency of the Government to enforce the provisions of the section and prevent the use of spirits distilled after September 8, for beverage purposes. It is also necessary for some agency of the Government to commandeer distilled spirits for redistillation for the use of the Army and Navy, so far as required by the Act.

I respectfully suggest that the Internal Revenue Department has the skill and technical knowledge and practically all the machinery necessary for the effective enforcement of the Act, and that it would cause duplication of effort, waste of money, and unnecessary confusion and conflict of authority, if such enforcement were attempted by the Food Administration. The administration of the sentence in Section 15, prohibiting the importation of distilled spirits, has already been undertaken by the Division of Customs in the Treasury Department.

I enclose, herewith, a tentative draft of Executive Order, showing the authority and the method by which these duties might be assigned to the Internal Revenue Department.

Respectfully yours,
HERBERT HOOVER

Recommendations for Fat Shortages

August 31, 1917

Dear Mr. President:

As I stated yesterday, I am greatly disturbed with regard to our whole situation as to fats. They fall naturally into three groups, namely, pork products, dairy products, vegetable oils and substitute fat products.

PORK PRODUCTS

The price of hogs has increased from about $8.00 per 100 lbs., pre-war normal, to $20.00, of which $10.00 represents the increase since January 1st, and $5.00 since July 1st. The causes are complex: high feed, inflation, etc., but more particularly we are exporting more than we can afford.

While the animals on the farms increased considerably in 1916, they are still only about 3 % over 1912, despite our increase in human population. There has, however, been an increase in amimals [sic] slaughtered from about 33,000,000 on a pre-war average, to 46,500,000 during the year ending July 1st, 1917.

The average pre-war exports were about 950,000,000 lbs. of pork products, while during the year ending July 1st, 1917, they were nearly 1,500,000,000 lbs. If we take 1910 as 100, then the animals stand this year as 103, the number slaughtered 171 and exports at 215. These figures are not quite true proportions to the productivity of the country, owing to the short life of a hog, but they are, with the increase in price, significant enough.

I wish to present for your consideration, the following recommendations:

1. That we do not reduce exports to the Allies.
2. That we should reduce them to neutrals.
3. That we should reduce to all neutrals alike.
4. That we should, for the present, reduce them to the three-year pre-war average of their imports, or to the average of 1916–17, whichever is the least.
5. The Exports Administrative Board should undertake the limitation and should inaugurate the necessary machinery to carry it out.

DAIRY PRODUCTS

During the past fiscal year we exported over 25,000,000 lbs. of butter against a pre-war net normal of something under 2,000,000 lbs. The high price of feeding stuffs has probably reduced our output. In any event, we are in no position to export to any quarter, more than the pre-war net normals, for butter is not only rising rapidly in price, but there are localities of actual scarcity. Fortunately, the Allies have lately been drawing but little butter.

Therefore, my recommendation is that for the present we should stop all butter exports and we can relax later toward the Allies if their necessities compel it.

Our exports of cheese and condensed milk have greatly increased, but there are other factors involved which are not wholly clear and may be solved by the embargo of butter. In any event, I should like to reserve any recommendation for the present.

VEGETABLE AND SUBSTITUTE FATS

The export of various vegetable oils, tallow and soap, and other fat products, are much above normal to many neutral countries, although below normal to others, and prices are rising. At any rate, these substitutes would come rapidly into demand to replace any reduction of pork and dairy products.

I should like to recommend that we should limit exports to neutrals to pre-war normal or to the average of 1916–1917, whichever is the lesser.

If these recommendations, or part of them, meet with your approval, will you kindly indicate as much to the Exports Administrative Board.

I remain, Your obedient servant,

HERBERT HOOVER

Carter Harrison and the Brewing Trade

Dr. Harry Garfield, President of Williams College and a trained economist, was chairman of a special committee of twelve, established at
Hoover's suggestion to determine a fair price for wheat. The committee reached its decision late in the afternoon of August 30 after a trying
ten days of discussion. Hoover's letter below vaguely refers to this
period where he makes enquiries about the equanimity of Carter Harrison and his ability to survive similar travail as chairman of a brewery
committee. Harrison was a 48-year-old lawyer in the real estate business
who had formerly been publisher and editor of the *Chicago Times*.
For five terms, spanning the years 1897–1915, he was mayor of Chicago.
This exceeded the four terms of his father whose life came to an un-
timely end at the hands of an assassin. For these and other reasons,
Wilson may have concluded that Harrison was too controversial a
political figure for Hoover's assignment. (See September 4 letter.)

August 31, 1917.

Dear Mr. President:

Would you advise me whether you think Mr. Carter Harrison, of
Chicago, would be a man of balanced mind and equanimity to handle
such situations as Dr. Garfield has gone through with during the past
week?

I especially want to suggest to you a committee to consider the whole
question of conservation in connection with brewing, as to whether we
should interfere with tbe [sic] brewing trade in any fashion, and I want
some gentleman of prime importance and open fairness of mind to assist in assembling such a committee and to act under direction from
you, if it pleases you to inaugurate such a measure.

Yours faithfully,
HERBERT HOOVER

Auditing Methods for the Food Administration

Hoover had learned from his early Belgian relief experience the wisdom of providing for careful auditing of the books. On October 14,
1914, one of his CRB associates had warned that "some day some
swine may rise up and say we either made a profit out of this business
or that we stole the money." Hoover accordingly enlisted a respected
independent firm to audit the books of the CRB. This prudent plan
provided Hoover with a firm defense when in 1917 his enemies charged

him with graft with CRB funds. The following letter reveals that he
was equally prudent in organizing the Food Administration. (*Memoirs,*
vol. 1, pp. 157, 248, 271.)

August 31, 1917.

Dear Mr. President:

Mr. McAdoo has kindly furnished me a copy of the letter he addressed to you on the 30th instant, with regard to the question of accounting for the funds of the Food Administration Grain Corporation.

As Mr. McAdoo does not see his way for the Treasury to make an
audit, I am proposing to engage a firm of public accountants to make
a monthly audit of the accounts in the form which they have to be filed
with the Clerk of the House and Senate, by way of reinforcement of the
very great accounting precautions already being taken by Mr. McGarrah,
who is the treasurer of the corporation.

My one desire is to surround this operation with all of the safe-
guards of which we are capable.

I remain, Your obedient servant,
HERBERT HOOVER

Praise for Auditing Methods

1 September, 1917

My dear Mr. Hoover:

I am very much obliged to you for your letter of August thirty-first
about the methods you are adopting with regard to accounting for the
funds to be spent by the Food Administration Grain Corporation. I feel
confident that I can rely upon you to take measures which will satisfy
you to the severest critic.

Cordially and sincerely yours,
WOODROW WILSON

Harrison and the Brewing Board

4 September, 1917

My dear Mr. Hoover:

On the whole, I think that Mr. Carter Harrison of Chicago is rather
too much of a politician to be entrusted with such matters as you had in
mind when you wrote your letter of August thirty-first.

After you suggested a certain college president to me, I was thinking over the men available of that kind and two men occurred to me whom I think you would find satisfactory in every respect. One is President Meiklejohn of Amherst; the other, Professor Henry B. Fine of Princeton.

I wish I knew someone to suggest for the function you had in mind for Mr. Harrison. On the whole, I think for the present we had better leave the brewing trade alone until the situation develops more clearly.

Cordially and sincerely yours,

WOODROW WILSON

Stimulation of Hog Production

A major difficulty faced by Hoover in realizing an increase in hog production lay in the fact that market speculation in the spring of 1917 had carried the price of corn along with that of wheat to hitherto unknown levels, while the price of hogs lagged behind. It thus became more profitable for the farmers to sell their corn than to feed it to their pigs, and consequently the stock of hogs was being depleted. In this letter Hoover proposed to Wilson a solution to this problem and invited comments. (For more information on pork production during World War I see *Pork.*) Wilson replied on September 7. (See p. 80.)

September 4, 1917.

Dear Mr. President:

Aside from placing some restrictions upon the export of fats as a temporary measure of solution to our shortage, it appears to me that we should consider a definite plan of stimulating the production of hogs. The world's demands for fats will increase steadily during the war due to the degenerating animal situation among the Allies, and after peace the additional demands from the Central Powers will be enormous and long continued.

I have, therefore, devised the following tentative plan which I wish to submit for your consideration:

1. Hogs in the United States are, in the last analysis, a corn product. The cost of production and price are interdependent as shown by the inclosed chart. When other feeds are used, it is because they are cheaper than corn and the predominance of corn tends to control the use of all other feeds.

2. Owing to the violent fluctuations in demand for corn and hogs,

there have been five periods since the war began in which it was more profitable to sell corn than feed it to hogs at the price of hogs, and three periods the reverse. There were practically only two such periods of unprofitable feeding in the previous eight years. The results of these unprofitable periods is to retard hog production, as the grower is discouraged during these periods from breeding, and these fluctuations due to war conditions are, I believe, the fundamental reason why our hog production has not increased in volume such as one would expect from the general upward trend of prices which we have had over the entire war period.

3. On preliminary investigation, it appears that the corn price ratio to hog is, roughly, ten to eleven bushels of corn to one hundred pounds of hog, and that his menu is spread over a life of eight months in, roughly, the following ratio:

1st month,	1.5 per cent.		5th month,	9 per cent.	
2nd "	, 3 "	"	6th "	, 20 "	"
3rd "	, 4.5 "	"	7th "	, 27.4 "	"
4th "	, 6.5 "	"	8th "	, 28.1 "	"

4. It appears to me that, if we should take the weighted average price of corn over this period of eight months, we should arrive at a figure which, if hogs could be marketed, would be welcomed by the producer as an absolute assurance to his industry. If by setting up some instrumentality, we should on the first of each month make this determination and fix this price for the succeeding month as the price to be paid by the packers, we should not only assure the producer from the day he bred hogs, but also assure him freedom from speculation in the stock yards at day of arrival.

5. The violent fluctuations in the price of hogs tends to lift the price of hog products to the consumer unduly, for at every rise the stocks in warehouses in the whole country are marked up, and thus the margin between producer and consumer increased. With a stabilization in price, this must tend to disappear and could effectually be made to do so if arrangements were entered into between the Food Administration and the packers for the fixing of a differential between hogs and their products. We have, or are in the course of carrying out, such an arrangement with the millers and sugar manufacturers, and, although complicated and filled with difficulties, is not, I believe, impossible with the packers, more especially as they are disposed to show the utmost good will in carrying out any programme of national interest.

6. The weakness in this chain lies in that some one [*sic*] must assure the packer a market for the products at the agreed ratio to the price he buys hogs. This, I believe, could be solved by a contract with the Allies to take the whole production in excess of domestic demands at the price above arrived at, such contract to be terminable upon, say, six months' notice on either side. This would give the producer notice of the break in the assurance.

7. There are thus three parties to be organized and consulted:

> (a) The producers.
> (b) The packers.
> (c) The Allied Governments.

Before, however, I open negotiations as to the acceptance of the principle with these elements, I wish to secure your approval. If the principle is agreed, it will be necessary to assemble a commission to determine the statistical basis upon which the plan is founded, and to set up a commission which will have the judicial function of determining the price each month, based upon such statistical determination. Also, some system of classification of hogs at the yards will need [to] be arrived at and a basis for determining the packers' ratio.

Would you be so kind as to express your views as to whether I should open the subject for discussion and determine the feeling of the three parties towards it?

I remain, Your obedient servant,
HERBERT HOOVER

Draft of a Proclamation

> The proclamation suggested in this letter was signed by the President on September 7 and sent to the State Department.

September 6, 1917.

Mr. President:

I hand you herewith draft of a Proclamation which applies the license provisions of the Food Control Act of August 10, 1917, to the importation, manufacture, and refining of sugar and the manufacture of sugar syrups and molasses.

I respectfully request that you make this Proclamation, and direct
the Department of State to attach the seal thereto.

Faithfully yours,
HERBERT HOOVER

Suggestion for Meeting Houston

> Hoover's letter of September 4 impressed Wilson and he suggested a
> meeting with Secretary of Agriculture David F. Houston. At 4:45 on
> that day H. A. Garfield came to Hoover's office and the two went to
> see Wilson. On September 9 at 1:45 Hoover met with Houston as the
> President had suggested in this letter of September 7.

7 September, 1917

My dear Mr. Hoover:

I have been very much interested in your letter of September fourth
about the hog supply in the United States. I was discussing the matter
this afternoon with the Secretary of Agriculture, since it so directly
affects the matter of production, and found his observations and suggestions so interesting that I am going to take the liberty of asking you if
you will not avail yourself of an early opportunity to see him and match
your views with his in this important matter.

Sincerely yours,
WOODROW WILSON

Wheat Price Demands

> Since Wilson was vacationing in New England, Hoover wrote to
> Joseph Tumulty, informing him of a telegram sent by Theodore B.
> Wilcox of Portland, Oregon. This protester asserted that farmers in
> the northwestern states would continue to hoard their wheat and
> would sell nothing to mills until the price of wheat, fixed by a com-
> mission according to law, was revised upward. Hoover asked that the
> President issue a statement affirming that no such action would be
> taken. He also requested a meeting with Wilson.
>
> The President returned to Washington Sunday evening September
> 16, and on Monday at 5:00 he met with Hoover. Perhaps the whole
> matter was then discussed. In any event, Wilson wrote a note to his
> secretary on September 17 asking him to get suggestions from Hoover
> on the kind of statement he wanted as a pacifier for the disgruntled

farmers and their congressmen. The note read: "Please find out from Mr. Hoover what form he thinks my statement which he suggests ought to take." The Food Administrator answered Wilson in a letter to Tumulty on September 18.

September 12, 1917.

Dear Mr. Tumulty:

Please find enclosed herewith a telegram from one of our people, which explains itself.

Various Northwestern Congressmen have called upon me and I explained to them that the prices laid down by the Committee could not be altered, but apparently the farmers have been advised that the matter is still under consideration. It is therefore most desirable that the President should send out some word, settling this one way, or another.

A further situation arises because of mass meetings being held by the North Dakota farmers,—apparently with a good deal of anti-war sentiment,—demanding that they shall have a higher price for their wheat, and something of the same kind is being done in Oklahoma. The net result of these activities is that the farmers over the country are getting the idea that if they hold out long enough they can get more money, and the arrivals of wheat in the market are very low.

The whole question is whether or not the consumer is to pay another $5.00 or $6.00 per barrel for flour in order to please a lot of malcontents, and if they are to pay this higher price, the problem will arise at once whether we can maintain tranquillity in the large industrial centers during the winter.

Even with the reduction effected by the Food Administration plan, the price of flour is 125 percent over normal. The Commission that fixed the prices, as you know, was in itself a majority of the farmers.

Under the circumstances, it seems to me that it is necessary for the President to send some word to the Oregon and Washington delegates that no change will be made, and after the President returns, I need badly to have a discussion over the entire situation.

Yours faithfully,

HERBERT HOOVER

Advice on Answering Bilbo

No indication is supplied in this short note from Tumulty as to the nature of the suggestions of Theodore Bilbo, governor of Mississippi, nor as to the person who rejected them. However, it would seem that both Wilson and Hoover were recipients of a Bilbo telegram, that Hoover replied the suggestions were unacceptable, and that Wilson agreed with this decision but wanted to solicit Hoover's reasons before answering Bilbo.

September, 17, 1917.

My dear Mr. Hoover:

Referring to the enclosed telegram from Governor Bilbo, the President has no doubt there were the best possible reasons for not accepting Governor Bilbo's suggestions, but he would be very much obliged if you would give him a tip as to how to reply to this message.

Sincerely yours,
J. P. Tumulty
Secretary to the President.

Answer to Wheat Protesters

The "memorandum" mentioned in this letter is not now in the Hoover or the Wilson Papers. In the afternoon of September 18, Hoover met with the President; it is possible he then spoke to him about the message contained in this "memorandum."

September 18, 1917.

Dear Mr. Tumulty:

With regard to your note of the 17th on the subject of the Pacific Northwestern protest as to the differentials affecting the Government purchase of the Northwestern wheat, I inclose a memorandum which I sent on the 8th to several of the senators and congressmen of the Northwest and which seems to me to cover the situation. I understand they are coming to see the President, and this will inform you of the matter as far as we are concerned.

I would add that the average yield in the Pacific Northwest was some twenty-four bushels to the acre as against only fourteen or fifteen bushels in the Mississippi Valley points, so it is quite evident that the farmers in the Pacific Northwest will make more money than those in the Mississippi Valley, even with a freight differential against them.

Yours faithfully,
HERBERT HOOVER

Money for Food Administration Building

In this letter to Woodrow Wilson, Hoover asks the President to allot
$400,000 for the erection of a temporary structure to house the offices
of the Food and Fuel Administration. The new wooden structure, built
in ninety days, stood near the Potomac River in a swampy area called
Foggy Bottom. It was one of several "temporaries" whose expected life
span was three or four years, while actually it continued to serve various government purposes for thirty-four years until it was pulled down.
Hoover wrote in 1951 that it was "abominably cold in winter and hot
in summer. But enthusiasm is little dulled by temperature." (*Memoirs*, vol. 1, p. 254.) In 1953 Lewis L. Strauss, Hoover's former secretary, sent his former chief a memento of this period of enthusiasm.
Salvaging a large ornamental plaster seal of the Food Administration
that had adorned the entrance to the building, he donated it to the
Hoover museum in Palo Alto, California. (Strauss, *Men*, p. 8–9.)
Hence it was transferred to the Hoover Presidential Library at West
Branch, Iowa, where it is now on display.

September 18, 1917.

My dear Mr. President:

In respect to our discussions as to office accomodation [*sic*], we beg
to set out formally the situation. The rapid expansion of the work of
the Food Administration and the more recent but equally urgent growth
of the Fuel Administration, the need for greater office space and more
efficient interlocation of the various departments, has become imperative.

We have, so far, been able to manage in temporarily leased quarters
scattered in a number of buildings, but with resulting loss of efficiency
and increase of expense. We see no way, however, in which the growing
needs of these two Administrations can continue to be met in this manner, and a proper regard for the effective carrying out of the work pre-
scribed for these Administrations by Congress would indicate the necessity of erecting suitable quarters in which all of the branches of the work
can be brought into efficient inter-relation.

A strictly temporary structure would be quite sufficient to meet the
requirements, as both the Food and Fuel Administrations are authorized
only for the period of the war.

Inasmuch as the appropriation made available by Congress for the
Food and Fuel Administrations contains no provisions which would permit of any portion of it being used for buildings purposes, we beg to

confirm our request for the allotment of $400,000.00 from the fund placed at your disposal under the Deficiency Act of April, 1917 for National Security and Defense, to be expended for the construction of a temporary building or buildings for the use of the Food and Fuel Administrations; this amount to be credited on the books of the Treasury Department under the title of appropriation "National Security and Defense, Food [and Fuel][1] Administration, Building."

Yours faithfully,

H. A. GARFIELD   HERBERT HOOVER

Approved and authorized

WOODROW WILSON [handwritten by Wilson]

21 September, 1917.

_____

1. Handwritten insertion.

Stearns's Appointment to the Food Administration

The appointment of Thomas Stearns of Colorado as coal and food administrator for that state caused Wilson some disquietude because of the opposition it provoked. In this letter he asks Hoover to inquire into the nature of this opposition. The concluding sentence in Wilson's letter clearly suggests that the item "enclosed" was a letter protesting Stearns's appointment and giving some adverse information about him.

18 September 1917

My dear Mr. Hoover:

I do not know anything about the appointment referred to in the enclosed letter except that I take it for granted that Mr. Stearn's [sic] name was one of those which you submitted to me on a list. Perhaps Vance McCormick was not fully informed in advising you about that particular appointment, but I suppose that water has passed over the wheel, and I would like a tip from you as to what you know about Mr. Stearns, that I may reply to the enclosed.

Faithfully yours,

WOODROW WILSON

Protests against Stearns

20 September 1917.

My dear Mr. Hoover:

The protests against the appointment of Mr. Stearns of Colorado as coal and food administrator for the State seem to me to have a great

deal of substance. If it is not too late to reconsider the matter, I am sure
that you will wish to take it up afresh.

Cordially and sincerely yours,

WOODROW WILSON

Approval of Sugar Controls

> The regulations submitted in the following letter were approved by
> the President on September 26.

September 22, 1917.

Mr. President:

I submit herewith for your approval certain regulations which I
have approved governing the conduct of the producers of beet sugar,
issued under the authority of your proclamation of September 7th.

As it may become necessary to prosecute criminally violations of
these regulations, I am advised that under the terms of the Act they
should be approved by you.

Faithfully yours,

HERBERT HOOVER

Defense of Stearns's Appointment

> Hoover inquired more deeply into the appointment of Thomas Stearns,
> as Wilson had requested in his letters of September 18 and 20, and then
> wrote the following letter to the President. In answer, Wilson himself
> or a secretary typed a brief note which said, "I think there is nothing
> else to do but let this stand as is." The message was telephoned to
> Hoover on September 26.

September 25, 1917.

Dear Mr. President:

With regard to the appointment of Mr. Thos. B. Stearns as Federal
Food Administrator for Colorado, I am, of course, entirely willing to
withdraw his name. I would be glad, however, if you could take a
moment to consider that Mr. Stearns was chosen for us and recommended by—

> The Democratic Governor, Julius C. Gunter
> The Democratic Mayor of Denver, R. W. Steer
> The State Council of Defense

I enclose copies of telegrams of September 22nd from the Governor and the Mayor of Denver on the subject, and also copy of a very manly letter from Mr. Stearns himself.

We were not aware of Mr. Stearns' politics until the protest of *The Denver Post* was received, but it does appear unique that he should be so strongly approved by responsible men of both parties.

We are totally at loss to substitute anyone for Mr. Stearns without getting into worse party conflicts which seem pretty acute in that region.

Faithfully yours,

HERBERT HOOVER

Sugar Rules and Regulations

October 1, 1917.

Mr. President:

I submit herewith, for your approval, additional rules and regulations governing licensees for the importation, manufacture and refining of sugar, sugar syrups and molasses. These rules supplement those recently submitted to you, and deal especially with the refining of cane sugar. The original copy as approved should be returned to my office to be filed. ["Orig retd 9–2–17" handwritten on letter.]

Faithfully yours,

HERBERT HOOVER

Food Administration Contracts and the Sherman Act

The Sherman Anti-Trust Act of 1890 forbade all monopolies and all contracts that would restrain trade in the stream of interstate commerce. The following letter deals with this law insofar as it concerned certain activities of the Food Administration. President Wilson responded by asking Tumulty to look up the Attorney General's opinion for use as Hoover thought fit.

Also on Saturday, October 6, Hoover made a request to see Wilson on Monday. Sometime that day Hoover jotted on the memorandum, "To-day—8th—at 5:00 W.W." The meeting took place as scheduled and may well have been the occasion for a discussion of the Attorney General's opinion on the Sherman Act and of the questions then being raised by some congressmen relative to certain contracts of the Food Administration.

October 6, 1917.

Dear Mr. President:

On the 23rd of August, the Attorney General addressed you a written opinion advising that certain contracts which we were making with various trades were not in violation of the Sherman Act.

Some questions have been raised in Congress, and we are desirous of furnishing to Congress, if occasion arises, a copy of the Attorney General's opinion. The Attorney General informs us today that he has no objection to our doing this, but as the opinion was addressed to you, he thinks it would be desirable that we should secure your concurrence before doing so. I should be glad to know if it meets with your approval.

I am, Your obedient servant,

HERBERT HOOVER

Permission to Use Opinion

This short note was dictated by Wilson to Charles L. Swem, his confidential stenographer, in response to Hoover's letter of October 6. It carries no date.

Dear Tumulty:

Please have this opinion looked up and, if you see no objection, tell Mr. Hoover that I am quite willing he should use it.

The President.

C.L.S.

Deferring Food Conservation Pledge Week

The four letters that follow concern Hoover's plan for a Food Conservation Pledge Week which Wilson asked him to defer because of a possible conflict with the Liberty Loan Campaign. Upon receipt of the President's request, Hoover went to the White House to discuss the matter. He, of course, acquiesced in the President's wishes but not without a pinch of chagrin as evidenced in his letter of October 10 to Tumulty.

After the Tuesday, October 9, meeting with Wilson, Hoover composed a "Dear Mr. Hoover" letter for the President who then sent it back to Hoover. It was calculated to soften the blow for Hoover's staff and workers. The first draft of this letter was included with one to Tumulty in which Hoover asked the secretary to take it to Wilson immediately. The President signed and returned the "Dear Mr. Hoover" letter, whereupon on October 11 Hoover answered his own letter, writing, "I am obliged for your favor of October 10th."

October Ninth 1917

Dear Mr. Hoover:

I think it is so exceedingly important that nothing should check or interfere with or divert the attention of the country from the Liberty Loan Campaign that I am going to take the liberty of asking you if you cannot defer your special Food Campaign until the week following, the twenty-seventh of October.

I hope that it would not cause any considerable confusion or embarrassment in your plans to do this. You may be sure I would not suggest it if I did not think it of capital importance.

Cordially and sincerely yours,
WOODROW WILSON

Chagrin over Deferral

October Tenth 1917

Dear Mr. Tumulty:

I had a discussion with the President yesterday about delaying our Food Pledge Campaign, and he offered to write me a letter which we can transmit to our some three-hundred thousand volunteers that we have worked on this job.

The deferring of this campaign not only means a good deal of loss of expense, but is likely to break the campaign down unless we can have a strong helpful letter from the President.

As Mr. McAdoo is very anxious to get this matter cleared up at an early moment, I want to ask you to bring it to the President's attention and ask him if he would be so kind as to sign this letter sometime today and make the alterations in it that he thinks desirable.

We have worked for two and a half months to prepare this great orgy in food conservation, and it hits us pretty hard. We set our dates on the early assurances of the Treasury that they would not come on with the new loan until November. We do not complain, but I want to be able to try to hold this organization together if I can.

Yours faithfully,
HERBERT HOOVER

Second Deferral Request

This is the "Dear Mr. Hoover" letter which Hoover wrote himself and asked the President to sign and send back to him on the subject of the deferred pledge week. It had much praise for the Food Administration staff and workers and thus was better calculated than was Wilson's own letter of October 9 to soften the blow of having to postpone their long-planned week.

10 October, 1917.

My dear Mr. Hoover:

The exigencies of the Treasury have required setting the final week of the Liberty Loan Campaign during the period of October 21st to October 28th. This, I understand, brings it into the same week as the Food Conservation Pledge Campaign. It seems to me undesirable in the interest of both these capital matters that this should occur. In all the circumstances, therefore, I would be glad if the Pledge Campaign could be deferred one week, that is, until October 28th to November 4th.

In asking this alteration of the plans of yourself and your associates, I should like to take this occasion to impress upon them that I in no way underrate the importance of their effort. If we are to supply our Allies with the necessary food, and are to reduce our own prices of food-stuffs during the coming winter, it can only be accomplished by the utmost self-denial and service on the part of all our people through the elimination of waste and by rigid economy in the use of food.

Therefore, I would be glad if you would convey to all of your staff throughout the country my feeling of the prime importance of their plans and their work. I wish particularly to express my great appreciation of the service which this additional tax on their time will impose upon the many thousand volunteers who have already deferred their own concerns to public interest in this important work. I ask them not to allow this alteration in programme to dampen their fine enthusiasm, but, rather, to redouble their energies in their very great branch of national service.

Cordially and sincerely yours,
WOODROW WILSON

Agreeing to the Deferral

October Eleventh 1917

Dear Mr. President:

I am obliged for your favor of October 10th.

We, of course, have taken the necessary steps to comply with your wish as to deferring the final week of our Food Conservation Pledge Campaign until the week of October 28th to November 4th. You will, of course, realize that we may be unable to reach some of the more remote districts.

I have no doubt that the five hundred thousand workers who have enlisted to this service will loyally respond to your request for a greater and longer continued exertion. Your emphasis on the national importance of the Conservation Campaign should stimulate our large body of devoted workers to the utmost effort during the new week.

I am, Your obedient servant,
HERBERT HOOVER

White and the War Trade Board

The President immediately gave his approval of Hoover's nomination of Beaver White as a member of the War Trade Board.

October 12, 1917.
My dear Mr. President:

Referring to the Executive Order of the President establishing a War Trade Board, to be composed of Representatives, respectively, of the Secretary of State, of the Secretary of the Treasury, of the Secretary of Agriculture, of the Secretary of Commerce, of the Food Administrator, and of the United States Shipping Board, I hereby nominate Mr. Beaver White, and, subject to his appointment by the President, designate him as a member of the War Trade Board, to be the Representative of the Food Administrator on said Board.

Faithfully yours,
HERBERT HOOVER

Thanksgiving Proclamation

The President made no response to this letter, so Hoover prodded him once again on October 25. The sequel to this second prodding raises some unanswered questions that are discussed later with the treatment of the October 25 memorandum.

October Thirteenth 1917

Dear Mr. Tumulty:

I would be glad if you could let me know about what time the President will be formulating his Thanksgiving Proclamation. This year, I would like to suggest to him that it should be formulated on the lines of the world's necessity for food, our abundance, and our obligations in this matter, and if you will give me due warning, I shall try to take the matter up with him.

Yours faithfully,

HERBERT HOOVER

Suggested Food Administration Nominees

Since Wilson was always careful to exclude controversial political figures from Food Administration posts, Hoover assured him that Arthur Williams, about whom there was some concern, had not been a participant in the campaign to elect the mayor of New York City. This assurance was particularly necessary to qualify Williams for the post because the Tammany congressional delegation had threatened to oppose the war program unless Wilson maintained a neutral attitude in the mayoralty race. Accordingly, federal office holders in the metropolitan area were enjoined from openly supporting any of the candidates. The incumbent, John Purroy Mitchel, technically a Democrat but supported by such Republican stalwarts as Roosevelt, Root, and Hughes, was defeated by the Tammany candidate. (*Politics,* p. 106.) Wilson had reason to fear a Tammany man in the mayor's seat, and he had been urged to give Mitchel his public support. But on October 29 he declined to do so, writing that he had "lost confidence in Mayor Mitchel of late," so that "it is a Hobson's choice." (*Life and Letters,* vol. 7, pp. 333–34.) On October 23, the day after writing this letter, Hoover met with Wilson at 5:15. He had actually requested a meeting for October 22, but the President had replied that it was "literally impossible today, but I can see him at 5:15 tomorrow, the 23rd."

October 22, 1917.

Dear Mr. President:

Please find enclosed suggestions for Federal Food Administrators for the District of Columbia, Hawaiian Island, New York State and New York City.

I understand that Mr. McCormick has already spoken to you regarding Messrs. Cooke and Williams and that the point was raised that possibly Mr. Williams was participating in the New York City Mayoralty Campaign. I find that Mr. Williams has never taken an active part in politics and has had no connection whatever with the present Mayoralty Campaign in New York.

Trusting that the above suggestions for Administrators will meet with your approval, I beg to remain

Your obedient servant,
HERBERT HOOVER

Approved
WOODROW WILSON [handwritten by Wilson]

King Albert and Whitlock

> Hoover had been on close terms with the Belgian King Albert during 1914–17 while engaged in Belgium on relief work. In his *Memoirs* (vol. 1, p. 186) Hoover recalls that the king confided to him that "the happiest period of his life" was when as heir apparent he visited America to learn about the railroad business and worked as a fireman in Montana on Hill's Great Northern. Brand Whitlock was the American ambassador to Belgium, also known by Hoover from the 1914–17 period, who was in Le Havre in October 1917 attached to the Belgian government in exile. The cablegrams mentioned below were answers to an anxious message sent by King Albert to Wilson on October 18. He sketched a pitiful picture of suffering Belgium and implied that America was not doing its utmost to bring relief. "The President was somewhat nettled," Hoover observed, when he asked the Food Administrator to draft a reply. Wilson accepted Hoover's composition but put into it "more emphatic expression" before dispatching it as his answer to King Albert. Hoover also composed a cablegram for Secretary of State Lansing, intended to be sent to Whitlock, explaining the herculean efforts of America on Belgium's behalf. (*Epic,* vol. 1, pp. 340–43.)

October Twenty-Fourth 1917

Dear Mr. President:

I send herewith draft of a cablegram to King Albert, in reply to his cablegram of October 18th, the original of which I am returning, and, also, a draft of a proposed cablegram to be sent Mr. [Brand][1] Whitlock through the State Department.

I am, Your obedient servant,
HERBERT HOOVER

---

1. Handwritten insertion.

Louisiana Sugar Producer

The Food Administration was constantly harassed by contentious producers of sugar. The Louisiana producer mentioned in this letter is
not further identified in any of Hoover's correspondence, thus one
might reasonably conclude that he did keep "the bargain." But such
cooperation was not always forthcoming as letters for March 1 and 5,
1918, clearly demonstrate.

October 25, 1917.

My dear Tumulty:

Sometime during a breathing spell, if you have them now-a-days,
will you inform the President that after a prolonged struggle we settled
with the Lousiana [*sic*] sugar producer—provided he keeps the bargain.

Yours faithfully,

HERBERT HOOVER

Thanksgiving Proclamation Reminder

On October 13 Hoover wrote to Tumulty asking him about the annual
message the President issued prior to Thanksgiving and suggesting
that it mention "the world's necessity for food." On October 25, he
reminded Wilson again through a memorandum to Tumulty on which
the President wrote: "Please ask Mr. H. for his suggestions. W.W."
Hoover obliged immediately by sending the two-paragraph message that
follows the memorandum. Wilson changed one word with his own
pen and signed the Hoover proclamation. A copy in the Library of
Congress notes that the original was signed and returned to Hoover
on October 26. If this is true then it is difficult to explain Hoover's
letter bearing the October 27 date. It seems far more likely that
Hoover included his suggested proclamation in this letter and that
Wilson signed and returned it the same day, that is, on October 27.
(The original copy has an October 27, 1917, date written in by hand.)

But for some reason or other Wilson changed his mind, for when
his proclamation was issued on November 8, it was quite different from
the one prepared by Hoover, although there was a brief reference to
humanitarianism and America's "abundance" as suggested by Hoover.
(*Times,* Nov. 8, 1917, p. 3.)

October 25, 1917.

Memorandum for the President:

The last Thursday in November falls on November 29th, and this is to remind the President that it has been customary to issue the Thanksgiving Proclamation about a month in advance of the day set aside.

The President will recall that Mr. Herbert Hoover would like to have an opportunity to make some suggestions to the President as to the form the proclamation might take.

[unsigned]

Humanitarianism in Message

October Twenty-Seventh 1917

Dear Mr. President:

With regard to the Thanksgiving Proclamation, I have the idea that it would be of great purpose if the tone of the proclamation could be directed towards the saving of our food and other supplies in provision for the many millions of people who are dependent upon us now more than ever before in our history; that, perhaps, it might be placed on a basis of humanity rather than for miltary [sic] necessity.

I have the feeling that in our particular organization, we harp too much on the military and war ends to be gained, and too little upon the humanitarian phases of supporting millions of people who are now isolated from their normal supplies and the burden of which we must have carried whether we had entered the war or not.

I am Your obedient servant,
HERBERT HOOVER

Hoover's Proclamation

This draft of a Thanksgiving Day proclamation to be used by the President was apparently prepared by Hoover sometime around October 27. Wilson signed it, but as mentioned above, did not use it for his Thanksgiving message.

October 27[?], 1917

The chief part of the burden of finding food supplies for the peoples associated with us in war falls for the present upon the American people, and the drain upon supplies on such a scale necessarily affects the prices of our necessaries of life.

Our country, however, is blessed with an abundance of foodstuffs, and if our people will economize in their use of food, providently confining themselves to the quantities required for the maintenance of health and strength; if they will eliminate waste; and if they will make use of those commodities of which we have a surplus and thus free for export a larger proportion of those required by the world now dependent upon us, we shall not only be able to accomplish our obligations to them, but we shall obtain and establish reasonable prices at home. To provide an adequate supply of food both for our own soldiers on the other side of the seas and for the civil populations and the armies of the Allies is one of our first and foremost obligations; for if we are to maintain their constancy in this struggle for the independence of all nations, we must |also| [first][1] maintain their health and strength. The solution of our food problems, therefore, is dependent upon the individual service of every man, woman and child in the United States. The great voluntary effort in this direction which has been initiated and organized by the Food Administration under my direction offers an opportunity of service in the war which is open to every individual, and by which every individual may serve both his own people and the peoples of the world.

We cannot accomplish our objects in this great war without sacrifice and devotion, and in no direction can that sacrifice and devotion be shown more than by each home and public eating place in the country pledging its support to the Food Administration and complying with its requests.

WOODROW WILSON

---

1. Word between | | deleted by hand, followed by handwritten insertion in [ ].

Food Rules and Regulations

October Thirty-First 1917

Dear Mr. President:

I enclose herewith for your approval rules and regulations governing the importation, manufacture, storage and distribution for domestic trade of food commodities by persons subject to license under your proclamations of August 14, September 7, and October 8, 1917. These regulations have been prepared under my direction. They consist of general regulations relating to all licensees and a series of special regulations dealing with the different industries. It will be necessary to supplement the regulations from time to time to meet conditions which may arise.

They have been evolved after a great amount of study, consultation with trade representatives, and some scores of conferences with representatives of trade bodies.

If they meet with your approval, will you please sign the original on the last page and return them to this office?

I am, Your obedient servant,
HERBERT HOOVER

Approval of Food Regulations

1 November, 1917

My dear Mr. Hoover:

I cheerfully accept your judgment in the matter of the rules and regulations which you submit to me concerning the importation, manufacture, storage and distribution of food commodities for domestic trade by persons subject to license, and take pleasure in returning the same with my signature.

Cordially and sincerely yours,
WOODROW WILSON

The Food Administration and the Civil Service

In this letter Hoover explains how seriously the Food Administration would be handicapped if it were forced to operate under the strictures of Civil Service regulations. The President apparently was convinced, for on November 7 he had Joseph Tumulty ask Hoover to prepare a draft of an appropriate executive order on Civil Service exemption. Hoover complied on November 12; Wilson signed the order the same day and had it forwarded to the State Department. On November 13 Hoover sent a letter to Tumulty thanking him for information about this action. The following letter of November 5 was also signed by Harry A. Garfield, the United States Fuel Administrator.

November Fifth, 1917

Dear Mr. President:

We are encountering great difficulty in operating under the Civil Service regulations. Our associates are men accustomed to control large industries and they feel that in the interest of economy and efficiency, the present handicap which we as an emergency organization are under should be removed. Our position is vastly different from that of the the older and permanent Departments of the Government, as we cannot well secure the ordinary type of Government employee; because of the temporary nature of our work we cannot offer the inducement of permanent employment, and especially because of the necessity of selecting for most positions men whose ability is personally known to us.

The enclosed brief, intended only for our own information, has been prepared by our Appointment Division and seems to be conclusive in its findings. I am wondering whether it will be possible for you to alleviate this condition by absolving us from the obligation to secure our force through Civil Service. It is quite evident that the whole of our organization will be disrupted if we strictly conform to all of the Civil Service rules. We have a great appreciation for the officials in the Civil Service Commission, who have given our requests uniform, courteous and careful attention, but have been helpless to remedy the unfortunate conditions governing our work.

Faithfully yours,

H. A. GARFIELD   HERBERT HOOVER

Food Savings by Bakers

The proclamation mentioned here as formulated by Hoover was signed by President Wilson and sent to the State Department on November 7. For the ordinary person these legalities were translated into such strictures as "Victory Bread," which contained less wheat than ordinary white bread. If they ate out, people found that the proclamation meant no bread until after the first course.

Eventually a large number of "less" days were proclaimed in the name of conservation—breadless, gasless, meatless, etc. Secretary of the Interior Franklin K. Lane, who apparently had a sweet tooth, wrote on March 7, 1918: "Hoover can only commit one fatal mistake—to declare a taffyless day." (*Letters of Lane*, p. 272.)

November sixth, 1917

Dear Mr. President:

We desire to put the bakers of the country under license with a view to effecting a number of savings, particularly by giving them certain maximums for ingredients whereby we should be able to save something like 100,000,000 pounds of sugar, 60,000,000 pounds of lard and a great deal of milk. In addition thereto, we wish to standardize the bread as to weight in order that we may focus competition on the question of price instead of allowing it to have four or five variables as at present, owing to the thirty-seven different sizes of bread baked in the United States. We also wish to eliminate certain trade wastes which we compute will make a saving of something like 6,000 or 7,000 barrels of flour per annum.

The whole of the regulations which I will forward to you in a few days have been worked out to a large degree with the bakers themselves with the co-operation of the Federal Trade Commission and the Agricultural Department.

I send you herewith the proclamation for your signature if you approve of this course.

I am, Your obedient servant,
HERBERT HOOVER

Arsenic Proclamation

> The proclamation referred to here was signed and sent to the State Department on November 15.

November Twelfth 1917

Dear Mr. President:

I inclose a proclamation licensing the arsenic industry. There are only a dozen people to be licensed, and therefore it needs no publicity.

The situation is that there is so large a demand for our domestic production in the glass and other trades that we are unable to supply the amounts needed for insecticides, and unless the matter is taken in hand, we shall lose a large amount of foodstuffs next year.

We propose to use the licensing power to restrict the use of arsenic to this critical purpose so far as may be necessary.

I am, Your obedient servant,
HERBERT HOOVER

Data on the Crop Situation

> Sometime after their 3:30 meeting on November 15, Hoover sent Wilson the data on crops about which they had spoken.

Fifteenth November 1917

Dear Mr. President:

In the matter of my conversation today it may be of use to you to have the data itself. As you are aware, our harvest has not been up to hopes and our statistical position without regard to savings by conservation is as follows:

Harvest of 1917, plus
carry-over on July 1, 1917 . . . . 704,797,000 bushels

Average yearly domestic consumption
for the past three years 615,189,397   "

Additional seed requirements
this year 10,190,288   "

Essential carry-over 50,000,000   "

Total exports since July 1, 1917 33,790,055   709,169,740   "

Deficiency, November 1st 4,372,740   "

Against this purely statistical position we have to consider the better grade of the wheat this year and the savings by conservation.

The practical famine in corn during the last three months and consequent higher cost of corn meal than of flour has greatly interfered with conservation. At the utmost we can count on a saving of only 15% of the wheat, especially in view of the high wage level of the country, and this only with forced measures in mixing meal with the flour. Even so it would increase our exportable supplies by about 100,000,000 bushels of wheat. This however is a speculation on conservation measures and prudence demands we should only allow export month by month as we may be able to gauge conservation.

The Allies require a minimum of 350,000,000 bushels during the next eight months under the most drastic of rationing and substitution of other cereals, or an average of about 45,000,000 bushels per month. A large part of this must come from the Argentine and will not be available in Europe until the end of January. The Canadian surplus yet available is about 100,000,000 bushels, or, about a two-months' supply. The Canadian surplus is not available at the rate of 45,000,000 bushels— for reasons of internal collection and transportation. The Allies must be fed pending the availability of Argentine wheat and it appears that we must supply 75,000,000 bushels to attain this end, some of which we might or might not recover from Canada. This is simply a gamble on conservation. We must also furnish some wheat or flour to adjacent countries.

In these circumstances I can see no alternatives to the following courses:

1. As soon as corn is available to put the country on a mild war bread, containing about 20% of other cereals than wheat.
2. Refuse wheat (and flour) exports to all neutrals except Cuba.
3. Reduce Cuba to the minimum.
4. Instruct the Allies that they must secure all wheat from Canada, India, Australia and the Argentine and that any further exports from the United States must be replaced from Canada or the Argentine.

There is one domestic factor that we must not overlook. If we came out 10% short in our prime food this shortage would fall mainly upon the city and industrial classes as the producer always protects himself. It thus becomes 20% of their supply and as the well-to-do always live, it means 30% or 40% shortage to the poor—and our tranquility endangered.

Furthermore, it is hopeless for us to anticipate continued control of price if we are to operate food ourselves on an absolute shortage. Up to date, due to the firm control of wheat by the Food Administration, we have managed to control prices upon a visible circulating stock of wheat of only 10% of the usual amount, but it represents only ten days' supply of bread to the country and fills us with constant anxiety. We have however risked this so far in order to keep Allied ships loading without delay.

Some of the economic results of the Grain and Flour and Bread Control may interest you,—Briefly, the price of wheat is today 27% greater than the farmer realized last year and 109% over a three-year pre-war normal. The price of flour at the mill is 30% less than the day the Food Bill was signed. The price of cash bread in Washington for the full one-pound loaf is six to seven cents against eight to nine cents. The farmer is today receiving 40% of the price of the loaf against under 20% in pre-war times,—the result of total elimination of speculation and extortinate [sic] profits.

Your obedient servant,
HERBERT HOOVER

Rules and Regulations for Bakers

The sixteen rules drawn up by Hoover and enclosed in the following letter were approved by Wilson and returned to Hoover November 16.

November Sixteenth 1917

Dear Mr. President:

I am inclosing herewith for your approval the Rules and Regulations governing licensees manufacturing bakery products.

This provides the necessary machinery for putting into operation the policy outlined in the Proclamation of the 7th of November.

I am, Your obedient servant,
HERBERT HOOVER

Food Administration Conflict with New York State

This letter reveals the difficulties caused by the insistence of certain New York officials that the Food Administration share its authority with the state food commission. The John Mitchell mentioned by Hoover was not Mayor John Purroy Mitchel, who had written Hoover on June 17 pledging that his government would "voluntarily cooperate" with "any plans for food conservation which you have in mind." Hoover's brief answer thanked him for his "splendid offer" and promised to "take advantage of it." The following letter concerns Hoover's plan for resolving the disturbing problems that arose despite this early profession of goodwill and cooperation from New York City.

Seventeenth November 1917

Dear Mr. President:

We have a difficult situation in New York state with regard to the organization of the Food Administration there. The State of New York has passed special legislation and created a commission comprising Mr. John P. Mitchell, Chairman; Dr. Jacob Gould Schurman and Mr. Charles E. Wieting, and has given this commission an appropriation of $1,300,000. Its duties are practically identical with the Federal Administration and it has been necessary for us to find some basis of co-operation in order to prevent conflict and overlapping of activities and to secure the benefit of the State appropriation for common purposes.

After lengthy negotiation we have made an agreement, subject to your approval, by which we are to nominate two men to be added to the New York commission, these gentlemen being: Mr. Arthur Williams, who has already been approved by you as the Food Administrator for New York City and who is doing a very efficient work, and Mr. Charles Treman of Ithaca, New York, a member of the Democratic Committee for New York who has been Chairman of our State Campaign Committee on household enrollment.

The new commission will elect its own chairman and apportion the duties of its various members. It is agreed, however, that Mr. Williams will remain in charge of the Federal Administration work in New York City directly responsible to the Food Administration here. Mr. Charles Treman will be directly responsible to the Food Administration here for the up-State.

The above plan is somewhat complicated but it seems to us the only solution for an otherwise very difficult situation and we have confidence that the character of the men involved will enable them to work out satisfactory relationships.

I would be glad indeed if you could give me your views on this plan as early as possible as some busy-bodies have already started gossip as to conflict between the state and federal authorities. The plan has the great advantage that it attaches the responsibility to state authorities in the whole matter of food control in the state of New York; and this state, as you can imagine, is one of our most difficult problems. One object of the arrangement set up is to separate the consumer's problems in the city from the producer's problems up-State.

Your obedient servant,
HERBERT HOOVER

Food Administration Arrangement for New York

19 November, 1917

My dear Mr. Hoover:

I have your letter of Saturday about the New York situation and hasten to say that the arrangement you have suggested seems to me the best practicable in the circumstances.

Cordially and sincerely yours,
WOODROW WILSON

Memorandum on the Crop Situation

The memorandum referred to here was possibly based on an exhaustive twenty-page report published October 25 as Bulletin 10 of the U.S.

Food Administration. But Wilson more than likely had in mind Hoover's four-page letter of November 15 which presented the President a survey of the crop situation.

19 November, 1917

My dear Mr. Hoover:

Thank you very much for your memorandum of November fifteenth about the crop situation. It will be very serviceable to me.

In great haste, Cordially and faithfully yours,

WOODROW WILSON

Trouble with Pinchot and Lasater

Two members of the Food Administration, Gifford Pinchot of Pennsylvania and E. C. Lasater of Texas, grew impatient with the methods and progress of the programs and resigned in November 1917. They forthwith began a public campaign against the organization. Hoover brought the matter to Wilson's attention with the following letter. The President responded the following day.

November 19, 1917

Dear Mr. President:

I have unfortunately had a tea-pot storm in my department. Mr. Houston and I appointed a joint committee to undertake propaganda for the stimulation of animal production. I selected, amongst others, Mr. E. C. Lasater, a Texas cattle-man, and Mr. Gifford Pinchot for the committee. Mr. Pinchot, whose views are followed by Mr. Lasater, instead of confining himself to stimulation of production in a patriotic way, and devising methods for a better distribution of our young cattle and other portions of the program, took upon himself to advise me with regard to financial measures to be undertaken and more especially that we should take over the packing plants in the country and operate them for the Government, and other radical measures. These measures were practically all outside the powers of the Government aside from their visionary character. After some time he resigned and his resignation was followed by that of Mr. Lasater on the ground that we were not conducting the Food Administration for the public welfare. I have declined to answer any of their newspaper propaganda.

The fault is of course mine for having even placed them on a . . . committee, although my one justification was that their personalities could be turned to good account in this emergency.

I merely wished to inform you of this as I do not propose to take any action whatever in the matter.

HERBERT HOOVER

Comment on Gifford Pinchot

20 November, 1917

My dear Mr. Hoover:

Thank you for your memorandum about Mr. Gifford Pinchot. The same thing happens wherever he is involved.

In haste, Faithfully yours,
WOODROW WILSON

Three Percent Beer

Hoover had sent the President a memorandum on the agitation of temperance advocates for restricting the manufacture and sale of alcoholic beverages and Wilson responded in the following letter. As for Hoover's personal views on the matter of prohibition, Secretary of the Navy Josephus Daniels, himself a prohibitionist, noted that on May 7, 1917, he had a "long talk with Hoover" who asserted that "no wheat or barley should go into intoxicants. As an ethical question he believed in it, but he advocated it purely as a war plan." (Daniels Diaries, p. 147.) On June 4, 1918, Hoover wrote Democratic Senator Morris Sheppard of Texas that "I have been a life-long believer in national temperance." However, he also thought as "a purely administrative officer of the government that I should not enter into any contentious matters" but should await "definite action by the American people or by Congress to whom the ultimate responsibility in such questions belong."

The "memorandum" mentioned by Wilson in this letter is given in digest form in Hoover's Epic (vol. 2, pp. 116–17.)

20 November, 1917

My dear Mr. Hoover:

Thank you for your memorandum about the relations between the food supply and the brewing industry.

I am fully in sympathy with your suggestion that the percentage of alcohol in beer should be reduced to three per cent., and I think probably it would be wise to reduce the amount of grains used by each brewer, but I am inclined to think that fifty per cent. reduction is too severe, at any rate for a beginning, because I take it for granted that such a reduction would by reducing the supply greatly increase the price of beer and so be very unfair to the classes who are using it and who can use it with very little detriment when the percentage of alcohol is made so small.

This other question arises in my mind: Is the thirty per cent. of the grain value really being saved for cattle feed systematically and universally, and if not, are there not some regulations by which we should make sure that the full saving was effected and made available in the right way?

Cordially and sincerely yours,
WOODROW WILSON

Food Control Act Investigator

Twenty-third November 1917
Dear Mr. President:

In the perfection of organization for the enforcement of the Food Law I have gradually developed a division for inspection and control, this instrumentality to receive complaints, make investigations and prepare cases for legal action. I have had the assistance of Mr. R. W. Boyden of Boston in the development of this work and I now wish to suggest Mr. Boyden to you for confirmation, to take charge of this special branch of the work. I may mention that Mr. Boyden is a personal friend of Mr. Houston who commended him to me highly.

Yours faithfully,
HERBERT HOOVER
Approved
WOODROW WILSON [handwritten by Wilson]

Continued New York Problem

The conflict with New York officials, hinted at in Hoover's letter of October 22 and elaborated upon on November 17, was still a source of distress to him on November 23. In a letter with that date he speculated that the governor, Republican Charles S. Whitman, was responsible for the irritating situation. The Hoovers invited the Franklin Roosevelts to dinner at 7:30 on the night of November 23. Perhaps on this occasion something was said about the New York situation that was causing Hoover "a great deal of anxiety" and about which he had written the President that day. (See Wilson's letter, p. 111.)

(See Wilson's letter, p. 111.)

Twenty-third November 1917

Dear Mr. President:

The New York situation fills me with a great deal of anxiety because there are many forces at work of obviously political interest. I have had some days' conference with Mr. John Mitchell who is President of the New York State Commission and his attorney, and we finally proposed to them a form of organization for New York State set out in the enclosed memorandum. They so far refuse to accept this form of administration and demand that it shall be condensed to the following statement :

"To the end that there may be a united food administration within the state of New York, and that the interests of the people of the state may be harmonized with the interests of the nation; it is agreed as follows: —

1. That a joint Food Board is hereby created comprising the three members of the New York State Food Commission and the two federal food administrators for New York state appointed by the President.

2. That the purposes of the joint Food Board are:

First: to be the federal food administrators for the state of New York, subject in every respect to the superior control and direction of the United States Food Administration at Washington.

Second: to act in an advisory capacity with respect to the execution of the powers vested by law of the state of New York in the State Food Commission."

The selection of a board in New York state to control food activities, the majority of whom look towards the Governor for their inspiration is very distasteful to me and in any event, as you have so often said, boards generally do not make for efficient administration. The New York State Commission informs us that they will resign unless we are prepared to accept their views as above and my opposition to it is that we practically hand over the domination of our activities in New York state to their tender mercies. As near as I can make out the real reason behind the scene is that the Governor wishes to dominate everything in New York state and if the Food Administration is a success he wishes to add it to his laurels and if it brings criticism he wishes to be in position to lay the trouble up to the Federal Administration.

I recognize that the difference between creating a board to co-ordinate activities of two organizations and creating a board to take over the activities of one and advise the other is perhaps not very much of a differentiation on paper but already it takes on the appearance of an attempt to dictate to the Federal Government in a way that I greatly resent. I have nothing to propose to you in the matter except that I fear that the State Commission may resign and try to create the feeling in New York state that the Federal Government is not acting in public interest and place themselves in the safe position of critics.

Yours faithfully,
HERBERT HOOVER

Commissions to Control Milk Prices

Twenty-third November 1917

Dear Mr. President:

There has been a steady rise in the demands of the milk producers and distributors in many of our large cities and all attempts at conciliation and proper settlement [sic] of the matter by state authorities have been a practical failure. Further rises in the price of milk had been agreed between the producers and distributors and prosecutions had been contemplated by the Attorney General and state authorities which would result in the destruction of the Producers' Association if successful. I therefore felt that it was necessary for us to intervene as I believe these associations are intrinsically of importance to the protection of the producer, if they were under proper control, and the situation was likely to develop, through either collusion or disagreement between the producers and distributors, to one of great distress to the consumer.

The Administration has been for some time in negotiation with all parties concerned. We have, in order to stop the agreed further rises in prices and in some states to secure an immediate reduction in price, undertaken to form regional committees to be appointed by the Administration, who will conduct open hearings as to all phases of the industry and who will determine the price. We have secured the agreement from the producers and the distributors and the approval of municipal and state authorities to this course and are now engaged upon the appointment of these commissions. We have in the main asked each one of the various parties interested to nominate three people to us of which we have chosen one and have distributed the choice in such manner as to represent each class in the community from the complete socialist at one end to the complete Tory at the other, together with trade representatives. I have taken upon myself to finally approve the names of the commission in New York, which are as follows:

Mr. John Mitchell, New York State Food Commission,
Dr. L. P. Brown, New York City Board of Health,
Dr. W. H. Jordan, Director New York Agricultural Experiment Station,
Mr. John T. Galvin, New York Board of Water Commissioners,
Mr. Jacob Schiff, New York City,
Miss Mabel Kittredge, New York City,
Mr. Eugene Schoen, New York City,
Mr. Charles M. Dow, Jamestown, N.Y.,
Mr. Bradley Fuller, Utica, N.Y.,
Mr. C. S. Shedrick, Buffalo, N.Y.,
Mr. Arthur Williams, ex officio, Federal Food Commissioner.

I trust it will meet with your approval. Similar commissions will need to be set up in New England, in the Middle-West and in the South.

Yours faithfully,
HERBERT HOOVER

Executive Order on Brewing

Twenty-third November 1917

Dear Mr. President:
    In the matter of restrictions on brewing, I am having an executive order drawn on the lines of your suggestions and am consulting the Treasury and the Department of Agriculture as to the technology and administrative measures involved. The Internal Revenue [Department] will need to take over the enforcement of the regulations.

Yours faithfully,
HERBERT HOOVER

Requisitioning Feed for Cattle

November 24, 1917.

Dear Mr. President:

An important question has arisen in connection with the functions and powers of the United States Food Administrator under the provisions of the Act of Congress approved August 10, 1917, known as the Food Control Act, upon which I feel that it is necessary to obtain the official opinion of the Attorney-General, if this course meets with your approval.

Section 10 of the Food Control Act authorizes the President from time to time "to requisition foods, feeds, fuels, and other supplies necessary to the support of the Army or the maintenance of the Navy, or any other public use connected with the common defense, and to requisition or otherwise provide storage facilities for such supplies; and he shall ascertain and pay a just compensation therefor." At the present time there is a great shortage of cattle feed in the western part of Texas, to such an extent that the cattle in that region are dying of starvation in spite of every effort made to preserve them. There is now in storage at Texas Gulf points approximately 15,000 tons of cottonseed cake, a valuable feed, which was destined for shipment to neutral countries but for which an export license has been refused. Under the circumstances, it is essential that this feed should be used immediately to preserve the cattle herds of Texas and insure a proper meat supply for the country. We are endeavoring to reach an agreement with the owners of this feed, but up to date they have refused to sell.

The question which I wish to submit to the Attorney-General is whether the President, acting through the United States Food Administrator, has power to requisition this feed. From time to time it is probable that other situations will arise requiring the immediate disposition of foodstuffs held in storage.

Faithfully yours,
HERBERT HOOVER

Cuban Demand for High Sugar Prices

November 24, 1917.

Dear Mr. President:

As you know, we have formed a joint committee with the Allies for the united purchase and division of Cuban and other foreign sugars. In the meantime, we had fixed a price agreement with our own sugar producers. On the basis of our domestic price the International Committee should pay approximately $4.80 per 100, delivered New York, for Cuban sugar. This is an increase of $1.30 per 100 pounds over 1913, the year before the war, and an increase of 25 cents over 1917, and in our view fully takes account of any increased production costs in Cuba and leaves a very wide margin of profit to the producers.

The English members of our committee contended for a price of about $4.30 New York, but, in an effort to conciliate, we offered and persuaded the English members to agree with us in offering the excessive amount of $4.90.

President Menocal has intervened and is endeavo[u]ring to force a price which works out from $5.05 to $5.25 New York and has dispatched a committee to New York to negotiate.

The President of Cuba, we understand, refuses to accede and claims he will force us to agree through the American Government. We have endeavoured to keep the entire matter simply a commercial transaction, but they insist on interjection of governmental pressure.

I feel that we can not, in justice to our consumers or to our own producers, accede to their demands. It means on maximum figures demanded, about $40,000,000 to our people, and likewise a large increase of similar amounts to our Allies, which we will probably have to finance. Cuba only obtains a minor part of this huge sum because an increased price to them automatically raises the price of all the sugar of the whole world.

I trust we will, if the matter arises, have your support in our views.

Faithfully yours,
HERBERT HOOVER

Approval of Action on Milk Prices

> Hoover's November 23 letter outlined his plan for controlling milk prices. The President responded on November 26 with his general approval.

26 November, 1917

My dear Mr. Hoover:

Acknowledging your letter of November twenty-third, I am glad that you have made the beginning of a success in handling the milk question. I do not feel confident to judge the steps you have taken because, of course, I have not been in at the conferences which led to them, but I take pleasure in approving what you have done.

Cordially and sincerely yours,
WOODROW WILSON

Comment on Conflict with New York

In his lengthy communique of November 23, Hoover had complained of an attempt by certain persons in New York to harness the Food Administration to a state commission. He sketched his objections to such efforts and explained why he would insist upon the supremacy of the federal organization even though he agreed to cooperate with the state food commission. On November 26 Wilson gave a stamp of approval to Hoover's plans.

26 November, 1917

My dear Mr. Hoover:
I do not wonder that you are disturbed about the Food Administration situation in New York. I am afraid that you must insist upon your plan. I do not think it would do to yield to the New York people, because it is clear that we are in duty bound to keep the matter in our own hands and would not be justified under the laws under which we are acting in sharing the responsibility in any way. I am very sorry and very much disappointed.

I regret very much that the gentlemen in New York who are dealing with this matter are not in sympathy with us, and I hope that when it becomes evident that you must maintain your position they will yield.

Cordially and sincerely yours,
WOODROW WILSON

Food Administration Use of State Defense Councils

26 November, 1917

My dear Mr. Hoover:
Since the United States declared a state of war against Germany, all of the states of the Union have organized councils of defense. So far as I have been able to learn these councils are made up of thoughtful and energetic men sincerely desirous of rendering any service, whether local

or national, that may fall within their sphere. The organization of these state councils has been extended into the counties and the towns in nearly all cases, and the town and county organizations are in most instances made up of the most efficient men in their communities. By means of their direct contact with the people throughout the country, they constitute a nation-wide organization peculiarly fitted to bring home to the people the knowledge of the needs of the Government and to enlist them in its service.

It occurs to me to suggest, therefore, that it would be very serviceable to the Food Administration to make use of these organizations wherever it is possible to do so. Much duplication of work might thus be avoided not only, but an additional energy and spirit of service infused into the state organizations, which I am sure would be not only willing but glad to cooperate when invited to do so.

I venture to think this suggestion worthy of your most serious consideration.

Cordially and sincerely yours,
WOODROW WILSON

Limiting Excess Profits

> Charles L. Swem scribbled a few words on this letter which reveal that the draft enclosed and mentioned in the letter was signed and returned to Hoover on November 27.

Twenty-sixth November 1917

Dear Mr. President:

As you are aware the keystone of the Food Law in its provisions as to control of distribution rests on the provisions against "unjust, unreasonable, unfair . . . profit". Now that we have the principal trades under license the interpretation of what is "unjust, unreasonable, unfair . . . profit" is arising daily.

I should like to recommend to you the adoption of the following principle for guidance of the Food Administration. That principle to be "that any profit in excess of the normal pre-war average profit of that business and place where free, competitive conditions existed is deemed to be unjust, unreasonable, unfair profit".

We have given much thought to this subject and have proposed it as a tentative principle in the great number of trade conferences held in formulating regulations and securing the co-operation of the trades in their administration. The very large profits earned from war conditions prior to our entry into the war have established a fictitious basis of commerce and at the opening of our work this principle was most strongly resented in many quarters but I believe that our steady propoganda [*sic*] on the line no one has a right to take an extra profit from America at war has now proceeded so far as to enable its adoption in the food trades without consequential opposition.

If you are able to agree with this basis of interpretation it would be of the greatest help if I could have an instruction from you in somewhat the terms of the enclosed draft.

If this is done I should like to ask the Federal Trade Commission to make determinations of what pre-war or normal profits were in some of the larger trades—to be determined in either of four ways as the particular business may dictate as the most facile for guidance.

1. Return upon capital invested.
2. Profit per unit of commodity.
3. Percentage upon the "turn over" of specific commodities.
4. Positive differentials for handling certain commodities between purchase price and sale price.

Yours faithfully,
HERBERT HOOVER

Executive Order on Excess Profits

27 November, 1917

My dear Mr. Hoover:

In signing the enclosed Executive Order I am acting, and acting willingly, upon your judgment, because I cannot pretend to the knowledge of the case which you have. I should have assumed that possibly it would be fair to allow a somewhat increased margin above the prewar margin, because these dealers, like all the rest of us, have to adjust themselves to an enhanced cost of living so far as their own personal support is concerned, but I have no doubt you have taken that into consideration along with the other matters affecting your judgment.

Cordially and sincerely yours,
WOODROW WILSON

Problems in New York and Cuba

The New York problem arose over the possible conflict between its own state food commission and Hoover's food administrator. The arrangement for avoiding such a conflict was explained to Wilson in Hoover's letter of November 17. The Cuban problem developed after establishment of the Sugar Equalization Board with authority to purchase the entire Cuban sugar crop and to pool it with the U.S. cane and beet production.

Twenty-seventh November 1917

Dear Mr. President:

I have to report two troubles settled—or quieted for a time.

The New York State Commission has accepted our views.

After "breaking off relations" with Cuba over sugar they have renewed negotiations upon our basis of price.

Faithfully yours,
HERBERT HOOVER

State Councils of Defense

Wilson's letter of November 26 had suggested that the Food Administration make use of the many state councils of defense and thus avoid much duplication of effort and waste of manpower. Hoover's response was a clear but brief explanation of why such an arrangement was not feasible.

Twenty-eighth November 1917

Dear Mr. President:

In the matter of your note on the State Councils of Defense, I should like to say frankly that we originally endeavoured to act through them. In the matter of the home enrollment for conservation they secured about 1,700,000 homes over the entire country. With our own organization we renewed the campaign and enrolled 12,000,000. In fact our work has come to require the undivided attention of a State Food Administrator and his staff in hourly communication with us, a relationship impossible with any Council or Board. In some states our Administrator is a member of the Council.

The Councils are in many states strong and admirable bodies for consultation, but of sporadic value as executive officers. Furthermore, many of the Councils embrace men interested in food trades and they

are therefore incapable of the action we require, for we are daily enforcing the law against traders and making trade agreements.

Yours faithfully,
HERBERT HOOVER

Suggestions for New Legislation

The second session of the Sixty-fifth Congress was to open at noon on
Monday, December 3, 1917. (Not until the Twentieth Amendment was
added to the Constitution in 1933 did sessions begin on January 3.)
Wilson's state of the union message was presented on Tuesday, December 4. To help in its preparation, he requested suggestions from all
cabinet members and from Hoover and Garfield. (*Life and Letters*,
vol. 7, p. 380.) Hoover responded December 1.

28 November, 1917

My dear Mr. Hoover:

I would be very much obliged to you if I might have a memorandum
from you as to any legislation which you think it imperative should be
considered at this session of Congress.

I assume that the Congress will prefer to confine itself entirely to
matters directly connected with the prosecution of the war, and in my
judgment that is the policy which it should pursue. My request, therefore, concerns only such matters as you think should be provided for at
once and cannot be postponed.

Cordially and sincerely yours,
WOODROW WILSON

Response to Solution of Problems in New York and Cuba

Hoover's brief letter of November 27, reporting a happy solution of
the New York and the Cuban crises, brought relief to the President
who expressed his satisfaction in a letter of November 30. The Mr.
Gonzales mentioned by Wilson was the Cuban representative who was
highly cooperative in resolving the problems of the price of sugar.

30 November, 1917

My dear Mr. Hoover:

I am very glad to receive your letter of the twenty-seventh about the
acquiescence of the New York State Commission and the renewal of
negotiations with Cuba about the sugar.

I must say that Mr. Gonzales made a very considerable impression on me with regard to the price of Cuban sugar. I took the liberty of sending him with a card to you and I am sure you were interested, as I was, in what he had to say.

Cordially and sincerely yours,
WOODROW WILSON

Gonzales and Cuban Sugar

First December 1917
Dear Mr. President:

The purpose of Mr. Gonzales' visit is now necessarily modified by acceptance by Cuba of the terms which we proposed and as the Cuban Commission has expressed it is well satisfied I do not assume that any further opposition will be exerted. Mr. Gonzales' views were identical with those of President Menocal but I cannot bring myself to believe they were based upon such searching investigation of the cost of production as we had previously made and the figures with regard to which were practically agreed [upon] by the Cuban producers themselves.

I was very glad indeed to see him and to outline some of the difficulties that we would have to face with Cuba in the necessity to reduce the exports of bread stuffs from this country. As I have a feeling that inasmuch as every ounce of wheat products exported from the United States from now on must be by sacrificing consumption by the American people, we would be perfectly correct in asking the people of Cuba to undertake the same ratio of sacrifice, that is, approximately twenty-five per cent. of their normal wheat product consumption.

Yours faithfully,
HERBERT HOOVER

Packers and Profit Limitation

Hoover suggested that he was applying regulations on profits with some consideration of the particular firms concerned lest small dealers be unduly hurt. In this he seemed to agree with Wilson. But at the gargantuan dealer, J. Ogden Armour, Hoover cast a shaft sharp of sarcasm: "I have the feeling that . . . [he] can manage to live all right." Time did not soften Hoover's attitude toward the group

Armour represented. In his letter to Wilson on February 21, 1918, he observed, "I have no great love for the packers and they have been very difficult to deal with."

1 December, 1917.

Dear Mr. President:

As to regulating food handling concerns on a pre-war profit basis, I agree that it would work hardship if applied rigorously to small dealers. On the other hand, I have the feeling that our chief opponent to this plan—J. Ogden Armour—can manage to live all right. Therefore, we will try to apply it with consideration.

We have been for two months endeavoring to come to some settlement with the packers as to regulations governing that trade. Finally we were compelled to use our own judgment as to their profit limitations. We based this judgment upon pre-war conditions with an increase of $\frac{1}{2}\%$[1] for certain extra expense considerations in borrowing capital. The packers today came in a body to protest and I have written them the inclosed letter in confirmation of our discussion. I trust I have your approval in the course laid down.

Yours faithfully,
HERBERT HOOVER

---

1. Changed by hand from 1%.

Hoover's Suggested Legislation

Wilson's letter of November 28 inviting Hoover to suggest material for his December 4 address to Congress prompted the Food Administrator to reply with five pages of recommended legislation. The major portion of the address by the President concerned itself with the "objectives" of the war and a call for a declaration of war against Austria-Hungary. Only five short paragraphs were devoted to recommended pieces of legislation. Hoover made four suggestions, the major one being for a general price-fixing power. The President accepted this suggestion using words in his address to Congress strikingly similar to those found in paragraphs two and three of Hoover's December 1 letter: "Recent experience has convinced me that the Congress must go further in authorizing Government to set limits to prices. The law of supply and demand, I am sorry to say, has been replaced by the law of unrestrained selfishness. While we have eliminated profiteering in several branches of industry it still runs impudently rampant in others. The farmers, for instance, complain with a great deal of justice that, while the regulation of food prices restricts their income, no restraints are placed upon most of the things they must purchase; and similar inequities obtain on all sides." (*Messages*, p. 452.)

1 December 1917

Dear Mr. President:

With respect to your note of November 28 on the question of legislation to be considered at this session of Congress, I have the following views:

I[1]

It appears to me that it has now become critical, in mobilization of our productive power, our transportation, the control of labor, and the stimulation of production, that we have a general price-fixing power vested in yourself or in the Federal Trade Commission. At present, except for coal, there is no such power in the government; and by implementing exports, imports, embargoes, purchasing power for our own government and the Allies, and by making first one voluntary agreement after another, we are playing around the fringes of the problem and setting up great currents of injustice. For instance, the farmers justly complain that by these implements their income is restricted and no restraints are placed upon the goods they must purchase.

The law of supply and demand has been replaced by the law of selfishness; and while I am confident that we have eliminated profiteering in food trades it still runs rampant in other branches of commerce.

We cannot hope to restrain the constant demands of labor, with its reactions on national efficiency, unless we can bring the advances in price to a stop—and we can not do this in the food trades unless the materials of production are also controlled.

We could greatly increase the efficiency of the transportation system if we could zonalize distribution of great primary commodities, by controlling their distribution area, but as such a course would to some degree stifle competition it cannot be done without prior fixation of price. We are today saving 25% of the transport of wheat and flour by such a system, and it could be applied to the other great staple commodities.

My own views upon the economics of this question are that they should be based upon a determination of the fair price for the limited list of primary raw materials with the added power to fix the profits or differentials to be added by the various subsequent links of manufacture

---

1. Section numbers I, II, III inserted by hand after the letter was typed.

and distribution. Further, that this power should be backed by authority of the government to buy and sell these primary commodities if it becomes necessary to maintain regular and seasonal flow. Such legislation would enable the retail trader to be dealt with, – not now possible in the food trades.

I feel strongly that the fixing of such prices should be in the hands of somebody who can establish some sort of unity between the animal, mineral, and vegetable kingdoms, and that it cannot therefore rest in the hands of such a department as mine. It would appear to me a logical function for the Federal Trade Commission; the administration of such judgments as they might enter upon these subjects being left in the hands of the various departments which are concerned with the commerce in these commodities.

I have also the feeling that the Federal Trade Commission, being a semi-judicial body, holds the skill and independence to fix these prices, free from the great pressure to which administrative departments are now constantly subjected, and that if legislation on this line were applied for to the Federal Trade Commission it would be free from a great deal of the congressional opposition and prejudice that must arise against any particular organ of the government. We can not disguise the fact that such administrations as mine must, if we are to act with independence and justice to all sections of the community, excite the most violent opposition from individuals and minorities and that these are reflected by the direct representatives of these trades and minorities in Congress and that such prejudice would greatly color legislative action.

II

The next great problem confronting us is the stimulation of production. This rests primarily upon the fixation of prices of primary commodities at stimulative levels with consequent assurance of market at profitable levels, which would be covered by the foregoing proposals. In addition, however, I am convinced that some definite action must be taken as to agricultural labor. There will undoubtedly be a very considerable decrease in production if any further draft is made; and furthermore, the attraction of high wages in munitions plants is drawing labor from the farms. Beyond exemption from further draft, it appears to me more powers in the establishment of labor exchanges should be given to the Department of Labor, and other constructive mobilization of labor undertaken.

Another field of necessity for action has arisen if we are to promote production to its necessary level. Three sequent failures in wheat crop in the Northwest and some other points and the great drought in the Southwest with consequent cattle afmine [famine] all require constructive handling if production in those quarters is to be maintained. I would suggest a considerable appropriation, placed at the disposal of the Farm Loan Board, for advances against crops and animals. The Board at one time had worked out a constructive plan of local guarantee association.

III

The other point upon which I am convinced that emergency legislation is necessary is to give to you some general powers to control waste, to require substitution of one commodity for another in consumption, and to limit actual consumption of commodities. In other words, a broad conservation measure, capable of expression in few words, and enforcible [sic] by executive order. The necessity for forced food conservation in public places, in manufacture and distribution is evident enough; and the same necessity exists as to our other primary commodities, such as metals, and even to transport.

Such a course is the necessary complement to stimulation of production. No such powers exist today.

Yours faithfully,

HERBERT HOOVER

Innes for Food Administrator

Another Hoover nominee for the Food Administration received instant confirmation from President Wilson.

December 5, 1917.

Dear Mr. President:

Dr. Henry J. Waters, who as you know has been serving for several months as Federal Food Administrator for the State of Kansas, is about to change his headquarters from the Agricultural College at Manhattan, Kansas to Kansas City, Missouri, where he is to become the Editor of the Kansas City Star.

Careful consideration has been given to the selection of a successor to Dr. Waters as Federal Food Administrator for Kansas, and I now wish to recommend for this position —

MR. WALTER P. INNES of Wichita.

Mr. Innes is the head of the George Innes Dry Goods Company, the largest concern of its kind in Kansas and has had a long business experi-

ence which, in my opinion, qualifies him for the important position of
Food Administrator.

Mr. Innes is well known throughout his State and is strongly endorsed for the position of Food Administrator by Governor Capper,
Hon. Jouett Shouse and Hon. W. A. Ayers; also by Dr. Waters and
many other leading citizens of Kansas.

Mr. Innes is here today and has assured me that if appointed to this
position of responsibility he will serve the country as a volunteer to the
best of his ability.

At your convenience I shall appreciate a word from you in regard
to the above as it is desirable that Mr. Innes, if approved by you, get
into harness at the earliest possible moment.

Yours faithfully
HERBERT HOOVER

Approved
WOODROW WILSON [handwritten by Wilson]
6 December, 1917.

Avoiding Use of Word "Allies"

> Wilson's comments on Hoover's use of the word "allies" recalls a
> Hoover letter written to Colonel House on February 13. Among seven
> points in this letter "in case we go to war" was the following: "I trust
> that the United States will enter into no political alliance with the
> Allied Governments, but will confine itself to naval and military co-
> operation." It is thus clear that he shared Wilson's views on our
> relationship with the "allies." (Ordeal, p. 5.)
>
> George Creel, chairman of the Committee on Public Information,
> had also written the President that numerous critics, "undoubtedly pro-
> German," were protesting against the use of the expression, "our
> allies." On December 10, Wilson told Creel that he should reply that
> the words had "no significance" and were "merely used for short."
> (Life and Letters, vol. 7, pp. 402–3.)
>
> On December 12 Hoover saw Wilson at the White House at 5:30.

10 December, 1917

My dear Mr. Hoover:

I have noticed on one or two of the posters of the Food Administration the words, "Our Allies." I would be very much obliged if you
would issue instructions that "Our Associates in the War" is to be
substituted. I have been very careful about this myself because we have

no allies and I think I am right in believing that the people of the country are very jealous of any intimation that there are formal alliances.

You will understand, of course, that I am implying no criticism. I am only thinking it important that we should all use the same language.

Cordially and sincerely yours,
WOODROW WILSON

Statement on Senate Inquiry

In mid-December 1917 the Senate Committee on Manufactures undertook an investigation of the sugar shortage. Two implacable foes of Hoover, Republican Senator Henry C. Lodge of Massachusetts and Democratic Senator James Reed of Missouri, had introduced the resolutions calling for this inquiry, and throughout the hearings they were persistently sharp in probing into actions of the Food Administration. Since the testimony heard by the committee seriously damaged the organization, Hoover asked for a personal appearance to answer his critics but he was given no opportunity to do so. This much disquieted him, especially since the committee's adjournment over the holidays meant that for several days he would be deprived of a suitable forum in which to give exposure to his side of the matter. Therefore, at this juncture in the controversy he approached Wilson with the request that his statement be released immediately. The President acquiesced and on December 26 he issued Hoover's defense as coming from the White House. (*Times,* Dec. 26, 1917, p. 1.)

Hoover's action greatly chagrined Lodge and Reed. On December 28, two days after Wilson released the statement, Hoover received a telegram asking his attendance before the committee. He failed to appear at the time stipulated, which only sharpened the hostility of Senate critics when he did come before them in early January 1918.

Reed's animosity dated from early May when he assumed an adamant posture against the Food Control Act and the Food Administration that it authorized. Actually, Lodge's critical eye had singled Hoover out as early as 1914, soon after establishment of the CRB. This organization, the Massachusetts Senator alleged at that time, was among other things a violation of the Logan Act, which prohibited attempts by private citizens to influence American international policy by dealings with foreign countries. (*Memoirs,* vol. 1, pp. 199–202.)

Senator A. A. Jones, mentioned in Hoover's December 23 letter to Wilson, was a Republican from New Mexico who seems to have been generally favorable to Hoover. On March 23, 1918, he denounced Lodge for his attack on Hoover for wheat policies of the Food Administration. (*Times*, Mar. 23, 1918, p. 14.)

23 December 1917

Dear Mr. President:

As you are aware, the Senate inquiry on the sugar shortage has been in session for a matter of ten days. I have repeatedly requested permission to appear before the Committee in order that I might make a complete statement of the matters at issue from the Administration's point of view and give the very cogent reasons for each step taken in the protection of the American people from profiteering and excess prices. I was informed yesterday that I should be heard today at twelve o'clock and had prepared a complete and impersonal statement of the entire sugar question, copy of which I have already sent to you. I was informed late this morning that I would not be heard and that the Committee had adjourned over Christmas. I thereupon sent the statement to the Committee and asked that it be introduced into the record and through Judge Lindley requested that it might be given to the public in order that many mis-impressions might be dispelled.

Senator Jones moved that the Committee place it in the record and give it to the public but the Committee refused and also refused to say whether they would consider it discourteous or not if we issued it to the Press. I cannot but feel that here is a double attempt to stifle truth and to leave prejudice in the minds of the public. Senator Jones authorizes me to say to you that he thinks this statement should be given to the Press and that nothing will alter the mind of the majority of this Sub-Committee.

May I request that if you can spare a moment to glance over the statement to witness its impersonal nature, and if you find it in order, that you would consider whether or not it could be issued as from you through Mr. Creel's bureau to the public, as the statement was forwarded to you as much as to the Senate Committee.

Yours faithfully,
HERBERT HOOVER

Statement for Next Inquiry

The statement mentioned in this second letter of December 23 contained the testimony Hoover intended to give when next called by the

committee. In all probability it was not the same as the public statement referred to in the other letter prepared by Hoover as the presentation he would have made had he been allowed to appear. This also
was sent to Wilson on December 23 and then released by the White
House for publication on December 26. The *New York Times* called it
"unprecedented" for the President to intervene but thought that Wilson felt justified because of the committee's denial of Hoover's request
to appear and answer charges that would hang over the Food Administration during the Christmas holidays. (*Times,* Dec. 26, 1917, p. 1.)

23 December 1917

Dear Mr. President:
  Herewith a complete statement of the sugar question from the
Administration's point of view which contains the gist of what I shall
have to say to the Senate Committee.

Yours faithfully,
HERBERT HOOVER

Elliott for Food Administrator

December twenty-second 1917

Dear Mr. President:—
  Mr. David R. Coker, Federal Food Administrator for South Carolina, has resigned on account of ill health and pressure of other business.
He has found that the duties of Federal Food Administrator, Chairman
of the State Council of Defense, and Director of the Federal Reserve
Bank for his District, have been too much for him.
  Mr. William Elliott of Columbia, South Carolina, is strongly endorsed by Governor Manning, Mr. Coker, and many others, as the
best possible man to succeed Mr. Coker. Mr. Elliott is a prominent
lawyer and business man, and is Vice-Chairman of the State Council of
Defense. Investigation convinces me that he is fully qualified for the
position of Federal Food Administrator for the State.
  A wire today from Governor Manning urges the prompt appointment of Mr. Elliott, as there are several matters of importance which
should be attended to at once. I shall be pleased to hear from you at
your convenience in regard to Mr. Elliott.

Faithfully yours,
HERBERT HOOVER

Approval of Elliott

26 December, 1917

My dear Mr. Hoover:

I write to say that I am very glad to approve the appointment of Mr. William Elliott of Columbia, South Carolina, in place of Mr. David R. Coker, as Federal Food Administrator for South Carolina.

Cordially and sincerely yours,

WOODROW WILSON

Resignation of Legal Counsel

26 December 1917.

Dear Mr. President:

Judge Lindley, who has been Chief Counsel for the Food Administration, cannot, I fear, any longer stand the nervous strain of the work and he and I both think that we must consider someone else for the active head and that we continue to enjoy Judge Lindley's help in consultative capacity.

I feel that in this peculiar and dominant position in the work I must have someone whose long-established political and personal loyalty to yourself is beyond question and who has had no relations with the associated villanies [sic] of the country. Furthermore, some lawyer of national importance would no doubt tend to protect the Administration from such wickedly designed plots as this sugar investigation.

The only name suggested to me so far is Judge Lehman of St. Louis, formerly Solicitor-General. Could you advise me as to the matter or suggest some other men whom I could approach.

Yours faithfully,

HERBERT HOOVER

Untermyer for Legal Counsel

Senator James A. Reed of Missouri continued to be a painful thorn in Hoover's side with his nagging investigations into activities of the Food Administration. (See letters of August 23 and 24.) But the Grain Corporation had a resourceful lawyer, Judge Curtis H. Lindley, in its legal department who was well able to defend it against all obstructionists like Reed. Unfortunately, for health reasons, he resigned in

December 1917. Thereupon President Wilson suggested to Hoover in
a December 28 letter that Samuel Untermyer, Democrat and prominent
New York lawyer, be appointed. Actually the name may well have
been first mentioned to Wilson by his secretary Joseph Tumulty. In
any event Tumulty supported the choice in a typewritten undated note
which began "Dear Governor," the term he always used when referring
to Wilson. He then continued with words that the President took
almost verbatim for his December 28 letter to Hoover: "Perhaps this
suggestion may surprise you, but I suggest Samuel Untermyer, for the
very reasons that might be urged against him. The man who is going
to fight Hoover until this war is over is Jim Reed. There is but one
man in America who can meet him and who can beat him, and that
is a man of the Untermyer type. In fact, it would stop many of these
threatened investigations if men like Reed could understand that in
the various departments some attorney like Untermyer can be loosed."

26 December, 1917

My dear Mr. Hoover:

In reply to your request for a suggestion as to a successor to Judge
Lindley, I am going to take the liberty of suggesting Mr. Samuel Untermyer of New York. Of course, we now know that the man who is going
to fight you until the war is over is Senator Reed of Missouri. Mr. Untermyer is one of the few men who can beat him. I believe it would stop
many investigations of the type which Senator Reed is conducting if it
could be understood that in the various departments there was some
lawyer like Mr. Untermyer who is genuinely to be feared. We have
nothing to fear from investigations conceived in the right spirit, and we
have every right to defend ourselves against the other sort.

Cordially and sincerely yours,

WOODROW WILSON

Objections to Untermyer

Samuel Untermyer, Wilson's choice as legal counsel for the Food Administration, had an enviable record as a lawyer and a government advisor on trusts and income tax law. Unfortunately, he had been accused by New York politicians of pro-German sympathies and, although he had denied all accusations of disloyalty, Hoover still considered him too controversial a figure for the post involved.

James H. Covington, mentioned in the letter below, was a former Maryland congressman and at the time a federal district judge in Washington. Before recommending Covington, Hoover consulted Justice Louis D. Brandeis, who in 1916 had been appointed to the Supreme Court by Wilson in the face of resolute opposition from many who judged him far too liberal on economic and social issues. During the war Wilson frequently sought his advice, especially on labor problems. (*Daniels Diaries*, pp. 322, 456; *Life and Letters*, vol. 7, pp. 53, 120, 242, 401.) In 1920 Brandeis supported Hoover for President, writing that he was "the biggest figure injected into Washington by the war." (*Men*, p. 24n.)

However, on January 2 Hoover received a letter from Colonel House evidently containing a new suggestion, and Hoover forthwith wrote Tumulty asking him to ascertain "the President's views as to Mr. [William A.] Glasgow." On January 30 Glasgow became general counsel of the Food Administration. On January 18 Covington was appointed by McAdoo as a member of the Railroad Wage Commission.

Hoover's statement that he had "originally mentioned the name of this gentleman [Untermyer]" seems to conflict with Wilson's letter of December 28, 1917.

January 1, 1918

Dear Mr. President:

With regard to your letter of the 28th ultimo, on the subject of Mr. Untermyer,—since I originally mentioned the name of this gentleman to you I have found that his German associations prior to our going into the War were most intimate. While he is a perfectly loyal citizen I am afraid it would bring a great deal of criticism on an Administration so much founded on voluntary devotion of the extreme, patriotic type. There is in the Food Administration an idealism amounting almost to a crusader's spirit and I am afraid that the appointing of Mr. Untermyer where he would be in such intimate relation with all of these men would not tend to maintain this spirit, which is so vital to successful work.

On the other hand, the attitude taken by Senator Reed needs the course so wisely suggested by you. I have taken the opportunity of discussing the entire matter with Mr. Justice Brandeis. He strongly urges that Judge Covington should undertake the position as his Congressional experience, high legal ability and ideals so perfectly fit him for the work. Justice Brandeis is alive to the necessity, from the whole Administration's point of view, that the ideal man should be chosen and he authorizes me to say he would be glad, if you wish, to discuss it with you. He considers that Judge Covington would gladly resign and undertake the work upon request from you.

I would indeed be glad if you could take a few moments of your precious time to further consider the matter.

Yours faithfully,
HERBERT HOOVER

Glasgow for Legal Counsel

January Second, 1918.

Dear Mr. Tumulty:

I am enclosing, herewith, a letter just received from Col. House, and would appreciate your ascertaining the President's views as to Mr. Glasgow.

Yours sincerely,
HERBERT HOOVER

Approved
WOODROW WILSON [handwritten by Wilson]

An Opinion by the Attorney General

On January 2 and 3 Hoover was closely questioned before a Senate committee investigating the sugar situation. When Democratic senators James Reed of Missouri and James Vardaman of Mississippi accused him of violating the Food Control Act by fixing the price of sugar and wheat, his rejoinder was that his actions were in conformity with the spirit of the law and had the President's approval. Thus it is possible that, before or after the investigation, he requested an opinion from the Attorney General on the matter and that Wilson enclosed it in the following letter.

As for his performance before the Committee, he was cheered by the people when he left the witness stand (*Times*, Jan. 4, 1918, p. 6) and he won editorial approval from the *New York Times* which remarked that Reed's motto was "Skin 'em alive" and that his success was based on "nagging." (Jan. 8, 1918, p. 14.)

Hoover's later comments on his several appearances before congressional meetings make interesting reading. In his *Memoirs* (vol. 1, p. 248) he writes thus: "The bare idea of anyone interfering with the food rights of the people, especially in the land of milk and honey, came as a shock to many members of Congress. Some violently opposed us and I spent a vast amount of breath and time both on individual Senators and Congressmen and on their various committees making clear the need of action and the methods we proposed. It was my first intimate contact with a legislative body. I learned that even in such an august institution there was the same minority of malicious and dumb that there was in the rest of the world, and their opportunity was greater. When I ran up against Senator Reed and a few others, I concluded some were also expert in the practice of malice beyond the average."

A postwar observation on Senator Reed was penned on February 3, 1920, by F. W. Taussig, the Harvard economist who was chairman of the Tariff Commission during Hoover's days as Food Administrator. In a letter to Hoover on February 3 Taussig wrote: "I should vote for you on any ticket whatever, republican, democratic, new faith, socialistic, or Bolshevik. New Faith would suit me best. . . . I see Senator Reed has again got at it, and I hope you appreciate the credit you get with all the world from being abused by him. We all love you for the enemies you make." (*Pre-Commerce Papers.*)

3 January, 1918

My dear Mr. Hoover:

I know you will be glad to get the enclosed opinion of the Attorney General. I am glad to send it.

Faithfully yours,
WOODROW WILSON

Mitchell for Food Administrator

January 5, 1918.

Dear Mr. President:

Mr. Edmund Mitchell of Wilmington, Delaware, is endorsed by Governor Townsend, Senator Saulsbury, and many leading citizens of the State as fully qualified to act as Federal Food Administrator for Delaware. Mr. Josiah Marvel, who has been acting Food Administrator, also favors the appointment of Mr. Mitchell as Federal Food Administrator.

After careful investigation I am pleased to recommend Mr. Mitchell for this position. His name was one of four passed by Mr. McCormick.

Mr. Mitchell is Vice-President of the Wilmington Gas Company and is prepared to undertake the work if appointed. He is about fifty-five years old, and is described as forceful, a good organizer and favorably known throughout the State.

I shall appreciate hearing from you at your convenience in regard to the above.

Faithfully yours,
HERBERT HOOVER

Approved
WOODROW WILSON [handwritten by Wilson]

Letter to Wheat Export Company

Sir Herbert T. Robson was one of the British representatives on the Wheat Export Company in New York, which was the grain marketing agency for the Allies. Because of the dearth of wheat in Europe at this time, the Allies had asked the United States for an advance of supplies which could be replaced from Canadian stocks when spring would open river and lake navigation. This request prompted Hoover to write Sir Robson a letter on January 1, a copy of which he sent to Wilson on January 5. (*Grain Trade*, pp. 194–95.) In this letter, Hoover agreed to make the requested advance of wheat but underscored the fact that this was to be replaced by Canadian wheat if and when that became necessary. However, he assured Sir Robson that "no such demand" would actually be made by the United States unless it became "critically necessary."

5 January 1918
Dear Mr. President:
   As indicative of the Allied cereal situation and our action therein, I enclose herewith a letter which I have written to their Agency in New York.

Yours faithfully,
HERBERT HOOVER

Request for Additional Funds

January seventh, 1918.
My dear Mr. President:
   This is to advise you that we are filing with the Secretary of the Treasury a revised budget for the United States Food Administration for the fiscal year ending June, 1919, in which we ask for $5,000,000 in addition to the $5,000,000 requested on October 16.

   The licensing and control of commodities, together with the decentralization of the work, indicates that the expense of the State Administrators will be largely increased. This additional sum will be necessary to provide for the proper carrying out of this branch of the organization.

Faithfully yours,
HERBERT HOOVER

Approved
WOODROW WILSON [handwritten by Wilson]

Inter-Allied Food Committee

> On October 28, 1917, Colonel House left for Europe as head of the American War Mission. On that day Wilson wrote the colonel, "I hate to say good-bye. It is an immense comfort to me to have you at hand here for counsel and for friendship. But it is right that you should go. . . . I hope that it will be only weeks that will separate us." (*Life and Letters,* vol. 7, p. 331.)
> The need for a conference of Allied leaders had long been recognized; all felt that greater cooperation would result. When House and his staff arrived in England on November 7, the "situation was perhaps the gravest which the Allies had faced since 1914." (*Intimate Papers,*

vol. 3, p. 210.) The Italian army at Caporetto had collapsed and the Bolsheviks had come to power in Russia.

One pressing problem concerned food and shipping. On October 27, Hoover wrote to House on this matter and explained the approach that the Allies should take at the conference. (*Epic*, vol. 2, p. 125.) He also sent his own personal representative, A. E. Taylor, to the War Mission. (*Epic*, vol. 2, pp. 125–26.) In Paris, House met several times with the prime ministers and foreign secretaries of England, France, and Italy. (*Intimate Papers*, pp. 260–319.) He returned to America on December 15, 1917. On Monday, December 17th, he was in Washington and late that afternoon met with the President from 5:00–7:00 just after Hoover left Wilson's office. Secretary of State Lansing had been there for a conference a few minutes before. (*Life and Letters*, vol. 7, p. 414.)

On Saturday, December 22, Taylor came to report to Hoover. Once again at 10:00 in the morning, Saturday, January 5, the two discussed the Committee on Alimentation, or the Inter-Allied Food Committee, which had been established at the recent Paris Conference.

Sometime during the day of January 7, Hoover requested a meeting with Wilson. This would have been quite difficult to arrange since the President was preparing for his Fourteen Points address to Congress for the following day. Thus he must have kept his appointments for January 7 and 8 to the very minimum. He replied that he had "been caught up today. . . . Ask Mr. Hoover if he could come in at 3:30 tomorrow," i.e., January 9.

The subject of the discussion on that day can only be guessed at. However, very probably one topic high on the list was the Inter-Allied Food Committee. Moreover, on the previous Thursday and Friday Hoover had been questioned in a most searching manner by a Senate investigating committee and had invoked the authority of the President to defend himself. Therefore it is very possible that this inquiry was also touched upon during their meeting.

7 January 1918

Dear Mr. President:

One of the resolutions passed at the Paris Conference was to the effect that a committee should be set up comprising two members each from the United States, Great Britain, France and Italy, who would sit in Paris and investigate, from a scientific point of view, the food programmes of the Allies and suggest to the various Governments the measures which they would deem useful.

I consider that this is a constructive step and that we should undertake it. It carries no obligation but merely the proper formulation of data with a view to economy in transport and consumption.

I would like to suggest to you, Professor Graham Lusk of Cornell, and Professor R. H. Chittenden of Yale, as the American members of this committee. These gentlemen would have to have some liberal allowance for expenses and I presume it can be made out of either the appropriation of your own fund to the Food Administration, or from the Congressional appropriation, although we are running short in our whole work and may have to call upon you for further assistance later on.

I would indeed be glad if you would kindly let me have your views as to this matter.

Yours faithfully,
HERBERT HOOVER

Approval of Lusk and Chittenden

In the afternoon of January 9, Hoover met with the President at 3:30 and at 4:30 he went to the office of Secretary of War Newton Baker for a "war conference." This was the day after Wilson had delivered his "Fourteen Points" address to a joint session of Congress. Sometime that day the President sent the following letter to Hoover giving his approval to the pair of nominees suggested by the Food Administrator on January 7.

Taylor was apparently merely Hoover's representative at the December conference. Lusk and Chittenden were the two permanent appointees to the food committee with headquarters in Paris.

9 January, 1917 [1918]
My dear Mr. Hoover:

I have your letter of the seventh and entirely approve of your deputing Professor Graham Lusk of Cornell and Professor R. H. Chittenden of Yale as the American members of a committee to sit in Paris for the purpose of investigating from a scientific point of view the food programmes of the Allies and suggesting to the various governments the measures which they would deem useful, and I would be obliged to you if you would let me have, when you can, an approximate estimate of their probable expenses.

Cordially and sincerely yours,
WOODROW WILSON

Proclamation on Food Licenses

Wilson signed the proclamation referred to in the following letter and had it sent to the State Department on January 10. Section 5 of the Food Control Act provided for licensing "the importation, manufacture, storage, mining, or distribution of any necessaries." Exempted were those companies whose business did not exceed $100,000 a year. Hoover was empowered to revoke the licenses of profiteers or of those who otherwise violated the rules or regulations binding their particular trade. Fines and even imprisonment could be imposed as penalties. Actually arrests were made in only two or three cases and rarely if ever was a license revoked, for Hoover was highly successful in getting the voluntary compliance of most men. There were some violations of regulations, of course, but in place of fines, most violators were persuaded to make contributions to the Red Cross. (*Grain Trade,* pp. 373–86.)

January 9, 1918

Dear Mr. President:

I submit herewith a proposed Proclamation requiring a license for eight classes of business dealing in food products.

The largest class consists of all feed dealers, the control of whom is, in my judgment, essential to assure to the dairymen, the stock raiser, and the farm community in general, animal feeds at proper price levels.

Class 2 includes maltsters, whose purchase of barley for brewing purposes it is essential to reach.

Classes 3, 5, 6, 7, and 8 cover persons engaged in businesses which were licensed under the former general Proclamation, but who were then exempted. It has been found that their inclusion is necessary in order effectively to work out the controls already instituted.

Under Class 4 are included substantially all salt water fishermen. Federal control and licensing of these fishermen will enable us to remove many of the local restrictions which now hamper production, and it is hoped that in this manner the supply of fish may be increased by 50% over last year's production.

I enclose two extra copies of the Proclamation.

Faithfully yours,
HERBERT HOOVER

Mr. Hoover, the Chairman of the Commission for Relief
in Belgium,has approached me with regard to difficulties which
have arisen in the conduct of that great humanitarian work,
in which he feels he needs the support of an enlarged Committee
of gentlemen of large experience to co-operate with him in
settling and conducting the Administration of the Branch of
the Commission in the United States.

I am *So much* impressed with the importance of this institution,
on which the lives of so many people are dependent *and I would*
be glad if you could see your way to join such a Committee.

The other gentleman with whom I am communicating in
this particular ,are Messrs. Alexander Hemphill, Otto T. Bannard,
S. Bertron, Oscar Strauss, Melville Stone, Herbert S. Eldridge
and John Beaver White, *and Of* course you may wish to add others
to your number,either from the Officers of the Commission
or otherwise.

On November 3, 1915, Hoover met with Wilson to
ask him to enlist the financial support of American
businessmen and philanthropists for Belgian Relief.
A rough draft of Wilson's letter of solicitation is
shown here. (See p. 15.) *Reproduced from the Library of Congress collection.*

ackgt
6/15/17

Dear Tumulty

Could I impose
on your good offices
to bring this idea before
the President at an
early moment

H.C.H.

July 18, 1917.

Dear Tumulty

Herewith a note
to the President which
I would like very much
if you could get to
his attention

Tumy
H.

A handwritten note to Joseph Tumulty, Wilson's private secretary, was a method frequently employed by Hoover for reaching the President directly and with dispatch. (See p. 31.) *Reproduced from the Library of Congress collection.*

2. Sept. '18

THE WHITE HOUSE,
WASHINGTON.

My dear Hoover,

The conclusions and plans stated in the enclosed have my entire approval

Woodrow Wilson

This note was written by Wilson in answer to Hoover's letter of August 29 (pp. 238–41) containing his plans for the purchase of Cuban sugar. *Reproduced from the collection of the Hoover Institution on War, Revolution and Peace, Stanford University.*

26 October, 1918.

Dear Mr. Hoover:

The probable early evacuation of Belgium brings us face
to face with the problems of this distressed people, not only
~regard to~
in continued food relief, but ~in the bread issue~ *also with regard to the many questions* of economic
rehabilitation.   The initial task of preserving the bare lives
of the people during German occupation, undertaken four years
ago under your direction, is now nearing completion.   I ~conceive~ *believe*
that the American people will willingly accept a large
share of the burden ~in their continued assistance to~ *of assisting in this now all important work* reconstruction and rehabilitation, pending their re-payment for injury
by Germany.

In order that such assistance should be exerted in the
most liberal, efficient and comprehensive manner, I feel that
it should be organized under a single agency, that it may co-
ordinate the whole effort of the American people or the government, in the furnishing of supplies, machinery, finance, exchange,
shipping, trade relations and philanthropy.   I also feel in
this matter that such an agency, in addition to being the sole
vehicle of supplies, should also have some proper participation
in the expenditure and distribution of this assistance.   Such
unity of administration
~consolidation~ should give much greater assurance of proper
assistance and ~present day~ *should be effective in preventing* profiteering ~in this situation.~

Two drafts of the same letter are reproduced here to
show how carefully Wilson worked over the documents needed for important work by men in his administration. Wilson's handwritten alterations are
shown on the original draft of a "Dear Mr. Hoover"
letter the President was to sign for Hoover's use with
foreign governments on the subject of the restoration
of Belgium. The second draft shows the final polish-
ing; since no changes were made on the closing page,
it is not included. The final product is shown on pp.
285–86. *Reproduced from the Library of Congress
collection.*

The large experience of the Belgian Relief Commission,
the character of its organization without profit, its shipping [use of shipping,]
and the sympathetic bond which it [now forms] forms, after four years of
co-operation, with the Belgian people, [naturally] point to its continuation
and enlargement as the [natural] logical agency for this purpose. I [of the Commission]
should therefore be glad if you and your colleagues would under-
take this extended work. [it is also the wish and purpose]

I understand that the sentiment of the English and French [Carnys]
people is to also participate in this burden. It would seem
to me desirable to inquire if these governments would not therefore continue and enlarge their present support to the Commission to these ends, so that we may have a comprehensive and
efficient agency for dealing with the entire problem on behalf
of all. [importance]

It is of course [of] primary that our assistance in this expenditure and organization shall be built upon co-operation with
the Belgian government and the use of such internal agencies and
methods as may be agreed [upon] with them, to whom our whole solicitude
is directed.

It is also of first importance that the expenditure of all
[the philanthropic aid] philanthropy, of the American people toward Belgium, of whatever
character, should be conducted by or under the control of the
Commission, if duplication and waste are to be avoided.

With a view to the advancement of these ideas, I have addressed a note to the various departments of ~~this~~ our government,
indicating my ~~direction~~ wish that all matters relating to these
problems should be undertaken under your guidance and that they
should give to you every co-operation.

I wish ~~for~~ you to proceed at once with the undertaking so
far as it relates to the United States and I should be glad if
you would, through the proper agencies, take up a discussion
of these matters with the Belgian government and with the
English and French governments as to their relationship and
participation.

~~Yours etc.~~

Cordially & sincerely yours.

November 6, 1918.

Dear Mr. Hoover:

The probable early evacuation of Belgium brings us face
to face with the problems of this distressed people, not only
in regard to continued food relief, but also with regard to
the many questions of economic rehabilitation.   The initial
task of preserving the bare lives of the people during German
occupation, undertaken four years ago under your direction,
is now nearing completion.   I believe that the American people
will willingly accept a large share of the burden of assisting in the now all important work of reconstruction and rehabilitation, pending ~~their~~ re-payment for injury by Germany.

In order that such assistance should be exerted in the
most liberal, efficient and comprehensive manner, I feel that
it should be organized under a single agency, ~~that it~~ which may co-
ordinate the whole effort of the American people ~~or the~~ and government, in the furnishing of supplies, machinery, finance, exchange, shipping, trade relations and philanthropy. is aid. I also
feel ~~in this matter~~ that such an agency, in addition to being
the sole vehicle of supplies, should also have some proper
participation in the expenditure and distribution of ~~this~~

assistance. Such unity of administration ~~should~~ *would* give much greater assurance of proper assistance and should be effective in preventing profiteering.

The large experience of the Belgian Relief Commission, the character of its organization without profit, its use of *Established* shipping, and the sympathetic bond which it now forms ~~after four years of co-operation~~ with the Belgian people ~~naturally~~ point to its continuation and enlargement as the natural agency for this purpose. I should therefore be glad if you and your colleagues of the Commission would undertake this extended work.

I understand that it is also the wish and purpose of the English and French people to also participate in carrying this burden. It would seem to me desirable to inquire if these governments would not therefore continue and enlarge their present support to the Commission to these ends, so that we may have a comprehensive and efficient agency for dealing with the entire problem on behalf of all.

It is of course of primary importance that our assistance in this expenditure and organization shall be built upon co-operation with the Belgian government and the use of such internal agencies and methods as may be agreed upon with them, to whom our whole solicitude is directed.

Report on the Food Administration for Congress

> The report mentioned in this letter was sent to the House on January 18 and to the Senate on January 21. The report is omitted here.

January 10, 1918.

Dear Mr. President:

I hand you herewith the Report of the United States Food Administration required by Section 21 of the Act of Congress approved August 10, 1917, entitled "An Act To provide further for the national security and defense by encouraging the production, conserving the supply, and controlling the distribution of food products and fuel," which Report is addressed to The Congress of the United States.

The financial statements accompanying this Report are complete up to and including December 31, 1917, and in order to make them for this period, it was necessary to delay the Report until they could be prepared after the close of our books on December 31st last.

Faithfully yours,

HERBERT HOOVER

Proclamation on Food Conservation

> In this letter Hoover refers to a "draft of a sort of proclamation" on "food conservation." No such draft appears with this letter, now in the files of the Hoover correspondence. Nor is there a letter from Wilson to Hoover with the draft reworked. However, on January 18, 1918, an executive proclamation on food conservation was issued. (*Proclamations,* p. 12.) This may be the proclamation to which Hoover referred; however, if so, both Wilson and Hoover must have worked with great dispatch to have it ready for issuing by January 18.

17 January 1918

Dear Mr. President:

I enclose herewith draft of a sort of proclamation which I am anxious to have issued from you on the subject of food conservation. As I explained to you, the demands now being made upon us are much greater than we can carry unless we procure a further reduction in consumption of certain commodities and, generally, of all foodstuffs.

I have no doubt that you will be able to improve its expression and I take the liberty of asking that we may have it at as early a moment as possible.

Yours faithfully,
HERBERT HOOVER

Complaint from McAdoo

In the summer of 1917 McAdoo had urged the establishment of an Inter-Allied Council located in Paris to determine what American money and supplies were needed by the powers in common conflict with Germany. In this letter Wilson makes reference to such a council as being McAdoo's suggestion for avoiding a situation that provoked the Secretary of the Treasury to complain "with some asperity" that the Food Administration's demands on the British government forced the British to make demands of the United States Treasury. (*Life and Letters*, vol. 7, p. 493.) Hoover answered Wilson on the McAdoo complaint on January 28.

As to the Inter-Allied Council, an Allied Food Council with Hoover as chairman was established in July 1918 during Hoover's visit to Europe. It surveyed the food needs of the neutral nations and the associated combatants for the forthcoming year and the available supplies and shipping for transport purposes. (*Memoirs*, vol. 1, p. 259.) It is possible, however, that the President's letter of January 23 refers to the Inter-Allied committee or council suggested by the Paris Conference in December 1917. But if so, then it is difficult to explain Wilson's mention of it here in view of the fact that on January 7 Hoover had already suggested two men for that council whom Wilson approved on January 9. In any event, Hoover wrote McAdoo on February 13: "With respect to your suggestion that I appoint someone to represent the Food Administration on the Inter-Allied Council, I believe that this is a constructive measure and I am taking the matter up at once." But he added that it was difficult to find a person properly equipped for the position.

23 January, 1918

My dear Mr. Hoover:

I would be very much obliged if you would give your careful consideration to the enclosed and let me have your confidential advice. The Secretary of the Treasury is, I think, right in the position he takes. The financial problems we are now handling and are facing in the immediate future are of such magnitude that I believe it is absolutely essential that we should avoid every ounce of additional weight that can be avoided. Whether the representation of the Food Administration in the Inter-Allied Council will accomplish just what the Secretary of the Treasury has in mind or not, I am not clear, but that there should be coordination of the most intimate sort in big transactions of this kind will, I am sure, be your judgment as it is mine.

Cordially and sincerely yours,
WOODROW WILSON

Advice on Answering a Letter

The letter referred to by the President was apparently returned to the White House, but it cannot be identified among the many items in the Wilson papers for this period.

24 January, 1918
My dear Mr. Hoover:
I have just received the enclosed letter and do not know what reply to make to it without first receiving your suggestion and advice.

Cordially and sincerely yours,
WOODROW WILSON

Rules on Food Conservation

Hoover speaks of delaying the matter of this letter "until after the coal storm had blown by in order that we might secure for it proper attention in the press." This was a reference to the coal famine of December and January that compelled Fuel Administrator Garfield to warn on January 11 that no section of the country would be able to have its normal supply of coal for 60 days.

The letter was addressed to Tumulty, but was clearly intended for the President's eye.

26 January 1918
Dear Tumulty:
I enclose herewith a summary of the Rules for conservation which we are proposing to send out tomorrow morning with the President's Proclamation. We have delayed this matter until after the coal storm had blown by in order that we might secure for it proper attention in

the press. As these are the rules referred to in the President's Proclamation and as we are sending them out under that caption, I am extremely anxious that they should be laid before the President today.

I apologize for not having had them ready yesterday, but we have been involved in large telegraphic correspondence with our State Administrators in an endeavour to arrive at measures that will take care of local situations.

I do not anticipate any unfavourable reaction of any kind from the country, as the ground work of this programme has been laid and it contains no privation, but rather, a stimulus to patriotic effort. There is in it no curtailment of trade relations of any consequence.

Would you be so kind as to help me out by asking the President if he could go over it during the course of today.

Yours faithfully,
HERBERT HOOVER

Answer to McAdoo Complaint

> Secretary of the Treasury McAdoo had complained that the British government had upset his financial planning by making unanticipated requests for funds to purchase an unusual amount of food during the winter months. The urgings to make such purchases had come from Hoover, who thus became the target of a sharp letter which McAdoo addressed to the President about January 20. Wilson sent this letter on to Hoover with one of his own on January 23. The following is Hoover's answer.

28 January 1918
Dear Mr. President:

I am obliged for your letter of January 23rd, in respect to Mr. McAdoo's communication on increased meat purchases.

The $61,000,000 which Great Britain asks should not be intrinsically an addition to their monthly allowances but simply an advance in time as a credit to buy food in excess of the immediate requirements, in our own as well as their interests, and should be so arranged as to relieve pressure later on.

The reasons why this is so, were not stated in the communications from the British Government, and are substantially as follows:

In order to feed our population as well as to feed our associates on the other side at reasonable prices, and in order to ensure that agricul-

tural production in the United States continue at high levels, I conceive that one of the prime functions of the government will be to
maintain, insofar as possible, a stability in food prices. Our herds are
considerably diminished and must be recuperated.

At this period of the year we always have a large run of cattle and
a large run of hogs. We are in the period of accumulation of hog products. In the spring the current supply will fall off, and we may not
have enough to keep pace with the demand for ourselves and our associates, unless we attain a large measure of conservation of consumption.
But, at the moment the runs are heavy, and we are having an extra large
surplus—with a prospect of very deficient supplies later.

The Food Administration asked the British Government to increase its purchases during this period of temporary surplus, so as to
reduce their purchases later, in the periods of comparative shortage.
And this was particularly important to us so that we should be able to
see that the packers paid fair prices to the producers above the minimum limits which we feel would protect recuperation of our herds.

Prices for live animals have dropped perceptibly since the fall, and
unless our temporary surplus is absorbed by the foreign demand we
shall have a further slump in prices, with consequent discouragement
to the producer at a critical period when he is deciding the extent of
his future operations. If this further slump in live stock prices came,
we should have to withdraw our conservation measures under pressure
from the producer, in order to secure the consumption of the surplus
amounts in the United States, and thus destroy our whole conservation
work. This is markedly true of beef, which is a perishable product.
There are no facilities in the United States to preserve any temporary
surplus of beef at this time. If it does not go abroad for storage it will
simply be eaten here by our people, who at this time have a supply
ample for their needs. After spring we will have a long and desperate
period to face as to our meat supply, in any event. These difficulties
would be doubled if we had to find anew, through a diminished supply,
the surplus which we can now offer.

Therefore, if we cannot take care of this temporary surplus we
shall have lost the constancy of our people in conservation, we shall
have discouraged the producer, and the necessary reaction of a shortage
would be higher prices for meat products in the summer and fall, and
we shall have lost our hope of maintaining stabilized prices.

As to the financial problem: We assumed that that would be taken
care of out of the Allied current income from the United States Treas-

ury. I did discuss the matter with Mr. McAdoo over a month ago, and made a recommendation as to Allied food finances,—in the main that the Treasury should stipulate the setting aside a regular and definite sum for financing the foodstuffs purchased here, instead of allowing their food purchases to become the football of the deficiencies created by the attempts to maintain exchange on neutral centers.

For the last three months we and the Allies own representatives have been totally at sea as to their purchasing power. We receive demands for future food programmes, based upon the necessities of their peoples, and after we adopt measures to meet them we find they are unable to consummate because we are told by their food agencies that their American funds have been diverted to the exchange market. The result has precipitated actual food shortages abroad.

If their representatives and ourselves had a definite budget we might often arrange to finance temporary surpluses such as the present one in meat with our own manufacturers.

Yours faithfully,
HERBERT HOOVER

McAdoo and Transportation of Food

On the same day that Hoover addressed the letter to the President on McAdoo's complaint about Great Britain's demands upon the United States Treasury for increased meat purchases, he pressed a complaint of his own about the lethargic movement of food by the American railroads, which had been taken over by the government on December 26 and placed under the direction of William G. McAdoo. (See *Grain Trade,* pp. 238–72, for a general survey of transportation problems.) In his *Memoirs* of 1951 (vol. 1, p. 262) Hoover mentions McAdoo only once. Speaking of pulling the railroads together by putting them under a director general, he adds this laconic comment: "Because of McAdoo's lack of railway experience, it was not well done." The January 6 letter mentioned below was a veritable jeremiad filled with lamentations over the failure to transport food from farms to ports and thence to Europe. The letter three weeks later was a case of twice-told woes with an offer of suggestions of how to ameliorate the ever deteriorating situation.

McAdoo, of course, had his own explanation of the food and shipping crisis that threw the blame on Hoover and quite vindicated himself. He expressed his views some twelve years later in caustic language. (*Crowded Years,* pp. 483–87, 522–23.)

28 January, 1918

Dear Mr. President:

I am enclosing herewith a letter which I have addressed to Mr. McAdoo today and a letter which I addressed to him on the 6th instant, with regard to food movement in the country. I had hoped that the situation would have ameliorated so as to have relieved me from bringing this additional anxiety to your attention. I do not, however, believe that I should be discharging my duty did I not present this matter to you.

I am, Your obedient servant
HERBERT HOOVER

Proclamation Licensing Bakers

The President gave his approval to this proclamation and the rules governing the bakers' activities and returned them to Hoover on January 30. This is revealed by these words written by hand on Hoover's letter: "Proc. sgd & to State [Department] 1/30/18. Rules etc. re licensing approved & returned to Food Ad. 1/30/18." For the substance of the proclamation, see the source book, *Proclamations,* p. 13.

January 28, 1918.

Dear Mr. President:

I submit herewith, for your approval, a Proclamation licensing bakers whose consumption of flour is less than ten barrels a month and more than three barrels a month. These bakers were formerly exempted, but in order to secure uniformity in our new rules, I consider it essential that they be included. The Proclamation also licenses the importation and distribution of green coffee, which I consider necessary in order to forestall speculation and excessive prices which may result from the action of the Shipping Board in taking the ships engaged in the coffee trade.

I also submit, for your approval, certain amendments and additions to the Rules and Regulations governing licensees. The original regulations issued November 1 have had to be modified and supplemented from time to time, and the recent Wheat Conservation Rules are included on pages 11 and 12. I ask that you approve the rules by signing them on page 18.

Faithfully yours,
HERBERT HOOVER

Bush's Complaint of Food Shortages

The Mr. Bush in this letter is probably Colonel Lincoln Bush, a New Jersey civil engineer, who was associate officer in charge of the Engineering Division of Construction of the United States Army and in charge of seven ports and fourteen warehouses. His complaint was an echo of that heard from Great Britain and other Allied countries. Ever since November 1917 they had been reporting "alarm," "consternation," "crisis," "grave urgency," "disastrous results," and "events of incalculable gravity" if more food were not forthcoming from America. (*Grain Trade*, pp. 184–92.) This problem was of course directly connected with the inadequate transportation facilities provided by the railroads. On January 24 Julius H. Barnes, president and director of the Grain Corporation, wrote Hoover a letter marked "urgent and confidential" and bluntly stated that "you should put the responsibility clearly where it belongs, which is on the management of our railroads." He then advised Hoover to tell McAdoo that "you decline to hold yourself longer responsible for the present lack of cereal movement." (*Grain Trade*, p. 255.)

29 January 1918

Dear Mr. President:

With regard to the letter from Mr. Bush, which I return herewith, I beg to say that Mr. Bush has never consulted any member of the Food Administration or he would not have taken your time with this correspondence.

The Government is not behind in any obligations it has undertaken. The English have made demands far beyond our original undertakings and we are doing our best to fulfill them. So far as the English are concerned, we have now reduced our wheat consumption to a lower level per capita than they have in England. It may interest you to read a current letter from myself to the Allied grain agent on these points.

The package goods largely refer to flour, and I beg to say that the firm policy of the Food Administration, entirely approved by Mr. Secretary Houston and the whole country, is that our wheat shipments to England should take place in the form of flour. The reasons for this are:

All the wheat that we ship from now on is a reduction of American consumption. If we ship wheat we should be destroying 30% of the business of our millers; we would cause a rise in the price of flour owing to their extra working cost; we should be denuding the country of 30% of its wheat-basis cattle feeds which are absolutely and critically necessary to carry on our dairy industry; we should have overnight a further rise in the price of dairy products and we would have a further disastrous marketing of our dairy cattle. By shipping flour we save 30% of the tonnage and there is no such acute need for cattle feed in England as there is in the United States. Beyond this fact, we have, in order to save transportation in months gone by, directed the shipment of wheat into the milling centers of the United States and it is now in storage at these points. It would mean that we would have to take the wheat out of the millers' bins if we were to supply the Allies with this bulk commodity. We have some 20,000,000 bushels of wheat in the terminals and this, I regret to say, is about one-third what we should have as a safety valve on food distribution in this country. With the present shortage of cars we simply cannot take the risk of depleting this reserve store which is our only security for adjustment against sporadic and local famines.

I may mention that the complaint of Mr. Bush is identical with that of the English shipping officials in New York and if I may make such suggestion, I would reply to Mr. Bush that he should consult the Food Administration officials in New York, with whom he is well acquainted, rather than the British officials.

I am, Your obedient servant,
HERBERT HOOVER

Discouraging Certain Industries

The day after writing this letter, Hoover held a conference with the press at 3:30. Thereafter, it became a regular practice for him to meet the newspapermen at the same hour each Saturday. This continued until September when he began to see them on Monday or Tuesday.

1 February 1918

Dear Mr. President:

There are a number of food industries, particularly flour mills, canneries, candy manufacturers, sweet drink manufacturers and some others, where the existing producing capacity January 1st was more

than sufficient to take care of all of the nation's needs. Due to the
profits earned in many of these industries during the last two or three
years there is a tendency to speculative expansion by extension of
equipment. The result is to spread the production over a larger amount
of machinery, thus to increase the cost of production by the decreased
output, to increase the demand for labor, for capital and for transportation. In many of these industries we can, through the Food Administration, discourage the establishment of such concerns. I believe that
it is very much in the national interest that this should be done and I
have tentively [sic] taken this view. I should, however, like your approval of this course. It would, of course, be applied only where there
are great numbers of units and no dominating groups.

I beg to remain, Your obedient servant,
HERBERT HOOVER

Approval of the Discouragement

> The day after writing this letter Wilson was visited by the French
> ambassador who presented a memorandum from the Allies on shortage
> of bread cereals from North America. On February 5 Hoover also
> requested a meeting with the President at which "the President prob-
> ably requested information on the cereal situation." (Life and Letters,
> vol. 7, p. 527.) Hoover sent him the desired information on February 9.

4 February, 1918

My dear Mr. Hoover:

I have your letter of February first in which you speak of the tendency on the part of flower [sic] mills, canneries, candy manufacturers,
sweet drink manufacturers, and some others whose productive capacity
is at present more than sufficient to take care of the country's needs to
enter upon a speculative expansion of their production with the result
of spreading their production over a much larger body of machinery
and thus increasing the cost of production by the decreased proportion
of the output, and also increasing the demand for labor, for capital,
and for transportation. If such expansion can be discouraged through
the Food Administration, it is clear to me that it is in the national interest that it should be discouraged, and I am very glad to confirm
your view in that matter.

Sincerely yours,
WOODROW WILSON

United States Cereal Food Position

In this lengthy report Hoover traces the critical cereal food situation in February 1918 to the failure to provide sufficient railway transportation for certain basic commodities. This is simply a restatement of his complaint of January 28. It also appears to be criticism of McAdoo, general director of railroads since December 26, 1917, although Hoover's thrust is softened by his final observation that the weather has been "insuperable." Nonetheless, Hoover had pressed his views strongly before the Council of National Defense on February 6 and was supported by Garfield, Houston, and E. N. Hurley, chairman of the Shipping Board. This quartet harmonized on the theme "transportation has fallen down," to borrow from the diary of Josephus Daniels, Secretary of the Navy, who reported that it was a "depressing meeting." Hoover complained of his unsuccessful prodding of McAdoo, and the council decided to name a committee to see McAdoo. (*Daniels Diaries*, p. 270.) On February 21, Hoover, Garfield, and Hurley told the council that since everything depended on transportation, there was no purpose in meeting unless McAdoo were present. (*Daniels Diaries*, p. 282.)

The Paris Conference, mentioned here, was the topic of Hoover's letter of January 7.

9 February 1918

Dear Mr. President:

I send the following response to your desire for a memorandum as to our cereal food position for your consideration of the cable from the Premiers of England, Italy and France:—

1. At the Paris Conference a definite cereal world programme was drawn up for the provisioning of the Allied countries during the year. I attach herewith a copy of the programme there agreed upon. The following table is a summary of the actual experience with this programme for the months of December, January and February, from which you will see that the failure in shipment amounts to 1,144,000 tons of cereals and of this failure,—35 per cent. falls upon Canada, 37 per cent. on the United States and 29 per cent upon other countries, such as the Argentine, India, et cetera. You will therefore observe that the failure in delivery falls, as to 64 per cent, outside of the United States. The problem, however, is one of practical character and simply means, in view of their statement, that we must increase our shipments to at least partially take care of this deficiency.

	December 1917 000 tons		January 1918 000 tons		February 1918 000 tons		TOTAL
Canada							
Programme	335		425		465		1,225,000
Actual Shipment		290		346		250	886,000
Deficiency			45		79		215	339,000
United States							
Programme	465		575		675		1,715,000
Actual Shipment		201		353		650	1,204,000
Deficiency			264		222		25	511,000
Other Countries							
Programme	220		350		300		870,000
Actual Shipment		131		235		210	576,000
Deficiency			89		115		90	294,000
Total Programme	1020		1350		1440		3,810,000
Total Shipments		622		934		1110	2,666,000
Total Deficiency			398		416		330	1,144,000

2. It must also be a prime consideration to protect our own population, as well as to increase the shipments to the point desired by the Allies. The following is a rough summary of our food situation.—

a. We have apparently a sufficiency of corn to meet both domestic and export requirements provided we do not lose it. On the other hand, the corn crop this year is anything up to 50 per cent. soft corn and much of it will be lost if not moved within six weeks. Inasmuch as some of the corn will probably not keep beyond the end of March the farmers are naturally desirous of selling it in preference to their better qualities. If it can be removed from the farms to the terminal elevators and dried, a great deal of it can be saved. This situation, however, has created a blockade in trade because the country dealers will not buy and store this corn on account of its dangerous condition, unless they can have complete assurance in advance, of railway cars for its instant removal. With the general car shortage and their repeated failure to secure cars, we have thus developed a complete block in its movement. I understand Mr. Houston's view is that it is desirable that the farmer should keep this corn and feed it on the farms and ship the better qualities of corn which he is now holding in reserve. I see no way to induce the farmer to bring out this better quality of corn.

b. In the matter of wheat, although we have exhausted our export surplus, we are continuing to supply the Allies with flour from approximately 12,000,000 bushels of wheat per month in the hope that we can reduce the consumption in this country by that amount. I am fearful, however, that with the general degeneration in the distribution of other foodstuffs, such as corn and potatoes, we will not be able to secure this conservation. This again becomes a question of car supply to get a sufficient distribution of the substitutes for wheat. In any event, I understand that you approve of the policy that we should ship this amount of wheat at least until the critical situation of the Allies has passed, regardless of the risk to our supplies later in the year.

c. We have an ample supply of oats of good quality and the problem is simply one of transportation.

d. Our stocks of rye are practically exhausted as we have but a small crop in any event and the drainage abroad has been very large.

e. The American people are today eating large quantities of barley in substitution for wheat. At the same time the Allies are buying large supplies in America partially for bread and partially for brewing purposes. Also, our own brewers are trying to accumulate large stocks of barley for fear that it will be absorbed by the other two markets.— The consequence is, the price of barley has gone to unheard-of figures and is causing great discontent throughout the country. I believe it is necessary to seriously consider some repression of the use of barley for brewing. We are now investigating what measures can be taken in this direction and I have the feeling, in the situation in which we find ourselves, that—with a subnormal wheat crop and with a corn that, through loss, is likely to be subnormal—neither we nor the Allies are warranted in the continued use of cereals for brewing purposes. I do not however believe that we should take any action in this matter unless similar action is taken in the Allied countries.

Altogether, I feel, despite the short wheat crop and the probable loss of corn, we can feed our own people and the Allies through the year. The Allies however must draw every grain possible from the Argentine and we also may need to import. I cannot disavow the fact that we may have a period of extreme domestic difficulty later in the harvest year.

3. Any study of our food situation will develop the fact that the do-

mestic situation is in critical condition as the cumulative result of transportation failure for the last three months. The following table of arrivals of four of the principal cereal commodities at terminals will indicate to you the degeneration of our cereal food distribution.—

- TOTAL CARS MOVED -
(Interior and seaboard terminal receipts)
Wheat, corn, flour, oats.

	THIS YEAR	LAST YEAR
November	94,202	116,849
December	75,120	96,073
January	64,945	112,065
	234,267	324,987

The result has been exorbitant prices for the uncontrolled corn and oats in the consuming centers and the danger of loss of the corn untransported. A further illumination of the domestic difficulty may be found in the volume of potato movements.

[4.] On the first [of] November we had in the principal potato raising territory, 138,000 carloads of potatoes, the distribution of which should be accomplished equally over a period of eight months, or approximately 17,000 carloads per month. The actual movement, however, was:

November	- 12,934 cars
December	- 6,798 "
January	- 9,841 "

Leaving a balance of over 23,000 cars per month which must be moved if we are not to lose a considerable portion of the potato crop. The incidental effect of a short supply of potatoes has been two-fold: to drive the population to eat more bread and cereals and to lift the price of potatoes in all of the consuming centers, yet to demoralize the price in producing centers so that today the farmer is clamorous to sell his potatoes at $1. a hundred, whereas the city populations are paying $2. and $2.25 per hundred when there should not be a differential of more than 40 cents.

5. A further indication of the lack of movement of our foodstuffs lies in the situation of our warehouse stocks. The following table shows the stocks of wheat, oats and corn in our terminal storage at the first of each of the months shown, by which you will observe that we have not at any time during this period had more than 30 per cent. of our normal reserves for immediate distribution. The failure does not

arise in any difficulty with the farmer in marketing his material for a stock-taking at the end of January of the cereals lying in country elevators shows 170,000,000 bushels of grain awaiting transportation to the terminals.

Total in Terminals
of
Wheat, Oats, Corn

	THIS YEAR	LAST YEAR
November 1st	21,291,000	89,462,000
December 1st	27,138,000	89,656,000
January 1st	31,885,000	89,130,000
February 1st	30,957,000	82,802,000

I think the above figures clearly indicate the great degeneration in transportation and they illuminate the economic situation in the country at the present time in our growing areas of short supply among the consuming centers, in the shortage of stocks in the larger cities and in the exorbitant prices of the uncontrolled cereals, that is, corn and oats. The price level in these grains are at such a basis as to stifle the livestock industry and to force rises of price in animal products, dairy products, et cetera.

6. Mr. McAdoo's assistants entirely agree that the fundamental dislocation is a very great shortage in cars available for the movement of grain in the western territory and that the prime cause for this shortage lies in the fact that the empty cars for this service are blocked in the eastern section. Measures have now been instituted to give preferences in the use of box cars for grain and grain products movement and measures of co-operation have been established with the Food Administration through which I hope for some amelioration and that we may be able to meet the present Allied demands. I and my associates have felt that these measures should go even further than now proposed but I entirely agree that their efficacy should be tested for a few days. I am confident that the degeneration in transportation would have been stemmed when the railways were taken over and Mr. McAdoo placed in charged but the weather has so far been insuperable. On the other hand the cumulative result makes it a serious consideration as to whether measures which might have been successful on January 1st will save the situation on February 9th,

I beg to remain, Your obedient servant,
HERBERT HOOVER

Bills to Raise Wheat Price

Hoover was anxious to stimulate wheat production by guaranteeing an attractive and fixed price to the farmers. The Food Control Act of August 10, 1917, set the price at two dollars per bushel. But in January and February 1918 certain legislators, in an attempt to curry favor with their agricultural constituents, introduced bills that would have guaranteed as much as three dollars a bushel. In the following letter Hoover directs his criticism at three February bills. Senator T. P. Gore, Democrat of Oklahoma, authored one of them. Republican Representative Patrick Norton from North Dakota and P. J. McCumber, Republican senator from the same state, introduced the other two. None of these bills survived committee treatment. (*Grain Trade*, pp. 317–18.)

14 February 1918

Dear Mr. President:

Three different bills have been introduced into Congress during the last few days, looking toward an increase in the minimum guarantee for 1918 wheat, from the $2.00 under the Food Bill to various sums up to $3.00. One of these has been introduced by Senator McCumber, another by Senator Gore and still another by Congressman Norton. There has also been organized in Washington a group of agricultural representatives called the "Wheat Growers Protective Association," whose energies are directed towards accomplishing this legislation.

It does seem to me that determinations of this type should be left to commissions to be appointed by yourself, to make necessary and proper inquiry in which all complexions of such problems can be considered and it was in our mind to suggest to you—some time next June— to assemble such a commission as sat last year, and obtain from them a view as to the price to be paid over and above the guaranteed minimum for 1918 wheat if in their view any increase was desirable. My present purpose, however, of addressing you is to express my extreme anxiety as to the results that will come from the agitation of such legislation. About 125,000,000 bushels of 1917 wheat are still in the hands of the farmer and we are depending upon this supply for the bread of our people for the months of April, May and June. An agitation of this character will surely create hopes in the minds of the farmer that he will receive a larger price next year for his wheat than is being paid this year ($2.20) and he will certainly hold his present wheat with the hope of mixing it with his 1918 wheat and securing the larger return.

I feel absolutely certain that if such legislation is passed or even pressed, one of two alternative courses will have to be pursued by the Government.—

The first alternative is to stop all Allied shipments instantly and to use force to secure at least a sufficient portion of the 1917 wheat from the farmer to complete our domestic supplies at the price that was established by the commission under your direction and which price was stated to be constant for the year. The second alternative would be to at once raise the price of wheat to the level of the enlarged guarantee. In so doing we will not only be acting unfairly to all of the agricultural community who have marketed their wheat on the assurance that it was a fixed and constant price for the year, but further than this, we would be practically helpless to prevent the same rise in the price of some 90,000,000 bushels of wheat in the hands of the thousands of country elevators and mills and some 20,000,000 barrels of flour in the hands of the distributing trades in the country. In other words, in such an event a tax of anything up to $200,000,000 will be placed upon the consuming community without one penny's benefit to the producer and to the sole benefit of the distributing trades. It is hopeless for us to expect to prosecute the 300,000 concerns engaged in the distribution of wheat and flour for profiteering, or to determine which of their particular stores were based on the old price and which upon the new.

You are perhaps aware that there has been planted this year 42,000,000 acres of winter wheat as against 40,000,000 acres last year and as against 33,000,000 pre-war normal. I take it that this has been planted because of the stimulation of the $2.00 guarantee and it is evidence in my mind—and I think in Mr. Houston's—that the guarantee is ample to produce the results desired. Moreover, the world food situation has developed to a point where it is almost a matter of indifference as to what cereal is planted. The Allied peoples are now eating such a mixture of wheat, corn, rye and barley that if the farmers in this country should decide that any other cereal is preferable to planting spring wheat, it would make but little difference in the world food supply.

I have every desire that justice should be done to the American farmer, that he should receive every stimulant possible to the utmost exertion, but I believe that our anxiety should be equally directed towards the position of the American consumer, for if the price of flour should be raised during this winter by $5. per barrel it would mean a rise of at least two cents a pound in the price of bread and, as you know, already our anxieties are sufficiently great as to tiding over our industrial populations with the present range of prices without disturbances.

I am, Your obedient servant,

HERBERT HOOVER

Opposition to Higher Wheat Price

> On February 19 Wilson wrote to Senator T. S. Martin, chairman of the Committee on Appropriations, and to Representative F. A. Lever, chairman of the Committee on Agriculture. He enclosed in each letter Hoover's four-page message of February 14. He observed that Hoover had "made a very strong case indeed . . . against legislative action to secure higher prices for wheat," and he solicited their aid in blunting the thrust of agitators for such action. (*Life and Letters,* vol. 7, p. 552.)

18 February, 1918

My dear Mr. Hoover:

I have your letter of the fourteenth and agree with you that the agitation of legislation for a higher price of wheat is a very serious mistake just now. I will see what I can do, though it is practically impossible, I fear, to prevent agitation of this sort.

Cordially and sincerely yours,

WOODROW WILSON

Cattlemen's Complaint of Packers

> Wilson's letter does not include identification of the men mentioned nor any information as to the date of their meeting with the President (but see Hoover's letter of February 21 on the subject). The "memorial" to which Wilson referred was "returned to the White House," according to a handwritten note on the following letter. The memorial and the personal presentation of the cattlemen must have touched the President deeply and could well have been the reason for the cutting edge of another letter of his on the same day concerning the packers. At 4:00 Hoover himself had been at the White House.

19 February, 1918

My dear Mr. Hoover:

The men who brought me the enclosed memorial struck me as sincere and straightforward, and they made the very definite statement that they were losing so much per head on the cattle they were raising and they ascribed as the reason the entire control of the price by the packers. I would be very much obliged if you would look over these papers and make any comments upon them that occur to you and any suggestions of practicable courses of action, because manifestly our supply of meat depends upon the solution of just such questions as this.

Cordially and faithfully yours,
WOODROW WILSON

Reprimand for Packers

The sharp words in the following short note may well have been provoked by the event alluded to in the previous letter of February 19. It is also interesting to refer to Hoover's letter of February 21 in which he writes that "I have no great love for the packers and they have been very difficult to deal with."

19 February, 1918

My dear Mr. Hoover:

May I not call your attention to this important point:

There is pressing need of the full cooperation of the packing trade, of every officer and employee, in the work of hurrying provisions abroad. Let the packers understand that they are engaged in a war service in which they must take orders and act together under the direction of the Food Administration if the Food Administration requires.

Cordially and sincerely yours,
WOODROW WILSON

Insufficient Boxcars in the West

Once again Hoover addressed the President on the persistent crisis in the rail transportation of foodstuffs. (His last complaint would seem to have been the lengthy report of February 9 and not February 8 as mentioned below.) The following short letter prompted Wilson to write a note to "My dear Mac" (son-in-law William G. McAdoo), with Hoover's letter enclosed, indicating that he sided with the Food Administrator in this running battle of the boxcars. McAdoo responded with a short but trenchant letter to Hoover clearly implying that Hoover and not he himself was at fault for any food shortage that might exist. (*Life and Letters*, vol. 7, p. 559.) There was a steady flow of such communiques throughout the ensuing weeks, which prompted Hoover to observe in his letter of March 5 to McAdoo that "I am afraid if we start exchanging complaints there will certainly be a fairly large correspondence."

On February 25 Secretary of the Interior Franklin K. Lane wrote in his cabinet jottings that "Hoover and McAdoo are at swords drawn. Hoover had a cable from the three Premiers . . . crying for wheat and charging us with not keeping our word . . . because we have not been able to get the wheat to the ships. . . . I asked Hoover about this on Sunday night, . . . and he said that a list of eight hundred cars had been on McAdoo's desk *for a week.* . . ." Lane then reported that somebody on the Interstate Commerce Commission "had said . . . today that he thought Hoover seventy-five per cent right." (*Letters of Lane,* pp. 265–66.)

19 February 1918

Dear Mr. President:

I addressed you last on the 8th instant as to our domestic transportation of foodstuffs. Since that date, by a preference in the use of box cars for grain in the western territory, there has been some acceleration in the movement of some of the grains to the terminals. On the other hand the number of cars have not been sufficient to maintain the food traffic from the west into the east and have not been sufficient to move Allied supplies of cereals and meat products. In consequence, we are faced not only with a renewed failure in Allied shipments, but also, our stocks of foodstuffs in the eastern states are steadily diminishing. The Allied Purchasing Commission reports to me that the situation has become now the most critical in which they have found themselves since the beginning of the War. There are still great numbers of box cars on the eastern lines which belong to the west and the movement in the eastern territory is still far below the necessities of the case.

I cannot but feel that we are approaching a very serious crisis and I feel greatly discouraged over the entire situation.

I am, Your obedient servant,
HERBERT HOOVER

Taussig and the Food Administration Investigation

Hoover had suffered much at the hands of congressional committees. He therefore suggested that the Food Administration should forestall an inevitable congressional investigation of the Grain Division by holding one of its own under the competent and responsible Professor F. W. Taussig, chairman of the Tariff Commission and professor of economics at Harvard University.

20 February 1918

Dear Mr. President:

I have not the remotest doubt but that the operations of the Grain Division of the Food Administration will come up for assault or investigation by Congress sooner or later, and it occurs to me it might be worth while taking time by the forelock and having an investigation of our own. I am wondering if you would mind my appealing to Dr. Taussig to secure assistance and make an investigation of the entire operations and write a report—this report to be made to yourself. We could then be armed to use it the minute we saw that such an investigation was brewing. I would not propose to make any public announcement.

I am, Your obedient servant,
HERBERT HOOVER

Approval of Investigation

President Wilson gave his blessing to Hoover's suggestion and Hoover contacted Taussig. In his February 25 letter to Taussig he noted that "investigations are the order of the day" and that there should be one into the operation of the Grain Division "by an independent man of knowledge and economic sense" with freedom to choose his assistants. An investigation was subsequently held under Taussig but with emphasis on the Milling Division. In June the fact-finding commission issued its report which had high praise for the Milling Division mingled with some criticism of its operations. (*Grain Trade*, pp. 126–30.)

21 February, 1917 [1918]

My dear Mr. Hoover:

If Mr. Taussig has the time, I should entirely approve of his investigating the grain division of the Food Administration as you suggest in your letter of yesterday.

Cordially and sincerely yours,
WOODROW WILSON

Packers, Prices, and Profits

Hoover's letter of February 21 and the eleven-page memorandum enclosed were most likely prompted by Wilson's letter of February 19 with its reference to the "sincere and straightforward men" who had just recently visited him. Dwight B. Hurd was one of these visitors. Hoover's letter and exhaustive enclosure would seem to absolve the packers from the charge of price-fixing that had occasioned the complainants to carry their grievance to the White House. Hurd was in all probability a cattleman who on February 14 appeared before the Senate Agricultural Committee to urge the creation of a commission to regulate the livestock industry. (*Times*, Feb. 15, 1918, p. 10.)

21 February 1918

Dear Mr. President:

I have received your letter of the 19th enclosing the memorial presented to you by Mr. Hurd and his associates. Most of these gentlemen have already discussed these matters at length with us. I do think, however, that it is desirable to set out this situation on the points raised by these gentlemen so far as we are able to penetrate into it. I therefore attach rather a full memorandum to that end and upon which you may desire to secure Mr. Secretary Houston's views before using, as it concerns production matters.

In addition to the statement contained therein with regard to the packers, I would like to say that, as you know, I have no great love for the packers and they have been very difficult to deal with. They do control prices in the sense that every group of middle-men operating in large units control prices to some extent, that is, they control prices more or less from day to day and in the particular sense as to the price they pay for individual cattle and sheep and the prices at which they make individual sales. On the other hand, in the long run, even they cannot control the great forces of supply and demand. By the methods which we have employed in limiting their profits we have endeavoured to restrain the large ones from driving the little ones out of business, and have tried by our large buying orders for abroad to keep the plants, both large and small, running at full capacity. We have not detected, and we are certain they have not been making excessive profit since November 1st, although they appeared to have made very large profits prior to that date. Their sworn statements to us as to their monthly operations show that they have operated at a very small margin, or even a loss, for the last two months. We are anxious that the Federal Trade

Commission should give us the use of their staff of accountants to check up these statements as it is a very involved and complicated matter in which their own staffs have already had valuable experience. This work is in the nature of cost accounting similar to that in certain branches of the government and I understand, if some direction were given by you to the Federal Trade Commission they would place their staff at our service. I am wondering if you would be so kind as to instruct them to undertake this work.

It is only fair to say with regard to the packers that they have performed an indispensable service for war purposes. We have studiously kept away from discussions as to their previous career and private character and I can say that they have advanced very far during the last three months in performing a work of national service.

Yours faithfully,
HERBERT HOOVER

Answer to Lord Reading on Food

Lord Reading had been the British ambassador for slightly more than a week when in a letter of February 22 he wrote that "nothing short of calamity" would fall upon the Allies if more grain were not shipped immediately. The Italian ambassador and the French high commissioner also signed the letter. On February 26 Hoover responded by promising 1,285,000 tons of corn, wheat, and flour for March, or 185,000 tons more than requested. He enclosed a copy of this letter to President Wilson. (*Grain Trade*, p. 192.)

The day before, at 11:45, Hoover went to see McAdoo at his office. Their conversation quite possibly concerned the subject of Hoover's subsequent letter.

26 February 1918

Dear Mr. President:

Please find enclosed herewith a letter that I have addressed today to Lord Reading with regard to the March programme of Allied shipments. I wish you to know that this shipment amounts to a very considerable diversion from our domestic demands and will sooner or later precipitate us into difficulties with our own supplies. We felt, however, that it was your wish that we should take care of their pressing necessities.

Yours faithfully,
HERBERT HOOVER

Spreckels's Lack of Cooperation

Claus A. Spreckels, head of the Federal Sugar Refining Company, caused Hoover considerable distress by his refusal to sign a contract with the Food Administration designed to protect the sugar supply and the sugar market. On December 14, 1917, he appeared before the Senate Committee on Agriculture and declared that Hoover had "created" the sugar shortage. (*Life and Letters*, vol. 7, p. 409.) Hoover issued a rejoinder without delay, releasing a press statement on December 15 in which he asserted that Spreckels was "sore at the Food Administration and would like to see it destroyed." He contrasted Spreckels's greed for profits with the spirit of the vast majority who besides foregoing profits, were "sacrificing more than their money—their sons." He concluded by stating that "the 900,000 tons of sugar in Java is as remote as cheese out of the moon—unless we wish to take bread ships from our own soldiers and the Allies to provide ourselves with candy." (*Times*, Dec. 16, pp. 1, 19.)

1 March 1918

Dear Mr. President:

You will recollect that I discussed with you the fact that Mr. [C. A.][1] Spreckels was raising difficulties over the signing of the contract for purchases of Cuban sugar. All the other refiners in the United States have signed this contract. It has been signed by the representatives of the Allied governments and by the representatives of the Cuban government. We have arranged a loan of $100,000,000 to finance the Cuban sugar crop and the American bankers have loaned the money on the faith of this contract. Mr. Spreckels has not, so far, refused to sign the contract, but he has raised one quibble after another and in a patient desire to settle the matter amicably, he has been supplied with sugar since the first of January pro rata with the other refiners.

I enclose herewith copy of his last communication. I would be glad—if you could see your way to do so—if you would now direct me—if he does not at once sign the contract—to give the necessary instructions to the War Trade Board and to the Shipping Board, to cease the issuance of licenses to him on one hand for import, and to cease providing him with transportation on the other. The necessity for this whole arrangement is receiving daily demonstration, as, for instance, owing to the shortage in overseas transportation, sugars have accumulated to large

1. Handwritten insertion.

quantities in Cuba and were it not for this arrangement and the finance behind it, the price of sugar would have absolutely collapsed in Cuba before this, the mills would have been shut down,—with all the possibilities of disturbance and dislocation—to say nothing of the total jeopardy of our sugar supplies not only this year but next year as well.

I may mention, for your own information, that the points Mr. Spreckels raises in the latter part of his letter are also quibbles. Every refiner has the right to act as a wholesaler if he so wishes, provided he complies with the regulations as to wholesalers. So far as purchases of sugar in Cuba are concerned, these are in the responsibility of the Cuban government who are managing that end of the work and not upon us.

As to two-cent extra freight rates to his refineries, you will also find enclosed letter of February 5th, addressed to Mr. Spreckels, which shows the dishonesty of this paragraph of his letter, for on this date the matter was settled as he wished.

Yours faithfully,
Herbert Hoover

Tyler for Food Administrator

> In the following letter Hoover presents a nominee for state food administrator with some of his qualifications and names of those recommending him. William S. Tyler, like most of those in the Food Administration (including its head), had volunteered to serve for nothing.

March 2nd 1918.

Dear Mr. President:—

Ex Governor James F. Fielder of Jersey City, New Jersey, is obliged to resign from the position of Federal Food Administrator for the State, owing to the great pressure of his personal affairs upon his time.

After careful consideration, I wish to recommend, as Mr. Fielder's successor, Mr. William S. Tyler, of Plainfield, New Jersey.

Mr. Tyler is strongly endorsed by Mr. H. W. Jeffers and Mr. Alva Agee, both of the State Board of Agriculture; he is also thought very highly of by Senator J. S. Frelinghuysen and other leading citizens of the State. He has been active in war work in the city of Plainfield for some time, and with his brother has run a very large dairy farm, largely in a charitable way. He is, however, willing to give all his time—as a

volunteer—to war work, although, besides these activities I have enu-
merated, he actively practises law in New York City.

Faithfully yours,

HERBERT HOOVER

Approved

WOODROW WILSON [handwritten by Wilson]

Cooperation with Baruch

The following letter carried the same message that Wilson also sent to
cabinet members and other heads of war agencies. It asked all to cooperate with Bernard M. Baruch whom Wilson had appointed as
chairman of the War Industries Board. (*Life and Letters*, vol. 8, p. 7,
n. 1.) The board had been created in July 1917 as the major in-
strument in directing the industrial side of the war; Baruch was its
third chairman.

4 March, 1918.

Dear Mr. Hoover:

I am taking the liberty of sending you a letter which I have just
addressed to Mr. Bernard Baruch.

I am sending you the letter for your information not only, but in
order to afford myself the opportunity of asking if you will not be kind
enough, whenever the occasion arises, to afford the War Industries Board
the fullest possible co-operation of your Administration.

I have the lively hope that this reorganization of the War Industries
Board will add very considerably to the speed and efficiency of our action
in the matter of war supplies.

Cordially and sincerely yours,

WOODROW WILSON

Congratulations for Baruch Appointment

Hoover's work as Food Administrator brought him into close contact
with Baruch during the war. From such contact he learned that "aside
from Baruch's ability to select men, he possessed a fine manner and
fine probity of character . . . a capacity for friendship and loyalty
and an ability to listen patiently to complicated discussions and in the

end produce a penetrating and successful solution of the problem."
(*Memoirs,* vol. 1, p. 265.)

Baruch had an equally high appreciation of Hoover. Writing in
1960, he said that he was "by all odds one of the ablest men in Washington." (Baruch, *Public Years,* p. 89.)

March 5th, 1918.

Dear Mr. President:

I congratulate you on the selection of Mr. Baruch to head the War
Industries Board. We have always enjoyed the closest co-operation, and
I am sure it will continue.

Faithfully yours,
HERBERT HOOVER

Action against Spreckels

Wilson was convinced by Hoover's letter of March 1 that Spreckels was
at fault in the sugar dispute. He therefore agreed to the punitive
action suggested by Hoover, and on March 5 he wrote Edward N.
Hurley, chairman of the Shipping Board, authorizing him "to refuse
all further transportation for the importation of sugar to . . . Mr.
C. A. Spreckels." Borrowing from Hoover's letter of March 1, Wilson
observed that Spreckels had raised "objections which were purely in
the nature of quibbles." The same instructions were sent to Vance C.
McCormick of the War Trade Board authorizing him to deny Spreckels
the licenses necessary for the importation of sugar. (*Life and Letters,*
vol. 8, pp. 12–13.)

5 March, 1918.

My dear Mr. Hoover:

I have your letter of March first and have considered the important
matter it lays before me. I am returning the correspondence which you
were kind enough to send with it.

I agree with you that Mr. Spreckels presents no sufficient reasons
why he cannot join the other refiners in signing the contract with you
and I therefore feel justified in issuing the instructions to which you
refer. I am issuing them today.

Cordially and sincerely yours,
WOODROW WILSON

Lemon for Food Administrator

March 6, 1918.

Dear Mr. President:

Mr. Henry M. Hoyt of Reno, Nevada, is obliged to resign from the position of Federal Food Administrator for the State on account of ill health. We are sorry to lose his services as he has done excellent work.

After careful consideration, I wish to recommend as Mr. Hoyt's successor, Mr. H. A. Lemon of Reno.

Mr. Lemon is strongly endorsed by Governor Boyle, Mr. Hoyt, and other leading citizens of the State. He is now Secretary of the State Council of Defense and is ready to give all his time,—as a volunteer,—to war work. His occupation in normal times is sales manager of the local power company.

Faithfully yours,
HERBERT HOOVER

Approved
WOODROW WILSON [handwritten by Wilson]

Reading and U.S. Sacrifice

> Hoover explained to Wilson as he had to Lord Reading, the British ambassador, that to continue shipping the present amount of food to the Allies would be possible only if Americans had their normal consumption of wheat reduced by 15 million bushels each month. He thought only the President should rule upon the justice and feasibility of imposing such a sacrifice on the American people. Wilson answered immediately that "there is no choice in the matter."

7 March, 1918.

Dear Mr. President:

I enclose herewith a letter which I addressed to Lord Reading and his reply thereto. The situation with regard to wheat supplies in this country gets more and more difficult as time goes on and if we succeed in delivering to seaboard the amount of wheat products that have been allocated to the railways for transportation during the present month, we will apparently have a residue of about 130,000,000 bushels available to carry our people for a period of four months.—And this assuming that we get every grain of wheat from the farmer except his seed. I do not presume that we can count on the last 30,000,000 bushels from the farmer and therefore we have now before us about 25,000,000 bushels a month against a normal consumption of 40,000,000 bushels. There is, in addition to this, a certain amount in transit and in retail stocks.

I have replied to Lord Reading that under these circumstances it seems to me it is a matter that requires your decision.

I remain, Your obedient servant,
HERBERT HOOVER

Sacrifice of Food by Americans

At 5:00 on the day Wilson wrote this letter, he had a private talk with Hoover at the White House. At 2:00 Hoover had met with the Federal Trade Commission and W. A. Glasgow, chief counsel for the Food Administration, on the subject of the commission's investigation of the packers. It seems very probable that Hoover's conversation with the President touched upon the matter contained in the letter to Lord Reading. Hoover had sent a copy of that letter to Wilson and it reached the White House on March 8. The President answered the same day but may have felt it wise to see Hoover personally.

8 March, 1918.

My dear Mr. Hoover:

I have your letter of yesterday and realize the very great seriousness of the prospect you point out, namely, a probable shortage for our own people of 15,000,000 [bushels] a month in the wheat supply, and you close your letter by saying, "It seems to me it is a matter which requires your decision."

I am not sure what it is you think I ought to decide. I suppose you mean that I ought to decide whether we are to continue our present scale of shipment of breadstuffs across the seas and so incur the shortage for our own people to which you refer. I am afraid there is no choice in the matter. The populations across the sea must be fed and have, as I understand it, no available substitutes for wheat, whereas our own people have at least substitutes and have them, I believe (have they not?) in adequate quantities. Personally, I feel confident that the spirit of our people would rise to the sacrifice and that, if there are adequate quantities of the available substitutes, they would be willing to use them. Is not that your own judgment?

Cordially and sincerely yours,
WOODROW WILSON

Meeting of the War Cabinet

In February 1918 Hoover suggested the establishment of what became known as a "war cabinet," composed of the heads of the departments and agencies that dealt with war questions. In the following letter President Wilson announces its first meeting for March 20. Thereafter it met each Wednesday, usually in the President's study. The war council or cabinet discussed not only economic matters but major military and international policies as well. Members mentioned in the letter were William G. McAdoo, Secretary of the Treasury and director general of railroads; Bernard Baruch, chairman of the War Industries Board; E. N. Hurley, chairman of the Shipping Board; Vance McCormick, chairman of the War Trade Board, and Harry Garfield, Fuel Administrator.

In his *Memoirs* (vol. 1, p. 263) Hoover states that his idea for a war cabinet was the product of his "experience with every European government at War, and our own muddle." He also confesses his early failure to convince Wilson of the need for such a war establishment, but he succeeded in winning over Garfield, and this long-time friend of the President's converted Wilson to the idea. Wilson's initial coldness to the idea might well be traced to a Republican-inspired plan for a war cabinet unveiled in mid-January. It provided for a council of "three distinguished citizens" to function independently of the regular cabinet but directly under the President. Wilson attacked the proposal with cold ferocity. This attack plus general public disapprobation resulted ultimately in its demise. (*Politics*, pp. 88, 93, 101.)

Actually the war cabinet meetings quickly assumed greater importance than those of Wilson's official cabinet. A reading of Josephus Daniels's cabinet diaries *(Daniels Diaries)* reveals how these latter meetings became occasions for discussing trivial matters and listening to the President's jokes. Secretary of the Interior Franklin K. Lane wrote thus about the March 12, 1918, meeting: "Nothing talked of at Cabinet that would interest a nation, a family, or a child. No talk of war. No talk of Russia or Japan. Talk . . . by President about giving the veterans of the Spanish War leave with pay, to attend their annual encampment. And he treated this seriously as if it were a matter of first importance!" And about the session of October 23, Lane wrote, "For some weeks we have spent our time at Cabinet meetings telling stories." (*Letters of Lane,* pp. 267, 293.)

Ray Stannard Baker has suggested that Wilson's reluctance to discuss serious matters at the regular cabinet meetings was due in part to his feeling that Lane was too indiscreet. Baker also observes that during the war period "much of the immediate business of the war was taken up at the meetings of the so-called 'war cabinet.' " (*Life and Letters,* vol. 4, pp. 297–98; vol. 8, p. 20, n. 1.)

As to the character of the war cabinet meetings and their value as seen by participants, Hurley has written thus: "The weekly meetings were like conferences of executives of large corporations reporting progress of their work to their president and submitting ways and means to carry on further. . . . In the thirty years of my business career, I never have been associated with a group of men who worked together so harmoniously and effectively." (Hurley, *Bridge to France,* pp. 178, 319–21.) McCormick wrote that the meetings had "immense value" and constituted "a clearing house of facts and of policy." (*Life and Letters,* vol. 8, p. 37, n. 1.)

16 March, 1918.

My dear Mr. Hoover:

I wonder if it would be possible for you to make it convenient to meet me at the White House next Wednesday at 2:30 to discuss a number of matters which I would like to discuss with you and the following gentlemen, whom I am also inviting:

Mr. McAdoo, Mr. Baruch, Mr. Hurley, Mr. McCormick, and Doctor Garfield.

Faithfully yours,
WOODROW WILSON

Return of the President's Letters

During this time many people who typed their letters often made no carbon copies. Thus Wilson was naturally concerned that all his official letters were duly returned by recipients along with their replies. This meant, of course, that files must often have been inadequate unless secretaries typed copies of all letters received, since no copying machines existed at this time. Wilson himself very frequently jotted "approved, Woodrow Wilson" on letters sent him by Hoover and then mailed them back to his Food Administrator without making copies.

March 20, 1918

MEMORANDUM:

Please drop a note to the offices of the different Cabinet members and to that of Mr. Hoover, requesting them to return with their replies the letters the President refers to their chiefs for advice or comment.

C.L.S.

Suggestions on a Telegram

The telegram referred to in this letter was from Colonel T. A. Hudson of Columbia, Mo., and concerned the price of corn as it affected the producers of animals for food. Wilson received it on March 20 and forthwith sent it to Hoover who prepared a suggested reply on March 22. The "conference" mentioned in Wilson's letter was a meeting of the war cabinet held on March 20 at 2:30 in the White House and attended by Baruch, McAdoo, Hurley, Garfield, McCormick, and Hoover.

21 March, 1918.

My dear Mr. Hoover:

I would very much like a suggestion from you as to the answer to be made to the enclosed telegram. Does it not afford an opportunity for correcting the impression that you stated in our conference yesterday?

Cordially and sincerely yours,

WOODROW WILSON

Suggested Reply to Hudson

In his suggested reply to Hudson's criticism, Hoover said that "no power existed to fully relieve the difficulties of the higher grades of beef, nor to lower the price of corn." He also underscored the fact that the high price of corn had "to some extent" been due to the transportation shortage during the blizzard months. This problem no longer existed; therefore the normal play of supply and demand would return. In addition, he said that the Food Administration was taking measures to assist the corn growers.

The second source of distress mentioned by Hoover in this letter of March 22 was a continuance of the attacks by certain senators who remained adamant in their opposition to policies of the Food Administration and to its head. The extract from the *Congressional Record* referred to in Hoover's letter was for March 21, pages 4105 and 4106. On that day Senator T. P. Gore, Democrat of Oklahoma, had a telegram read in the upper chamber from the Dazey-Moore Grain Company of Fort Worth, Tex., which, among other things, charged that "concentration and monopoly have superseded the open competitive market and producers and distributors are now at the mercy of one man. . . ."

The reading of this telegram prompted a bitter attack on the

Food Administration by Senator Gore, Senator Reed, and Republican Senator Gronna of North Dakota. On March 21, Hoover wrote to Senator Morris Sheppard, Democrat of Texas, who had received the telegram that sparked this attack. In answering the accusations of the company (referred to by Hoover as the Moon Grain Company), he wrote in part that if the company had "made any committments [sic] on behalf of the Allied buyers, I am sure these gentlemen will complete the bargain. If, on the other hand, they speculated against allied necessities, I am sure they deserve no sympathy."

Although Hoover had talked to Wilson about the beef and corn problem the day before during the weekly meeting of the war cabinet, he saw the President again at 5:30 on the day he wrote his reply to Hudson. At 6:00 he went to Representative Lever's office. It is very likely that he discussed with both the subject matter of that reply.

22 March, 1918

Dear Mr. President:

I return herewith suggested draft of reply to Col. Hudsons [sic] telegram of March 20th which you kindly sent to me for preparation. All these gentlemen are hard to please. They base their troubles in raising animals on the price of corn and when corn falls they complain about that commodity. In fact, many commodities are falling as the result of more nearly normal transportation and merchandising conditions and I seem to have mud slinging both ways. I enclose a page from the Congressional Record yesterday and my reply thereto which I would indeed be glad if you would read as it develops an incident of which more complaints will no doubt reach you. It also indicates the heart-breaking injustice of criticism based on reckless statements without even the human courtesy of a telephonic inquiry into truth.

Yours faithfully,
HERBERT HOOVER

SUGGESTED TELEGRAM:

During your recent conference with the Food Administration, Mr. Hoover explained to you fully that no power existed to fully relieve the difficulties of the producers of the higher grades of beef, nor to lower the price of corn, which was suggested by some representatives of livestock growers in Washington.

Certain suggestions were made at the conference as to a course of action by the Food Administration to try and relieve the situation in feeder cattle, and this is being done as far as the Food Administration's authority extends. Satisfaction was expressed by those present with the attitude and effort of the Food Administration and it will continue as heretofore to aid in relieving difficult situations whenever possible.

Mr. Hoover informs me that he stated to yourself and many others, as illustrating the difficulties in the situation, that either the prices for certain classes of animals were too low, or the price of corn and feeds was too high, and further that the price of corn was, in his view, due, to some extent, to the shortage of transportation during the blizzard months and the consequent under-supply to the consumer; that with larger railway movement the prices of corn would probably decline. The energetic moving of corn by the railways and consequent fulfillment of the accumulated and pressing demands of the domestic trade and the Allies has now apparently given play to the normal action of supply and demand.

The measures taken by the Food Administration to extend the domestic and Allied human consumption of corn must be of help to corn-growers.

Cereal Supplies and Lord Reading

On March 22 another letter heavy with statistics on cereal supplies was sent to Lord Reading, the British ambassador at Washington. Among other things, Hoover pointed out to Reading that measures were being taken to reduce wheat consumption in America for the rest of 1918 to 50 percent of normal. This would mean, he pointed out, that "our population will have to live on only two pounds of wheat bread per week against over five pounds to allied countries." Such an imposition could be defended before the American public, he concluded, only if severe restrictions were placed on wheat consumption in Canada.

In his March 22 letter to Wilson, in which the Reading letter was enclosed, Hoover concentrated on the shortage in shipping and other problems that complicated the bringing of relief to the Allies.

22 March, 1918.

Dear Mr. President:

Please find enclosed a letter which I have dispatched today to Lord Reading on cereal supplies during the next three months. Our office has worked out the most constructive method that we can think of to give further relief to the Allies. The problem revolves in fact on ship-

ping, because if enough ships were placed at once at the disposal of the
Allies, with sufficient pressure upon the Argentine, it appears to me that
we could be relieved of pressure here by the end of May. The following
figures will indicate to you approximately our present situation:

Wheat on Farms March 1st	111,000,000
" in Mills " "	36,700,000
" in Elevators do	47,500,000
Flour Mills do	10,000,000
	205,200,000

Less —		
Seed	30,000,000	
Farms Reserve ..	20,000,000	
Allies	50,000,000	100,000,000
		105,200,000
Five months to go at 21,000,000 =		105,000,000

In addition to the above we have a reserve of the floating stocks of
flour in transit and in wholesalers' and retailers' hands which might be
worked down to somewhat smaller dimensions, but this is but a small
marginal reserve.

We are confronted with four serious matters. The first is that a
compilation of the wheat marketed by farmers to March 1st, added to
the existing wheat on the farms according to the Department of Agriculture reports, indicates that last year's crop was 40,000,000 to 50,000,000
bushels lower than the estimate. This is not an abnormal difference in
estimate as all crop estimates are necessarily 10 to 15 per cent speculation, but, unfortunately, the difference is against us this year and adds
to the seriousness of the whole position. We really had no export surplus
at all, and we will by the end of March have exported about 100,000,000
bushels.

The second difficulty we are confronted with is the fact that in order
to even carry out this programme, we must secure a further marketing
of 60,000,000 bushels from the farmer, and I am afraid there is a great
deal of hoarding, stimulated by the agitation in Congress. I have recently sent out a strong appeal to farmers to market their wheat before
May 1st, and I feel that if we have not secured it by that date it may be
necessary that I should propose to you that we should requisition all
outstanding wheat. All of the loyal farmers will have marketed by that
time and such a requisition would be received favorably by the majority
of those.

The third difficulty lies in the fact that although we are getting a gradually increased substitute milling capacity by the conversion of wheat mills, we may have difficulty in keeping pace with the demand.

The fourth difficulty is our total lack of adequate authority to impose a competent control of distribution, that whatever we do must be based to a large degree on voluntary action and, to a secondary degree, on remote interpretation of the Food Bill.

A fifth difficulty lies in the present location of our wheat, we having dangerously exhausted those milling sections that must supply the industrial population. The programme outlined in my letter to Lord Reading supplies 800,000 tons per month from North America, against a total demand of about 1,500,000 tons. Their actual need by careful conservation and gradual expansion of stocks is probably 1,200,000 tons.

For all these reasons I feel we are not only taking great risks but asking the last mite from our own people.

Faithfully yours,
HERBERT HOOVER

Comments on a March 22 Letter

> It is not possible to relate this brief note of President Wilson to any particular letter written by Hoover on March 22 since it is a response that would have been suitable to more than one letter bearing that date. The "situation" discussed in the Hudson reply was "serious" as was that forming the subject matter of the letter to Reading.

25 March, 1918

My dear Mr. Hoover:

Thank you for your letter of March twenty-second. I see how serious the situation is, but there is no choice, I believe, but to go forward as best we can.

Cordially and sincerely yours,
WOODROW WILSON

Commission for the Meat Problem

> The hog problem had caused Hoover considerable anguish from the moment he assumed the duties of Food Administrator in May 1917. For three years the Allies had been slaughtering their cattle, sheep, and pigs to feed soldiers and civilians; but since Hoover deemed it

impractical to ship feed grains for the depleted herds, he urged American farmers to increase greatly their production of meats and fats. The following letters concern, among other things, the problems involved in guaranteeing swine producers a sufficient price so as to comply with Hoover's urgings. As a step toward solving these problems, Hoover suggested a special study commission. This suggestion was made at a conference with the President on Friday, March 22. (*Life and Letters,* vol. 8, p. 42.) Wilson approved the recommendation, and on April 1 the text of the detailed March 26 letter on the meat problem and news of Wilson's appointment of the "official board" appeared in the press. (*Times,* Apr. 1, 1918, p. 1.)

March Twenty-Sixth 1918.

Dear Mr. President:

I am sending you, herewith, a letter on the whole meat problem, in amplification of my conversation on Friday in asking for the appointment of a commission to study this subject.

As you have seen by the number of deputations to Washington, there is a great deal of discontent amongst the animal growers in the country, and I believe the appointment of such a commission would go far to quiet this matter and develop some constructive policy.

I feel that it would do a lot of immediate good, if you find yourself in accord with the proposal that I make, that I should issue the accompanying letter to the press, together with your approval of the appointment of such a commission; and my excuse for writing at such length is to set out with all the care that may be the whole problem to public view, as there is the greatest misunderstanding throughout the country as to the Government's activities in this instance.

Faithfully yours,
HERBERT HOOVER

March 26, 1918

Dear Mr. President:

I feel that we have reached a position with regard to the whole meat industry of the country that requires a reconsideration of policy. The situation is one of the most complex with which the Government has to deal, by virtue of the increasing influence that the Government purchasing has upon prices, by the necessity of providing for increasing supplies for the allies, and the consequent reduction of civilian consumption and, withal, the due protection of the producer and the civilian consumer. This change of policy may take the form of more definite and systematic direction of the larger packers as to the course that they are to pursue from month to month, or may even take the form of operation of the packing house establishments by the Government.

The general economic forces bearing on the situation appear to me to be—

1. The allied purchases for both civilian and military purposes in meats, as in many other commodities, have been consolidated by necessity of shipping conditions and by necessity of the Treasury arrangement for advances to the allies until private trading has been of necessity eliminated.

It is also becoming necessary for the Government to coordinate these purchases with those of our Army and Navy in order to prevent conflict in the execution of orders. This great consolidation of buying has to some extent, and will increasingly, dominate prices.

We have, since last September, recognized that the export purchases of pork products would affect prices, and after consultation with important committees of swine growers we last autumn gave a rough assurance to the swine producers of a minimum price which we felt that we could maintain from the export buying, and this has been maintained, although with considerable difficulties, and has been beneficial in stimulating production. The indications are that these purchases will now be further increased.

The beef purchases have not, up to the present time, been sufficient in volume to more than temporarily affect price, but the present indications are that for some time in the future they will be greatly increased and to a point where they may affect prices materially.

2. The increased quantities required for export must be obtained by either increased production or by reduction in civilian consumption—probably both.

The reduction in civilian consumption can be obtained much the most equitably by voluntary reduction by the consumer and by moderate restraints, such as meatless days, etc., and while it may be contended by some that a reduction in consumption may be obtained by increase in price, such conservation is obtained by the elimination of that section of the community with the least purchasing power. In other words, conservation by price becomes conservation for the rich and not for the poor; whereas an extension of the conservation policy now in force places reduction in consumption where it rightly belongs—on those who can save from plenty, not upon those who save from nourishment.

It appears to me also of the utmost national importance that we shall maintain through the country a complete sense in voluntary reduction in the consumption of all commodities if we are to provide the necessary surpluses either in money, man power, or material necessary to winning the war. On the other hand, the adjustment of conservation measures of this type and the surplus required from time to time is extremely difficult without these measures themselves affecting prices and developing discontent and criticism in sections of the producing community.

I recognize fully the well-founded objection to any theory of price fixing, but where the purchases of war necessities in a given commodity have reached such a volume that the purchase of these commodities trench into the domestic consumption, the operation of this purchasing power becomes a condition of price fixing and, to my mind, all theories go by the board.

3. The Government is thus faced with three alternatives in the matter of control of meats:
    a. To free the Government from all interest in price by abandoning direction of war purchases and to abandon conservation measures because these may also affect price.
This would be a relief to the Government, but with growing volume of purchases the price influence will be transferred to uncontrolled agencies who are themselves price fixing and carries the following dangers:

It will stimulate profiteering and speculation. Prices in the season of the year of large production can be manipulated downward and in the sparse season will ascend to the point where some classes will be eliminated from consumption. The cost of living thus subjected to abnormal fluctuation will reflect in wage discontent and instability. It will destroy systematic saving of the commodity by individuals, and this saving in consumption is a vital national policy. The producer will go through erratic periods of discouragement and of stimulation which must undermine any systematic policy of national or individual increase in production, for every period of discouragement cuts off production of animals, which cannot be recovered.

    b. To continue as at present the direction of these large purchases with a mixture of partial national policy in production and day-to-day dealing with emergency.

This is an almost intolerable situation for any Government official in criticism from both producer and consumer, and with the growing volume of purchases this criticism must increase. It permits of no constructive policy in production.

    c. To stabilize prices based upon cost of production at a fair and stimulative profit to the producer and with stabilization to eliminate speculative risks and wasteful practices and thus some gains for the consumer.

If such a policy is adopted it also follows that it will have a most important bearing on and relation to policies of agricultural production and a long view can be taken and supported in assuring the producer of fair returns.

This course is also fraught with dangers. It leads either to a voluntary agreement with the packers as to prices to be paid producers and charged to consumers from time to time or to actual operation of the packing plants by the Government. In either case the Government will need to take some financial responsibility in speculative business. In such situation the Government will be under constant pressure from the producers for enhancement of price and from the consumer for reductions. It necessitates the constant action of a commission to determine such prices. It will mean that all the complaints of trade fall upon the Government. The choice of alternatives is one of determination of the maximum contribution to winning the war and the choice of the lesser economic evil between such alternatives.

The legal ability of the Government to give authority to such measures lies in the power to direct contracts for war necessities, to take over and

operate plants, and to make voluntary agreements to carry out a defini-
tive and constructive policy. When purchases are so large as to cut into
civilian consumption it becomes possible to insure manufacturers a complete market, thus eliminating their risk and thereby eliminating some
of the margin that they must take in the conduct of a speculative business, and it also gives sound reason for directing their policies.

For these very reasons it has been necessary to set up partial or complete
arrangements of this character in iron, steel, copper, explosives, wheat,
sugar, and some other commodities. None of these arrangements have
evolved out of any governmental policy of price-fixing, or any desire to
interfere with the operation of natural trade laws, but are simply the
result of the Government being forced into the issue of becoming the
dominant purchaser and thereby, willingly or unwillingly, the price
determiner in particular commodities.

We have been struggling as intelligently as possible with the situation
in the meat industries with entire inadequacy of definite national policy.
Our purchases hitherto have been sufficient to influence the market at
times, and in the case of pork products have been sufficient to preserve a
minimum price. We have been, however, powerless hitherto to properly
protect all branches of the cattle industry with its constantly changing
economic situation, or to give intelligent direction or assistance to cattle
production. As you know, I have never felt that when we arrived at a
point to determine the broad policy with respect to a commodity that
this should be determined at the opinion of any single individual, no
matter how sincere and earnest the application of intelligence might be.

I would therefore like to recommend to you to extend the policy which
you have already initiated in the matter of many commodities, by early
appointment of a board to study the entire situation with regard to the
meat industry and the steps that should be taken with regard thereto. I
would suggest that, following the precedent that you have already established, a committee should be set up embracing either the following
gentlemen or their delegates directly responsible to them—

> The Secretary of Agriculture as representing the producer.
> The chairman of the Federal Trade Commission as representing
> trade conditions.
> The chairman of the Federal Tariff Board as representing economic
> thought.

The Secretary of Labor as representing the civilian consumer.

The Food Administrator as having to carry out any given policy determined upon.

This commission should at once exhaustively consider the entire situation in all of its aspects and determine a positive national policy in meats.

I apologize for writing at such length but the subject permits of little brevity.

> I am, your obedient servant,
> HERBERT HOOVER

Barnes and Higher Wheat Prices

> Julius Barnes, president of the Grain Corporation, agreed with Hoover about the adverse effects that would ensue if Congress were successful in raising the guaranteed price of wheat from $2.00 to $2.40 a bushel. In a letter to Hoover he expressed himself on this matter and Hoover sent the letter on to Wilson who forthwith sent this acknowledgment. Hoover himself later set forth his views on the proposed increase in a July 8 letter to the President.

27 March, 1918

My dear Mr. Hoover:

Thank you very much for sending me the copy of Mr. Barnes' letter. He is certainly right and puts the case with all its force.

> Cordially and sincerely yours,
> WOODROW WILSON

Western Grain Exchanges

> In this letter Wilson refers to Hoover's "letter of yesterday." That letter does not seem to have survived, for neither the original nor a copy has been found in the Wilson or the Hoover papers. On Wednesday, March 27, the day he sent his answer, Wilson saw Hoover at 2:30 at the weekly meeting of the war cabinet.

27 March, 1918
My dear Mr. Hoover:
I have your letter of yesterday about the arrangements proposed with the Western Grain Exchanges, and in reply must frankly say that I have no judgment of my own about the matter. I do not feel that I am qualified to form one. I am quite willing to leave the decision in your own hands. I think it a very satisfactory feature of what is proposed that room is left for reconsideration and for checking speculation whenever it goes too far.

Cordially and sincerely yours,
WOODROW WILSON

Skinner for the Inter-Allied Council

The idea of concentrating authority in one commission for the purchase and shipment to Europe of war supplies was discussed in a cabinet meeting on May 11, 1917. The project appears to have originated with McAdoo. On December 13 of that year the commission was organized and Oscar T. Crosby, Assistant Secretary of the Treasury with residence in London, became its president and American representative. Wilson was frequently disturbed by Crosby's tendency to become involved in political matters instead of confining himself to financial business. A message to McAdoo expressed fear of "Crosby's inclination to go very much outside his bailiwick, an inclination of which I have many evidences." (Life and Letters, vol. 7, p. 460; see also pp. 64–65, 171, 247, 309, 341, 455, 459–60, 545–49, 559–60.)

In the following letter Hoover presents Colonel House's suggestion of Skinner to represent the Food Administration on the council.

27 March 1918
Dear Mr. President:
Mr. McAdoo has made the recommendation that the Food Administration should appoint a member of the Inter-Allied Council now sitting in Europe, under the Chairmanship of Mr. Oscar T. Crosby, in order to coordinate the financial activities of that council with the food buying activities of the Allies in this country.

Colonel House has suggested to me Mr. J. H. Skinner of Minneapolis and Mr. Skinner is prepared to accept the position as a volunteer. If this meets with your approval I would indeed be grateful if you would confirm Mr. Skinner's appointment by addressing the necessary letter to Mr. McAdoo.

> I remain, Your obedient servant,
> HERBERT HOOVER

Approval of Skinner for the Council

> Hoover must have been confident that his nominee for the Inter-Allied Council would win the President's approval, for on March 27, before receiving Wilson's confirmation, he wrote the Secretary of State that he had "secured the services of Mr. J. H. Skinner" who would be "leaving for Paris at an early date," and that he would be pleased if "you could facilitate his movements in any way."

28 March, 1918

My dear Mr. Hoover:

I have been very glad to confirm in a letter to the Secretary of the Treasury the appointment of Mr. J. H. Skinner of Minneapolis as the representative of the Food Administration on the Inter-Allied Council.

> Cordially and faithfully yours,
> WOODROW WILSON

Approval of a Meat Commission

> This brief note refers to Hoover's detailed letter of March 26 on meat problems and his recommendation for appointment of a commission to study them.

29 March, 1918

My dear Mr. Hoover:

I have read the enclosed letter which I take the liberty of returning and believe that it would be all right to publish it and to proceed with the plan for the appointment of a commission.

> Cordially and sincerely yours,
> WOODROW WILSON

Additional Remarks on the Commission

> On the same day that Hoover sent this letter it was announced that "on Hoover's recommendation the President has authorized a survey of the meat-packing industry." (Times, Apr. 1, 1918, p. 1.) At 1:00

Hoover had lunch with Secretary of Agriculture Houston; he met with Wilson at 2:30 for the regular Wednesday session of the war cabinet.

1 April 1918

Dear Mr. President:

In extension of your note of 29th March, approving of the appointment of a commission to consider the meat policy, would you be so good as to address a note to the Secretary of Agriculture, Chairman of the Federal Trade Board, Federal Tariff Commission and Secretary of Labour, asking them if they will sit in this capacity or select a representative for that purpose? Might I suggest that in such note you throw out the suggestion that whoever may be selected should have no personal interest in either production or distribution.

These gentlemen would probably understand the nature of the problem better if they had copies of the letter which I addressed to you and in case you should desire to adopt this suggestion I enclose herewith some copies of it to save clerical work.

I beg to remain, Your obedient servant,
HERBERT HOOVER

Replacing Taussig in Grain Division Inquiry

This letter from Wilson's pen was a disappointment for Hoover. It also presented him with somewhat of a task—that of finding a new chairman for the commission investigating the Grain Division of the Food Administration. Some six weeks earlier Hoover had first suggested to Wilson that an investigation by a hostile group could be headed off by initiating an inquiry under "an independent man of knowledge and economic sense," which qualifications he thought Taussig possessed in a preeminent degree. (Letter to Wilson, February 20, 1918; letter to Hoover, February 21, 1918.) How the problem was resolved is not clear. In his well-documented book, Surface speaks of the investigation as started and completed under Taussig's leadership. (*Grain Trade* pp. 126–29.) Hoover may have ultimately prevailed upon Wilson to let him keep this capable man in the chairmanship, but no letters on the subject seem to have been exchanged.

2 April, 1918

My dear Mr. Hoover:

I feel selfish to ask the question that I am about to ask, but I feel bound in duty to ask it. Mr. F. W. Taussig, the Chairman of the United

States Tariff Commission, has been acting not only in the important matter of the inquiry you have been conducting in connection with the Milling Division of your Administration, but also as a member of the Price Fixing Committee of the War Industries Board. He feels that it is inconsistent with his duties on the Tariff Commission to undertake both of these duties and, indeed, impossible to perform them in addition to his regular work and inasmuch as I feel that so many things in so many departments turn upon the determinations of the Price Fixing Committee, I am going to be bold enough to ask if you think you could replace Mr. Taussig in the milling inquiry.

I know this is asking a great deal, but I feel bound to suggest "priorities" in a case of this importance, and I am sure you will pardon me.

Cordially and faithfully yours,
WOODROW WILSON

Advice on Answering a Telegram

> The contents of this telegram are not identified. The telegram itself was returned to the President on April 4, 1918, with Hoover's answer which is printed below. Morris and Company was one of the largest in the packing industry whose activities presented Hoover with unending problems during the war years. On March 26 he had written the President a detailed letter on "the whole meat industry" and the "situation" which he called "the most complex with which the Government has to deal." Since early January the industry had been the subject of investigation by the Federal Trade Commission and this inquiry had provoked a long public controversy over the packers' business activities.

2 April, 1918

My dear Mr. Hoover:

Again I must resort to you, for the sake of cooperation, to ask what reply you would advise me to make to the enclosed telegram from Morris & Company.

Cordially and sincerely yours,
WOODROW WILSON

Suggested Treatment of Telegram

April 4 1918
My dear Mr. President:
Might I suggest that it would be advisable that no reply at all be made to the telegram from Morris & Company, which I am returning herewith.

Faithfully yours,
HERBERT HOOVER

Report from the Federal Trade Commission

4 April, 1918
My dear Mr. Hoover:
I do not know whether the Federal Trade Commission has supplied you with a copy of the enclosed report. If not, it certainly ought to be in your hands, and I take pleasure in sending it to you.

Cordially and sincerely yours,
WOODROW WILSON

Ames for Food Administrator

April 4th, 1918
Dear Mr. President:—
Doctor Stratton D. Brooks, of Norman, Oklahoma, has found it necessary, owing to the stress of affairs in connection with his activities with the University, to resign from the position of Federal Food Administrator for the State. We are sorry to lose his services as he has done good work in building up an organization throughout Oklahoma.

After careful consideration, I wish to recommend, as Doctor Brooks' successor, Mr. C. B. Ames, of Oklahoma City.

Mr. Ames is strongly endorsed by Governor Williams, Senator Owen, Congressman Ferris, and Doctor Brooks himself, together with having the recommendation of many other leading citizens of the State. He is at present Chairman of the Liberty Loan Committee, but after

April fifteenth will be in a position to give his entire time—as a volunteer
—to this war work. He is one of the leading lawyers of Oklahoma.

Faithfully yours,

HERBERT HOOVER

Approved

WOODROW WILSON [handwritten by Wilson]

5 April, 1918

Food Administration Nominees

4 April 1918

Dear Mr. President:

Subject to your approval, I should like to make the following important changes in staff arrangements in the Food Administration:

Dr. George H. Denny, President of the University of Alabama, to be head of the Cotton-Seed Division.

John R. Munn, a wool manufacturer, to be head of the Canning Division.

R. R. Williams, a banker, head of the Wholesale and Retail Division.

C. E. Spens, Vice-President of the Burlington Railroad, to be head of the Railway Transportation Division.

Prentiss R. Gray, Shipping Manager of the Belgian Relief, to be head of the Marine Transportation Division.

J. J. Stream, formerly a grain merchant, to be head of the Corn, Corn Milling and Feeds Division.

Miss Martha Van Rensselaer, Professor of Domestic Economy, to be head of the Home Conservation Division.

None of them have any financial interest in the trades with which they are to be concerned and all of them, with the exception of Dr. Denny, have been tried out in the Food Administration to first prove their adaptibility [*sic*] and capability for the work. All are volunteers except Dr. Denny and we share Mr. Gray's salary with the Belgian Relief.

I beg to remain, Your obedient servant,

HERBERT HOOVER

Thanks for Report of the Federal Trade Commission

6 April 1918

Dear Mr. President:

I am indeed obliged for your kindness in sending me the copy of the report of the Federal Trade Commission on Flour Milling. I have had the opportunity of reading excerpts from the report, but I am glad to see the whole of it.

Faithfully yours,
HERBERT HOOVER

Ships for Belgian Relief

Upon the declaration of war by the United States in April 1917, the American staff of the Commission for Relief in Belgium withdrew from Belgium and northern France and allowed Spanish and Dutch representatives to carry on the work of feeding the people in these German occupied territories. However, Hoover continued to act as chairman of the commission and his staff continued to deliver food and clothing to the borders.

As the spring of 1918 approached, a major transportation problem developed. The initial strategy of the Allies in 1917 did not envisage the use of large American armies in Europe. The United States was to provide massive quantities of food and equipment, the French and British troops were to hold the lines on the Western Front, and a tight blockade was to starve Germany into surrender. However, with the defeat of Russia in early 1918, Germany was free to withdraw her troops from the Eastern Front and to mount vigorous attacks against the French and British. Immediately a call went out for great numbers of American troops to bolster the lines in the west. Thus an unexpected demand was henceforth made on shipping, and this, coupled with renewed submarine attacks, created the transportation crisis that prompted Hoover's letter of April 8. Wilson was unable to relieve the situation, so Hoover made appeals to the highest authorities in London and Paris, and finally the Belgian relief commission was saved at least temporarily through the intervention of Clemenceau and Lloyd George. (*Epic*, vol. 1, pp. 355–73.)

8 April 1918

Dear Mr. President:

The War Council of the War Department has apparently decided that no shipping can be afforded to the Belgian Relief Commission. I fully appreciate the extreme gravity of the present situation yet I have the feeling that this decision was taken without consideration of the whole of its bearings and it does seem to me that it should be reviewed.

The Belgian Relief Commission has a fleet untouched by this decision which is able to transport to the population of Belgium and Northern France an average of under 60,000 tons of food per month. The amount of food which we have always considered as the minimum on which this population could be maintained in even reasonable health is about 120,000 tons of food per month. We have felt latterly that under this great shipping stringency and with the approaching spring, we could reduce it to 90,000 tons of food a month temporarily without bringing about a disaster; thus leaving 30,000 tons to be carried monthly by new shipping—needing, say, 65,000 tons deadweight.

In the original Dutch agreement we were to have 100,000 tons of Dutch shipping. Upon the failure of this agreement, Mr. Hurley undertook to do his utmost to supply the Relief Commission with some 70,000 tons of shipping at once and three Norwegian steamers have been assigned but under this last direction there is some uncertainty as to whether even these will not be taken away and no more be provided.

Aside entirely from its deep humanatarian [sic] aspects, the Relief problem has very great political importance. So great has the political aspect been regarded by the Allied governments that during the whole of these years they have not only supported it in shipping and money but at the recent Inter-Allied Council in Paris it was decided to be of such extreme importance that the Belgian Relief was given a priority in shiping, money and food, over all Allied needs. This political importance hinges around:

1st. The prevention of an agreement between the Flemish population and the Germans as to the establishment of a separate and independent government under German tutelage.

2nd. The fact that the Belgian government itself and the Belgian Army may consider the cost in sacrifice of life of their civilian population too great to pay for constancy in the war.

3rd. The loss of morale to the French people and the French Army by a debacle amongst their own civilians in the North of France. The French Premier has expressed himself vigorously on this point.

5th. There are some 2,000,000 workmen in Belgium who have, with the most extraordinary constancy, refused all these years to work for the Germans and even under the terrible suffering of actual forced labor they have so resisted as to give the Germans no adequate return for the measures they adopted in this manner.

I believe we can maintain the Relief and the whole of its objectives if we can have (a) No interference with our present fleet, including the three ships already assigned by the Shipping Board. (b) The assignment of five more ships promptly for April loading and four further ships for May loading.

The whole matter seems to me of such importance that it should at least be referred to the Supreme War Council in Europe for decision before any action of the nature proposed is taken here.

Yours faithfully,
HERBERT HOOVER

A Governor's Food Administration Nominations

Democrat Westmoreland Davis was elected governor of Virginia on February 1, 1918. Soon thereafter he and the Virginia congressional delegation became involved in a political dispute over the appointment of food administrators for their state. The controversy developed over the naming of a successor to Colonel E. B. White of Leesburg, Va., who is mentioned later in Hoover's letter of April 23. On April 9 Davis wrote a letter to Hoover protesting that none of the three men he himself had suggested for the post was then being considered, but that a certain Mr. McD. Lee was the current favorite upon the recommendation of the Virginia congressional delegation. A copy of the Davis letter was sent to Wilson who in turn mailed it to Hoover with this brief note of April 12.

In replying to the President, Hoover stated that he was trying to draw up another list of likely candidates for the Virginia post. On April 23 he submitted the name of Hugh B. Sproul who had won the support of the two Democratic senators from Virginia, Thomas S. Martin and Claude A. Swanson. Similar approval came from Democratic Representative Henry D. Flood. Hoover says nothing of the attitude of the other eight representatives, seven Democrats and one Republican. It seems legitimate to conclude that the nominee had not been endorsed by them nor by Governor Davis.

12 April, 1918

My dear Mr. Hoover:

The Governor of Virginia is evidently very hot about the matter referred to in the enclosed and I do not like to reply to him without knowing how the matter stands with you.

Cordially and sincerely yours,
WOODROW WILSON

Reply on Governor's Chagrin

April 12, 1918

Dear Mr. President:

I am very sorry to see you annoyed over the matter of appointment of a State Food Administrator in Virginia.

In our usual method of these appointments, we asked the Governor to suggest several men. We then submitted these names to the Virginia delegation in Washington and found that they approved of two of the Governor's nominees. Both of these gentlemen, however, were unable for one reason or another to accept.

The third did not meet the approval of the Virginia Senators and Congressmen. The delegation in turn recommended a fourth man, with regard to whom we again approached the Governor and in consequence created this storm.

We are now endeavoring to find another list of men on whom we can get approval on all sides before submitting them to you.

The Governor of Virginia does not apparently cooperate very much with the Congressional delegation. We will, however, try to solve the matter without friction.

Yours faithfully,
HERBERT HOOVER

Regulation of Fishermen

> The regulations mentioned here were approved and returned to the Food Administration on April 23.

April 20, 1918

Dear Mr. President:

I beg to enclose herewith license regulations governing salt water fishermen, and to request that if you approve thereof you sign them on the last page.

These regulations have been carefully prepared in cooperation with the Bureau of Fisheries and the various state fish commissions. They are designed to increase the production of fish on the Atlantic and Gulf Coasts by removing many state and local restrictions which now seriously hamper the operations of the fishermen. I am very hopeful that they will result in a largely increased production.

Faithfully yours,
HERBERT HOOVER

Sproul for Food Administrator

On April 22 Hoover met with Hugh B. Sproul in Washington and the following day proposed his name to Wilson for a Food Administration post. Sproul began to serve as a federal food administrator for Virginia on May 8, 1918.

April 23rd 1918

Dear Mr. President:—

Colonel E. B. White of Leesburg, Virginia, has resigned from his position as Federal Food Administrator as he is a candidate for election to Congress.

After careful consideration, I recommend Mr. Hugh B. Sproul of Staunton, Virginia, as Colonel White's successor. Mr. Sproul has signified his willingness to undertake this work, as a volunteer, if appointed.

Mr. Sproul is strongly endorsed by Senators Martin and Swanson, Representative Flood, and by many other influential citizens of Virginia. He has been interested in the coal business for many years and has also made a thorough scientific study of food production and distribution, and is, therefore, conversant with our problems, although not having been actually connected with the Food Administration up to this time.

Faithfully yours,
HERBERT HOOVER

Approved
WOODROW WILSON [handwritten by Wilson]
24 April, 1918.

Proclamation for Food Licensing

The proclamation was signed and sent to the State Department on May 14.

May 3, 1918.

Dear Mr. President:

I beg to submit herewith, for your approval, a proclamation licensing certain additional food operators excepted from prior proclamations. It has been found that, in order to carry out in an effective manner the regulations governing licensed operators, it is necessary to make these regulations affect all of those concerned in the industry.

Faithfully yours,
HERBERT HOOVER

Brooks for Food Administrator

May 6, 1918

Dear Mr President:

Mr James Hartness of Springfield, Vermont, is obliged to resign from the position as Federal Food Administrator for that state owing to the many demands upon his time and energy called for by the various war activities in which he is taking an active part.

After careful consideration I wish to recommend as Mr Hartness' successor, Mr Frank H. Brooks of St Johnsbury, Vermont.

Mr Brooks is strongly endorsed by Mr Hartness, the retiring Administrator. Governor Graham is favorable to his appointment as are many other leading citizens of the state. Until recently Mr Brooks has been President of the E. &. T. Fairbanks Company, but has now sold out his interest and is free to devote his time to this work. His principal activity outside of his own business has been in the educational line. He has been an active member on State Educational Commissions and Boards of Education for many years and is still a member of the State Board of Education. Mr Brooks is a man of great force and vitality as well as excellent judgment and tact and I am confident that he could administer the work in Vermont in a most satisfactory manner.

Faithfully yours
HERBERT HOOVER

Approved
WOODROW WILSON [handwritten by Wilson]

Transfer of Workers

8 May, 1918

My dear Mr. Hoover:

A good deal of embarrassment and dislocation in the administrative business of the Government has been caused by the transfer of clerks and specialists of one sort or another from the older and longer established departments to the new instrumentalities which have necessarily been created or greatly enlarged since this country entered the war, and I take the liberty of calling your attention to the fact, because it has often happened that employees of the older departments have been drawn away by offers of considerable increases of pay, to the very serious embarrassment, and sometimes to the serious weakening, of the departments which they were induced to leave. All this has been a very natural process. There have in fact not been trained men enough to go around, but I thought I might venture to speak of this to you, because I was sure your judgment would agree with mine that this process ought to be avoided wherever it is avoidable, and the new activities recruited from outside Washington. I write, therefore, to beg for your cooperation in seeing that we all act as a single family in this matter and restrain our subordinates from poaching in each other's preserves wherever it is possible to restrain them.

Cordially and sincerely yours,
WOODROW WILSON

Report on Packing Industry

In his March 26 letter Hoover outlined for Wilson the many problems of the meat and packing industries and recommended the appointment of a commission to study possible solutions. Seven weeks later he was able to send to the President the following letter together with the report drawn up by the commission on May 11.

13 May 1918

Dear Mr. President:

I enclose herewith the report on the packing house industry formulated by the committee appointed by you in response to my letter of the 26th March. The report has been approved by Messrs. Secretary Houston, Secretary Wilson, Doctor Taussig of the Federal Tariff Commission, by Governor Fort of the Federal Trade Commission and myself for the Food Administration. I wish to add that two members of the Federal Trade Commission are not fully in accord and are of the opinion that there is no solution to the problem short of government operation.

I should be glad to know if the course laid down in this memorandum meets with your approval.

Yours faithfully,
HERBERT HOOVER

R E P O R T :

11 May, 1918.

Having examined the suggestions of the Sub-Committee, we make the following recommendations to the President with regard to meat policies:

REGULATION

1. We recommend the continuation of regulation of the meat packing industry by the Food Administration and do not favour governmental operation of the industry unless it should be found impossible to enforce regulatory measures.

2. The auditing of the packers' bi-monthly profit returns to the Food Administration and the installation of uniform bases of accounts by the Federal Trade Commission should proceed as already settled between the Federal Trade Commission and the Food Administration. The present regulation by the Food Administration as to maximum profits should be continued to July 1st. In the meantime the Federal Trade Commission should report upon the reasonableness of these maximums. If found reasonable they should continue in effect until further notice. If found unreasonable such maximums should be made effective as facts warrant.

3. The packers should be required to report wholesale prices received for meat products and the transfer value of the principal by-products from their meat departments should be furnished by the packers to the Department of Agriculture for publication in their market reports as the Department may require.

4. The reports showing the wholesale prices of food dealers, now being made to the Food Administration, which includes the wholesale prices made by packers' branch houses, should be given local publicity to consumers.

5. The stockyards should be placed under license and regulation by the Department of Agriculture which should also establish a governmental system of animal grading under suitable regulations and methods of price reporting of actual transactions. Daily reports should be made on distribution and destinations of livestock, meats and other products from principal packing points.

GOVERNMENT AND ALLIED PURCHASES

1. The Food Purchase Board established last November by the Food Administrator, and the Secretaries of War and Navy, with the approval of the President, for the co-ordination of policies in purchases of official governmental agencies of certain food commodities, should extend its activities to the co-ordination of the purchase of packing house products by all official agencies.

2. It must be recognized that the meat purchases thus co-ordinated through the Food Purchase Board during periods of sparse marketing or during periods of extreme production broadly influence market levels in meat and in animals and, at such times as they do influence prices, they should be made in accordance with economic conditions as they affect both producers and consumers and at prices on one hand sufficiently stimulative to ensure production at a point necessary to furnish supplies of meat during the war period, and, on the other hand, at such ranges as will prevent extortionate prices to the consumer. The packers' profits should be controlled so as to prevent excessive charges and so that the policy already declared by the President in cases where war buying dominates the market, that "We must make the prices to the public the same as the prices to the Government", may be effectuated. Any changes in prices the Food Purchase Board proposes to pay from month to month should be referred to the price committee of the War Industries Board for review and any substantial representatives of producers or consumers should be heard by them thereon. The advice of the Agricultural Advisory Committee, for the producers, through its Committee on Livestock, and the Department of Labour, representing the consumers, should be sought in event any substantial changes are contemplated.

GENERAL

1. The Food Act gives no regulatory powers with regard to retailers. It is desirable, however, that an investigation should be made of the conditions of the retail trade with view to determination of some constructive effort that may be made in retail distribution and it is recommended that a committee should be created for thorough investigation of, and recommendation upon, the subject.
2. The privately-owned cars of the packing industry should continue to be controlled by the Director General of Railroads.

Cuban Sugar Ships for Belgium

On April 8 Hoover had written to Wilson of the peril that threatened Belgian Relief because of a shipping shortage, and in his May 17 letter to the President he revealed plans to lessen this peril, by diverting shipping from the Cuban sugar trade. He also expressed high hope that Lloyd George would supply enough additional tonnage to provide the needed transportation of food for Belgium. William B. Poland took over as the director of Belgian Relief following Hoover's return to America in May 1917 to become head of the Food Administration. On May 16 Hoover saw the President at the White House at 4:45 and spoke to him of the dangers that threatened Belgium because of the shipping crisis. (*Times,* May 17, 1918, p. 4.)

17 May 1918

Dear Mr. President:

Please find attached hereto copy of a telegram I have sent to Mr. Poland, who is Director of the Belgian Relief in Europe. I have seen Mr. Hurley this morning and he has given directions that such ships as can be diverted from the Cuban sugar trade shall be assigned to the Belgian Relief, as we shall have to justify this further shortage in sugar supplies on the basis of a contribution of the American people to saving life in Belgium.

I am in hopes that Mr. Lloyd George will see to it that the British authorities provide at least an equal amount of tonnage to that which will be supplied by these and other means on this side. I feel sure that we have an issue here that transcends in its moral and, therefore, in its eventual military significance the earlier despatch of soldiers to France and I am confident that on a definite consideration of the problem by Premiers Clemenceau and Lloyd George they will again adhere to this conclusion which has had to be debated in each crisis of the Relief so often in the past.

Yours faithfully,
HERBERT HOOVER

C A B L E :

16 May, 1918.

To

CREVOOH, Poland, [William B. Poland]
London.

Would like you to present the following with the British National Committee to Mr. Lloyd George as from me as head of the Relief, not as a government official—Quote—As Chairman of the Belgian Relief I wish to again ask your personal intervention upon behalf of these suffering people. Three years ago upon my personal appeal you intervened to save the Relief and established it firmly as an unparalleled enterprise in humanity with the full sympathy and generous financial support of the British peoples. That action, which cost much in sacrifice to the British people by its demonstration of their true and broad humane objectives in the war, became one of the most potent forces in the conviction of the American people of the Allies' just cause. At our adherence to the Allied cause our government considered its obligations included a participation in the maintenance of these people who have suffered first and continue to suffer most from barbarism and in so doing we have not only taken our share of a burden and humane duty but we have all of us in the midst of the freezing flood of war contributed to keep alive in the hearts of our peoples its higher aims. The problem today is ships. Our people have stripped to the bone to furnish transport of supplies and men for Allied support. We can furnish no tonnage unless sacrifice is made somewhere in these directions. The tonnage required is so pitiable either in transport of men or supplies in the vast totals as to seem to justify the risk. Today to consign the Belgian people to starvation after three and one half years of almost unendurable suffering and steadfast loyalty and service in the Allied cause is indeed a terrible fate and it will destroy an invisible but great spiritual force among our two peoples worse than the loss of a great battle. I feel that without Your Excellency's intervention and positive instruction the Relief cannot be saved and a direction from yourself to your authorities and a communication of your approval of necessary diversions to our President would yield solution by our joint shipping authorities.

HERBERT HOOVER

Lloyd George and Ships for Belgium

The German defeat of Russia in early 1918 compelled the Allies to reappraise their grand strategy and to ask for the immediate transport to Europe of huge American armies and great quantities of equipment. This naturally resulted in unexpected demands for additional shipping which in turn seriously imperiled the work of Belgian relief. On April 8 Hoover had written a detailed letter to Wilson justifying his position that none of the promised tonnage should be denied this charitable undertaking because of the fresh military needs. The "vigorous protest" which he made on April 10 "to the President and the State Department" (*Epic*, vol. 1, p. 367) may have been oral as well as written, the oral one being delivered possibly during his conference at the

White House at 2:30 that afternoon. The written protest is not to be found among the Wilson or the Hoover papers.

At 6:00 on April 10 Hoover met with Edwin F. Gay of the Shipping Board and Prentiss N. Gray, chief of Marine Transportation. At 6:30 he met with Gray alone. The following morning at 9:00 he was again closeted with Gray and Theodore F. Whitmarsh, the Food Administration representative on the War Industries Board. Hoover also saw Gray on May 15; on May 16 he was at the White House at 4:45 and at 6:00 spoke with Gray again. On May 17 he consulted with E. F. Carry of the Shipping Board at 5:30. Gray was also present for his May 17 conversation with E. N. Hurley, head of the Shipping Board, at 11:30. Hoover's letter on that day indicates that decisions made at this meeting with Hurley were highly consequential in meeting the shipping crisis. Thus it would seem more than likely that the same subject was high on the agenda of all these mid-May conferences.

No final solution ensued from all this energetic activity nor from the several remonstrances he addressed to European centers of power until the happy break of May 20, the day on which Hoover wrote Wilson of Lloyd George's promise to supply the necessary tonnage, provided America made a similar commitment. The President acquiesced and restored the necessary steamers for shipping 90,000 tons of food to Belgium. (*Times,* May 23, 1918, p. 14.)

20 May 1918

Dear Mr. President:

I am informed that my cable, which I dispatched to Lloyd George and of which you have a copy, was delivered to him on the 17th. I am also informed that he considers that the Belgian Relief should have priority over other war needs and in any event the British Government has acted at once by offering to find one-half of the tonnage necessary to support the Belgian Relief and has assigned already, for immediate loading, four ships. This is contingent upon the United States Shipping Board's assigning one-half the necessary tonnage *pari passu* with the British. Our Shipping Board has been directly advised of these arrangements.

I am happy to state that this apparently reverses the attitude of mind expressed from the inquiry sent through the various departments here to various departments in England and I am sincerely in hopes that you can see your way to complete the matter by giving positive directions to the Shipping Board that they should at once undertake to comply with this arrangement in preference to other war measures.

Yours faithfully,

HERBERT HOOVER

Colver's Plan for Packers

William B. Colver was one of the federal trade commissioners who, as indicated in Hoover's May 13 letter, dissented in part from the May 11 report and favored solving the packer's problems by having the government assume operation of the industry. Wilson's letter of May 20 suggests that he was inclined to Colver's "half-way course" which envisaged an experiment with government operation of one of the packing houses. Hoover answered the President on May 21 with a letter and a memo detailing his objections to the Colver proposal.

In addition to his suggestion regarding this proposal, Wilson apparently asked Hoover for consideration of another revision of the committee's May 11 report. This becomes clear from their May 27–28 correspondence.

20 May, 1918

My dear Mr. Hoover:

I have examined the enclosed report and before forming a judgment on it I would be very much obliged if you would read the letter from Mr. Colver which I also enclose. It struck me as containing some unusually interesting suggestions. Do you think that the half-way course he proposes is not feasible or advisable?

Cordially and sincerely yours,

WOODROW WILSON

Objections to the Colver Plan

21 May 1918

Dear Mr. President:

I enclose herewith a memorandum mentioning some of the objections to Mr. Colver's proposed experimental Government operation of one of the packing plants.

I have consulted Mr. Houston on this matter and he is strongly of my opinion that Mr. Colver's suggestion is directed more towards a determination of some permanent remedy of the faults of the packing industry than to meeting war emergencies.

Whatever our opinions may be as to the method for rectifying the packing industry, I am strongly of the view that we will have less interruption and disturbance to our present difficult economic situation through regulation of the packers than through any form of Government operation and that the permanent solution of this matter is one for legislation and not for experimental work under emergency powers.

I return herewith the report of the committee and I would be glad to discuss the subject at our next meeting.

Yours faithfully,
HERBERT HOOVER

MEMO:

Mr. Colver's interesting suggestion was before the Committee at the time the report was settled. The members of the Committee were in full agreement that the situation at the present time did not warrant any Government operation and that a determination should be made as to whether the war objectives of the Government could be attained by regulation without the necessity of Government operation.

There are two principal points of departure from the committee's report. — First, a proposal of limited and experimental operation by the Government, and, second, regulations impigning [sic] upon the producer.

As to the first, it must be recognized that this is one of the most complex and speculative industries in the country, due to the fundamental variations in every individual animal, the perishable character of products and the daily changing demands of the consuming public and from abroad. The Government, in operation of all five of the big plants, or even of one of them, would at once become the target of pressure on the part of both producers and consumers, and for an extended fixing of all factors entering into production and consumption. We should amass around ourselves an amount of political pressure and the ultimate definition of political issues between producer and consumer that would be most confusing and embarrassing during the period of the war.

To operate one packing concern, or all five large ones, means that the Government comes into competition with some hundred other packing houses in the country and is of course subject to the same methods of competition as exist between members of the trade. If the Government were to operate Wilson and Company's business alone and retain its volume of business—and it would be necessary to hold it if it is to become an experimental situation of any value—it must be prepared to take all of the risks of competition with the others and this competition drives into the price determination of every single animal bought and practically every commodity sold. There would seem to be serious danger that the other packers, if they were willing to sacrifice the money, could put the Government out of action in a month. We could not say to the people that they must consume Government meat at larger prices than private enterprise. Wilson and Company, roughly, do about ten per cent of the total business of the five big packers. This situation would be somewhat different if we took over all five packing plants, because we should have such a dominant part of the purchases as to fix prices even as against the other hundred packers. But if the Government forced them from business by competition the difficulties would be considerable.

Another factor in this matter that must not be overlooked is that the packers are engaged in many other avenues of activity than meat, such as fertilizers, leather, groceries and canned goods of all sorts, which they either pack themselves or buy under contract from other packers, and we should be entering competitive business upon all these lines.

Mr. Colver's plan also involves the control of the flow of animals to the markets and government advice to stock-raisers in the country as to marketing. It also involves the determination of prices for standard fed animals as a basis of all purchases, with an advance fixation of animal prices on the basis of the cost of feed. Aside from the fact that no government has the power to assure consumption at such prices, this would constitute an interference in the daily life of the producers that they would resent and carries price fixing to a degree hitherto not contemplated. One instance will illustrate a minor phase of difficulty.— The price of corn in Illinois today is $1., whereas in Kansas it is $1.50. If the Government attempted to fix the price of animals from Illinois for fifty per cent less than Kansas a situation would arise in Washington overnight.

Whatever the sins of the packers have been, the general fact that they have more than doubled the whole of their export business and at the same time cared for domestic consumption during the past few months, should be credited to them as an endeavour on their part to assist in the war situation. We are not satisfied that we need to despair in the control of their profits. It does seem that if the intelligence does not exist by which the profits of the packers can be controlled, it certainly does not exist by which the packing houses can be operated. To solve the whole problem of the packing monopoly would seem to be a matter for a permanent legislation, not for experiment under emergency legislation.

We are in intimate contact with the great majority of livestock associations in the country and, with the exception of one or two individuals out of many thousands of such representative men with whom we have been in contact, from no single association has there been any expression in favour of taking over and operating the packing houses for the Government. The only thing wanted is the proper operation of the packing houses to war ends and that there shall be a "square deal" to both producer and consumer.

Williams-Kennington Plan

John Sharp Williams, senator from Mississippi, was the third ranking Democrat on the Foreign Relations Committee. One of his constituents, Robert Kennington of Jackson, wrote the senator about a proposal to save food which envisaged the elimination of wheat bread from the American diet. Williams sent the letter on to Hoover.

On May 18 Kennington had addressed himself directly to Wilson proposing that the people in the South pledge themselves to eat nothing made of wheat except piecrust and that corn flour be substituted for all other products made of wheat flour. To prove the feasibility of this regimen, Kennington promised to send the President, each week, meal made at his corn mill.

In his second letter of May 25 to the President, Hoover discounted the need of such drastic action, although on the day before he had called for curtailing the consumption of wheat products by one-third of normal consumption. (*Times,* May 25, p. 7.) The "enclosed note" Hoover refers to was the second letter he wrote Wilson on May 25.

25 May 1918

Dear Mr. President:

I send you the enclosed note thinking perhaps it might serve to furnish the basis for a note to Mr. John Sharp Williams in respect to the attached letter from him.

Yours faithfully,
HERBERT HOOVER

Rejection of Kennington Proposal

25 May 1918

Dear Mr. President:

With respect to Mr. Kennington's proposal through Senator Williams, I beg to say that it is an admirable idea and has been put in force in certain of the states. On the other hand, we are now less than six weeks from the new wheat in the South and if the harvest is as good as we hope, there will be no occasion for the American people to do wholly without wheat bread, although we must still continue to wish for the most rigid economy in consumption. It is obvious that if we have a good crop we should make arrangements to establish reserves for years to come.

Yours faithfully,
HERBERT HOOVER

Closing Down of Breweries

A provision attached to the Food Production Bill in the House stipulated that appropriations would be available only if the President utilized the discretionary powers granted him under the Food Control Act of August 10, 1917, to forbid the use of wheat in brewing. Hoover personally favored prohibition, but he thought it should be realized by direct act of Congress rather than by this dubious circuitous method. Among several other adverse effects, he observed that since the Food Bill did not authorize the closing of saloons, the stopping of the flow of beer would merely induce drinkers to quench their thirst on the more potent drinks of whiskey, brandy, gin, and wine, the supply of which was still quite plentiful. Wilson agreed with Hoover, but in his undated memorandum sent to Hoover through Tumulty, he suggested that it was not politic "to fire this off just now." However on June 12 he finally stated his opposition to attaching prohibition riders to appropriation bills. (*Times*, June 13, 1918, p. 7.)

27 May 1918

My dear Tumulty:

With regard to the action of the House in stipulating for closing down the breweries, it seems to me that the time has arrived when some sort of statement on the subject might well be made from the White House.

I have drafted a short memorandum on the reasons for the action

hitherto taken by the Administration in this matter and I am wondering if you would see if the President thinks it desirable to make such
a statement; if so, whether you would issue it from the White House
with all the authority of that quarter behind it?

Yours faithfully,
HERBERT HOOVER

MEMO:

27 May, 1918.

As to the provision attached to the Food Production Bill in the
House, stipulating that the appropriations shall only be available if the
use of grain in brewing in the country shall be stopped under the provisions of the Food Bill.—The reasons why the Administration has not
exercised the discretionary powers in the Food Bill to close the breweries
are very simple.

All distillation of whiskey, brandy and other distilled spirits was
stopped under the Food Bill in September, 1917, but there are stocks of
these liquors in the country sufficient to last for a very long period. The
brewers' products, on the other hand, are not durable and if brewing
were stopped, there can be no stocks of consequence and brewed drinks
would practically cease to exist at once. The effect would be to place
the country entirely on a whiskey basis. The Food Act does not provide for closing the saloons and if brewing were stopped they would
remain open and be compelled to sell whisky [sic] and heavy alcohol
drinks only. The Food Administration has, under the direction of the
President, reduced the alcohol content of beer to a maximum of $2\frac{3}{4}\%$
and the amount of grain used in brewing by 30% and the closing of the
breweries has not been considered to be a real temperance measure
under these circumstances for it has been felt that the moral effect of
throwing the drinking class in the country entirely on a whiskey basis
would be intensely demoralizing and would constitute a constructive
monopoly of the most deleterious of all the drinks.

If Congress wishes that the country should go dry it will require
an entirely new act prohibiting the sale. The course proposed in the
House would have a conservation value in saving the use of grain by
the breweries and no one is so sympathetic with the saving of all grain
as the government, but the moral issues involved of stimulating the
worst form of drinking, have deterred any such action hitherto. | The

Administration is in no way opposed to any constructive prohibition measures. |1

---

1. Deleted by hand.

Caution on Brewery Suggestions

May 27, 1918

Dear Tumulty:

I think this ought to be reserved until it is necessary to give some reason why I cannot approve of the action of the House the other day in this matter. Mr. Hoover is entirely right about it, but probably it isn't necessary to fire this off just now.

The President.
C.L.S.

War Industries Price Board

Wilson must have made this suggestion for eliminating the Price Fixing Board from the proposed machinery for handling the packers' problems sometime during the two weeks between May 13 and May 27. However, no correspondence exists in the Hoover or the Wilson papers touching directly on this subject.

27 May 1918

Dear Mr. President:

I have now consulted the members of the committee on the packing industry and they are in entire accord with your suggestion as to the elimination of the War Industries' Price Fixing Board from the machinery proposed and I am sending you the report as amended.

I am extremely anxious that it should be issued to the public at the earliest moment as some indications as to its content have leaked out and it is a matter of great interest to a considerable portion of the public. If it now meets with your approval, in its present form, would you be so kind as to instruct that it should be issued to the Press?

Yours faithfully,
HERBERT HOOVER

Approval of Report

28 May, 1918

My dear Mr. Hoover:

I have your letter of yesterday containing the revised report of the members of the Committee on the Packing Industry, and take pleasure in approving the conclusions of that report, which I herewith return.

Cordially and sincerely yours,

WOODROW WILSON

Sheppard and Prohibition

Morris Sheppard, Democratic senator from Texas, wrote Hoover on June 2 to solicit his views on the conservation of foodstuffs by forbidding cereals in the production of intoxicating liquors, expressing his "hope that you will be able to work out some line of action by which we can prevent" the production of such liquors and "the sale of whiskey altogether." A few days earlier he had a conversation with Hoover on the same subject. On May 28 Sheppard received a letter from Wilson who expressed himself "distressed" over efforts by the House representatives "to put compulsion on the executive" by adding a rider to an appropriation bill that would withhold funds unless the President forbade the use of cereals for brewing purposes. Wilson wrote that he thought it wiser to do nothing until "I shall be apprised by the Food Administration that it is necessary." (*Life and Letters*, vol. 8, p. 176.)

The senator then approached Hoover and he also called upon the President on June 4 along with Democratic Senator Robert L. Owen of Oklahoma. In all probability, prohibition was discussed. That same afternoon Wilson saw Methodist Bishop James Cannon who was a crusader for the same cause. (*Life and Letters*, vol. 8, p. 190.)

Upon receiving Sheppard's June 2 lettter, Hoover decided to answer it with a statement that could be published to help quiet agitation that was detracting from the war effort.

5 June, 1918

Dear Mr. President:

Please find enclosed copy of letter that I have written to Senator Morris Sheppard, in response to one from him, which I also enclose.

I believe that the reply which I send herewith is in line with the views expressed by yourself. As you know, I have always favoured the saving of the grain from brewing but have felt with you that the moral issues involved, by the establishment of practically a whiskey monopoly, outweighed, for the time being, the conservation question. A great discussion has been launched in the country over the failure of the Food Administration to maintain consistency in this matter, with our strong urging to save grain, and is doing harm to all conservation measures. If you approve, I should like to give publicity to my letter to Senator Sheppard, as I believe it will go a good way toward clearing up the matter in the public mind.

Yours faithfully,

HERBERT HOOVER

Publishing of the Letter to Sheppard

At 2:30 on the day that Wilson wrote this lettter, he saw Hoover at the Wednesday meeting of the war cabinet. The letter Hoover had written to Senator Sheppard, and to which Wilson refers, was most likely the "statement" mentioned in Hoover's *Epic* (vol. 2, p. 117). Although he says he "issued" it on June 4, he undoubtedly meant that he wrote it on that day. For more on the beer problem, see Wilson's letter to Hoover on November 20, 1917.

5 June, 1918

My dear Mr. Hoover:

Thank you for letting me see your letter to Senator Sheppard. It is certainly convincing and I am perfectly willing, if Senator Sheppard is, that you should make it public.

In haste, Cordially and sincerely yours,

WOODROW WILSON

Reason for Trip to Europe

On the day before Hoover wrote this letter, he had met with Wilson and the small group of men who made up the war cabinet. One subject discussed was that of pooling American economic resources with those of the Allies. (*Life and Letters,* vol. 8, p. 207.) This is mentioned in Hoover's letter of June 13 as the fourth reason for his going to Europe in midsummer of 1918.

13 June 1918

Dear Mr. President:

Certain discussions have arisen with regard to Allied relations to the Food Administration next year that I do not believe can be solved without a joint meeting of myself with the Food Administrators of France, England and Italy.

First, we must determine an arrangement of a cereal program next year, based upon the real needs of the Allies, and its adjustment to shipping conditions. Beyond this, as you are aware, we have a guaranteed price for wheat, and I am anxious that the three European Governments should prepare large storage for wheat reserves, in order that if shipping conditions improve in 1919 they could transport our surplus to Europe as a safety reserve for themselves, and thus will relieve us from the necessity of carrying this large amount of wheat at great investment.

A second problem arises in that the European demands for meat at the present time are larger on the beef side than our production will stand without conservation methods further than we can carry on a voluntary basis. On the other hand, we shall have apparently a large surplus of pork, and I have failed in my endeavors so far to persuade the European Food Administrators to substitute pork for beef in sufficient quantities to take care of our excess production and at the same time relieve us of strain on the beef side.

The broad issue in this matter is that in order to increase the animal food supplies from the United States our only hope was through an increased production of pork, which we were able to do over a period of less than twelve months, whereas to stimulate the beef production in the United States would have required at least three years and would have been of practically no importance during the war. From an economic point of view the same food values can be had from pork at an expenditure of much less than the amount of feeding-stuffs.

Our policy has been absolutely sound in this particular and was informally agreed by myself with European Administrators. But the Administrators have changed and the force of national habit and the desire in Europe to proceed on the lines of least resistance has so far not secured the cooperation from them in this particular that is necessary. I believe that a personal conference would effect this, as I am able to present to them strongly that they must support production in this country if they are to be safeguarded in the future. Any failure on our part to find a market for our large increasing pork production would discourage our producers to a point which might become a national calamity in production.

Thirdly, it is necessary that we should improve the organization of the "Executives," who now handle the detailed cereals, meat, fats, sugar, vegetable oils and fiber on the lines that we have discussed with you during the last few days. In many of these commodities we are importers as well as the Allies, and we must have better cooperation in securing supplies and the elimination of competition in common markets abroad.

Fourth, I believe it will have a considerable effect on the psychology of the American production and consumption if we can present to the American people a definite statement that our food supplies must be pooled with the Allies' and set out to them a definite program we must fulfill and to be able to state to them accurately what this program is. Furthermore, it will, I believe, be of utmost importance in maintaining morale in the civil population in Allied countries if I could state on your behalf that the American people will make any necessary sacrifice to maintain their food necessities. There is nothing they can ask next year that with common-sense management will be beyond our capacity on present promise of production and conservation.

I propose to be absent from a month to five weeks and to set up in my absence a committee of the principal divisional heads in the Food Administration. I will obviously assent to no plans without the reservation of your approval, and I would like to add an assurance to you that I shall confine myself absolutely to food problems. I will be glad to know if this program meets with your approval.

Yours faithfully,

HERBERT HOOVER

Approval of Hoover's Trip

14 June, 1918

My dear Mr. Hoover:

I think that the reasons you give for your plan to go abroad and consult with the Food Administrators of France, England and Italy are entirely conclusive, and I believe that your visit to the other side will probably result in a better situation all around with regard to food supplies. My best wishes will certainly follow you.

Thank you for the arrangements you are making for taking care of the Administration during your absence.

Cordially and sincerely yours,

WOODROW WILSON

Report from States on Food Administration Work

June 14, 1918.

Dear Mr. President:

With regard to the monthly report on the activities of the Food Administration, I have asked for a report from each division head and from each State Food Administrator and will furnish these reports as an appendix to a short summarized report from myself.

I have instructed [that][1] the reports shall be prepared as quickly as possible covering the month of May, but the initial report will require a little more time for preparation than the subsequent one.

In order to have the matter constantly in hand, I have appointed Mr. Robert A. Taft, son of ex-President Taft, who is a volunteer in our Legal Division, to take charge of this reporting work. I trust that this will meet with your approval.

Yours faithfully,
HERBERT HOOVER

---

1. Handwritten insertion.

Wheat Purchase by the Grain Corporation

> On June 15 Wilson signed the executive order prepared by Hoover and sent it to the State Department on June 17.

15 June 1918

Dear Mr. President:

I enclose herewith an Executive Order for your consideration. As a consequence of the guarantee on the price of wheat it is technically necessary to designate some body to purchase wheat for the Government and for that purpose we are proposing the Food Administration Grain Corporation, which instrumentality has, as you know, handled the wheat problem up to this time.

The second feature of the Order is an authorization to the Grain Corporation to increase the price of wheat over and above the guaranteed price by an amount in compensation for the differences created by advance in railway rates. I have considered it was better not to increase the guaranteed price but that the Grain Corporation should purchase wheat at the necessary advance. The rates might conceivably decline and in such case it would not be possible to reduce the guarantee.

The third feature is the direction to increase the capital of the Grain Corporation. You will recollect that the present capital is $50,000,000. The total amount of appropriation under the Food Bill for purposes of carrying out the guarantee, et cetera, is $150,000,000. We will probably require the full amount at an early date.

From the present promise of the wheat harvest it appears that the surplus production which must be bought by the Government will be larger than can be compassed by $150,000,000. Mr. Glasgow has had some discussion with Congressional friends as to a further appropriation for this purpose. We came to the conclusion, however, that the present appropriation would be sufficient until some time late in the autumn at which time the pertinent necessity of Congress coming to the support of the guarantee would be more evident and there would be less likely to be tacked-on legislation interfering in price questions.

I hope the above plan and the Order may meet with your approval.

Yours faithfully,
HERBERT HOOVER

Approval of Wheat Purchase Plan

17 June, 1918

My dear Mr. Hoover:

I think the plan you propose is the right one and I shall be ready to supply the $5,000,000 capital necessary if the $50,000,000 appropriation in the pending Sundry Civil Bill goes through all right.

Cordially and sincerely yours,
WOODROW WILSON

Regulation of Malt Products

Wilson apparently had received a set of regulations from Hoover governing the production of malt, which he was asked to sign. But Wilson entertained some doubts about the necessity of such regulations and queried Hoover on the point. Perhaps Hoover answered the President orally, for no letter appears in which he alludes to the matter. Thus there is no evidence as to whether Hoover convinced Wilson and eventually persuaded him to sign the regulations.

18 June, 1918

My dear Mr. Hoover:

Before signing the enclosed, which I understand was prepared by your Administration, it occurs to me to ask this question:

You will remember that at the meeting of our Wednesday conference on the Wednesday before the last, it was provisionally agreed that on account of the necessity of conserving coal there should be an entire stoppage of the production of malt products. If that is to be done, I hardly see the necessity for issuing the amended regulations enclosed, and the question I want to ask is, Do these regulations represent an earlier conclusion?

Cordially and faithfully yours,
WOODROW WILSON

New Executive Order on Wheat

Wilson agreed to Hoover's request for a new executive order on the matter discussed in his June 15 letter and signed the order June 21 and sent it to the State Department.

20 June, 1918.

Dear Mr. President:

With regard to the Executive Order signed by you a day or two ago, constituting the Grain Corporation [as] the agency to effectuate the government guarantee on wheat.—A further study of this situation has led us to ask you to re-sign the Order, including an alteration making discretionary with the Grain Corporation as to whether the guarantee applies to the producer alone, or whether it applies to any sellers of wheat at all. This difference amounts to giving somewhat further control over the grain dealers in the country and has been done after further conference with our Grain Division.

If you can see your way to sign the new Order, we will destroy the previous one.

Yours faithfully,
HERBERT HOOVER

Brauer Complaint on Beef

In June 1918 Hoover announced new rationing regulations that would curtail the consumption of beef both in homes and hotels. (*Times*,

June 13, 1918, p. 24.) An adversely affected individual in the cattle industry, William Wallace Brauer, was distressed by these restrictions and apparently sent an alarming telegram to Wilson. He evidently sent it on to Hoover, who then offered his comments in this letter of June 26.

26 June 1918

Dear Mr. President:

I am obliged for the copy of [the] telegram from Mr. William Wallace Brauer who seems to feel that some grave national crisis has been brought about because we have asked for a voluntary restriction on beef consumption in public eating places so as to enable us to supply the very large military demands pending the fall marketing season.

He was formerly a shipper of live cattle to Europe. This trade is now impossible due to the shortage of shipping and the necessity to carry men and horses in the boats adapted to live cattle. As these boats are largely British, he perceives a conspiracy of the American packer to put him out of business and has been hitherto directing his energies by cable to Mr. Lloyd George and other prominent European officials. Mr. Brauer is naturally anxious to secure profitable business and we have been unable to help him.

There is scarcely a sentence in his telegram that represents the truth. The cattle industry has never been so profitable to growers as it is today. Any re-assurance upon this matter Mr. Houston can no doubt afford you.

As to Mr. Brauer's statement, "The democracy of the world is at stake. Please reply." I do wish to assure you that democracy has not been engulfed by our voluntary meatless meals in hotels.

I am entirely content that you should secure either the opinion of Mr. George Gordon Battle or Ex-Governor Stuart, to whom Mr. Brauer refers, upon him or his schemes.

Yours faithfully,
HERBERT HOOVER

Bradley for Alaska Food Administrator

June 29, 1918.

Dear Mr. President:

Owing to the sudden death of Judge Royal A. Gunnison, who had been acting as Federal Food Administrator for Alaska, it has become necessary to secure a successor.

After careful consideration I wish to recommend the appointment of Mr. Philip R. Bradley of Treadwell.

Mr. Bradley is strongly recommended by Governor Riggs, he is known personally to me, and in my opinion is an ideal man for this position. We understand that he has the confidence of all in Alaska. He is manager of the Treadwell property and is a man of force and excellent judgment and tact, and I am confident that he could administer the work in Alaska in a most satisfactory manner.

Faithfully yours,
HERBERT HOOVER

Approved
WOODROW WILSON [handwritten by Wilson]

Plans for European Trip

> The gloom that characterized the tone of many of Hoover's spring reports on the food problem began to dissipate with the advent of summer and its promise of "an abundant crop and the enormous savings of a spiritually mobilized people." The problem now was one of ships; to help solve this and other closely related problems, he decided upon a trip to Europe to meet with leaders of the associated powers. In the following letter Hoover presents his plans and purposes in greater detail than he did in his June 13 letter. Wilson indicated his approval by writing "okeh W.W." on the letter.
>
> The first proposal mentioned was immediately implemented upon his arrival in Europe by the establishment of an Allied Food Council. With Hoover as chairman, the council resurveyed the clothing, food, and medical supplies needed by the Allied and neutral nations for the following year. To carry these necessities to Europe, 2,000,000 tons of shipping a month was demanded; but here General Pershing intervened. Already planning a grand assault for September, he concluded that only 1,200,000 could be allotted for these needs. "I had a sinking feeling," Hoover recalled in 1951, "that food might lose the war, instead of, as represented in all our posters—'Food Will Win the War.' Had the offensive failed, we would have had a debacle." (Memoirs, vol. 1, pp. 259–60.)

29 June 1918

Dear Mr. President:

As I shall be leaving for Europe in the course of a few days, I am anxious to secure your approval to the plans I have in view:

First: I propose, in conference with the Food Administrators of England, France and Italy, to study the world harvest supplies, the Allied and United States requirements of the principal food commodities for the next twelve months and the distribution necessary at each point.

In order that these studies may be carried out expeditiously, I propose to make use of the staffs which the Food Administration has already in Europe and I propose to be accompanied by three or four assistants representing the technical side of different food commodity groups. Through these conferences I propose that we shall draw up as nearly as may be the general programme for the ensuing twelve months' requirements, sources and supplies in each commodity group.

After these preliminary programmes are drawn up, I would propose that they should be submitted to the International Maritime Council for consideration on the shipping side and, upon the settling of these issues, to the Inter-Allied Finance Council for their consideration.

Second: You will recollect that during the past year we have built up certain bodies for co-ordinated action, that is, an "Executive" for cereals, another for meats and fats, and a third for sugar. I propose to add to this a fourth, covering jute and hemp. We have also consolidated the direction of overseas buying into these bodies to eliminate competition. There is some complaint as to these "Executives" and we need more effectual relations to them as, in every commodity, our interest in distribution extends outside the United States. I propose therefore to endeavor to arrange that either these "Executives" themselves, or their policies, should be controlled by a committee representative of each of the four Governments; they, of course, operating within the programmes agreed.

For this purpose I propose to add somewhat to the staff the Food Administration already has in Europe so as to carry out this work efficiently. The necessity for these "executives" increases daily by virtue of our common interest in supplies from all quarters of the world. One point in having these "executives" is to have proper advice here as to the fluctuating requirements and supplies of the different Allied nations in order that we may properly formulate our production and conservation policies at this end.

It may prove necessary in order to obtain co-ordination between these different food "executives" that I should constitute some one of the gentlemen that I leave in Europe as the responsible head of our American food group, who can represent me personally in relations with the different Allied Food Ministers and who can represent in common the relation from our point of view with the American War Trade, Finance and Maritime representatives in Europe.

In all these programmes and arrangements I shall, of course, immediately submit any programmes for your approval, and if we consider it desirable to vary from the above form of organization, I shall, of course, secure approval first; and, as is customary, I shall assume it is my duty to approach the various European Food Ministers through and in co-operation with our Embassies abroad.

Third: I feel the food problem is for fundamental reasons a problem of marked distinction from all of the other Inter-Allied supply problems. This revolves around the points of psychology and morale which arise in this class of supplies as they so much affect the minds of the civil population both abroad and in the United States to a degree not touched by the more abstruse and less personal problems of war trade, finance and munitions.

During the whole of the past year we have built up a devotion of the American people to the issue that we must make any sacrifice of food short of damage to public health that the necessity of the Allies calls for. In other words, we have had morally and effectually a pooling of foodstuffs with the Allied peoples. The confidence this has inspired in Allied populations, of which I could furnish you many particulars, has been very great. I would therefore like to maintain this attitude in negotiation as being a direction from you that "the American people are gladly willing to make any sacrifice in consumption and production of foodstuffs short of damage to our own efficiency in the war that will maintain the health, comfort and courage of the people of the Allied countries. That we are, in fact, eating at a common table with them". I have in view endeavouring this year, if our supplies warrant, the establishment of a universal bread of about 20% other cereals than wheat over the United States and the Allied countries and to take off the quantity restrictions in Europe. This will be a much better bread than now prevails. It would give us a much better moral background here to effect economies and would have a great moral effect in Europe. It would also have a depressing effect in Germany where much comfort has been taken out of our bread difficulties.

In all this matter it seems to me fundamental that no financial restrictions should be placed upon the supplies of money for the purchase by the Allies of staple food commodities of United States production. Unless this can be assured, we cannot hope for continuity of policy in either production or consumption. On the other hand, problems will arise which are purely Treasury problems, as to the finance of supplies that may be purchased by the Allies from overseas sources outside the United States where they may want financial assistance.

I would indeed be glad to know if the above meets with your approval.

Yours faithfully,

HERBERT HOOVER

Okeh

W.W. [handwritten by Wilson]

Curtailing Nonwar Industries

> The war could not have been fought without vesting in government the authority to determine which products were essential and which nonessential to the Allied effort. The Priorities Board exercised such a power in America, and its activity is the subject of the following letter.
>
> Needless to say, decisions that certain products were nonessential brought profound grief to many manufacturers who must have at times agreed with the *Washington Post* that the board was the "vermiform appendix" of the war machine and should be cut off.
>
> The board's lack of unanimity in regard to the brewing industry, mentioned in the letter below, evolved from a very practical consideration, namely, the large tax revenues the government would lose from banning or curtailing the production of beer and other forms of alcohol. This loss had to be balanced against the gain in essential foodstuffs that would result from denying breweries and distilleries the grain necessary for their products.
>
> President Wilson signified his approval and returned the letter to Hoover. The following day Hoover saw the President at 2:30.

2 July 1918.

Dear Mr. President:

In accordance with your instruction that we should prepare for you a recommendation in connection with the systematic curtailment of nonwar industries, we have asked a special committee, comprising:

Messrs. Clarence M. Woolley of the War Trade Board
Edward Chambers of the Railway Administration

Edwin F. Gay of the Shipping Board
P. B. Noyes, of the Fuel Administration
Theodore F. Whitmarsh of the Food Administration
Edwin B. Parker of the War Industries Board.

to make a detailed study as to the general policy to be pursued in connection with such industries. The conclusions of this committee, to which we unanimously agree, except in those relating to the brewing industry, upon which subject we are seeking further information, pending possible action by Congress, are:

That the approach to curtailment of non-war industries should be made by way of systematic and scientific reduction in their activities rather than by total and initial annihilation. They do not find that there are any industries which should be instantly cut off but there are many which should be reduced in activities at the earliest possible moment. These gentlemen are all members of the Priorities Board of the War Industries Board. This problem, in certain phases, lies outside the present conception of priorities in the use of material.

As to further action in the matter, we recommend that the above committee be constituted a special committee of the Priorities Board to study each industry from the aspect of what can be curtailed and what is a desirable curtailment, and to make such recommendations to the Priorities Board from time to time, and that the Priorities Board should advise the various departments of the action of the Board and the departments which will effectuate the conclusions of the Board.

The committee has furnished us with a recommendation that the brewing industry should be curtailed to 50% of the normal barrelage. A copy of this report we enclose herewith. We have asked the committee to further consider whether, in addition to the curtailment at once of 50%, the industry should not be notified that no further foodstuffs are to be purchased and that, with the exhaustion of their present materials in process, they are to cease operation.

We are also asking the committee to make a further report, if possible, on the reduction that we recommend in connection with other non-war industries.

Yours faithfully,
HERBERT HOOVER

Okeh
W.W. [handwritten by Wilson]

Request to See Wilson

Hoover was anxious to see the President on Saturday, July 5, to discuss matters pertaining to his pending trip to Europe, but Wilson wrote this note on the memorandum: "If Mr. Hoover is to be here to-morrow (Sunday 7th [sic]) ask him to come in at 2:30." The meeting took place at that time.

Memorandum for the President:

July 5, 1918.

Mr. Herbert Hoover asks if he may see the President tomorrow. Mr. Hoover is expecting to leave Monday and is anxious to see the President before his departure.

[unsigned]

Federal Trade Commission on Packers' Profiteering

Hoover was ever alert to the dangers of unscrupulous war profiteers. On July 8 he suggested to Senator Furnifold M. Simmons that an excess profit tax be considered as a curb for these activities. Prior to this suggestion, the Food Adminstration had established a "maximum profits" for packers but the Federal Trade Commission disagreed with this ceiling and incorporated its disagreement in a written report. Hoover was prompted to formulate his own reply which he sent to President Wilson with the following letter. This reply is the "lengthy letter" that follows the one below. It likewise is dated July 8.

Ex-Governor Henry Stuart, mentioned below, was chairman of an agricultural advisory committee known as the "Farmers' War Committee." Bernard Baruch was chairman of the War Industries Board.

8 July, 1918

Dear Mr. President:

I am enclosing you rather a lengthy letter in reply to the Trade Commission's report on the Food Administration maximum profits allowed the packers. I have the feeling that if the Trade Commission report is made public then this reply, in justice, should be given co-incident publicity. I do not, however, believe that any useful purpose is served by public ventilation of inter-departmental disagreements as to governmental policy.

The matters at issue are matters of considerable importance and principle. If Congress passes sufficiently strong excess profits legislation, it will automatically correct the situation and meet the views of both the Trade Commission and ourselves. If Congress does not do so, I am afraid you will need to make some decision in matters of principle.

My proposal is, therefore, that the whole matter shall be laid aside until the action of Congress is determinable. If, however, you think it desirable to have the matter inquired into at once, I would like to suggest that the Trade Commission report, together with the letter which I enclose should be submitted to some independent person, say Mr. Baruch, or ex-Governor Stuart of Virginia, both of whom could advise upon the matters of principle involved, without necessarily entering into details of fact.

Yours faithfully,
HERBERT HOOVER

Refutation of Federal Trade Commission Report

The second paragraph of this letter, the "lengthy letter" Hoover mentions above, proved to be prophetic of what was to happen in January and February 1919 when congressmen engaged in sharp attacks on Hoover's policies relative to the packing industry. On February 19 of that year Hoover at length prevailed upon Wilson to release his September 11, 1918, statement in which he had objected to the proposal of the Federal Trade Commission for government operation of the packing companies. Both Wilson and Hoover previously had believed that no useful purpose would be served by releasing the statement and had therefore held it up out of fear of the dismay that might well ensue from a public airing of a "family" disagreement. (See letters below for more on this matter.)

8 July, 1918

Dear Mr. President:

I beg to acknowledge the report of the Trade Commission, which you have so kindly forwarded to me, upon the effect of the Food Administration regulation of the packers' profits.

I realize fully that in the discussion of this matter, any sentence uttered that can be interpreted as in support of profits to the packing industry subjects one to the charge of corrupt influence and, on the other hand, I recognize equally the easy road to popularity through de-

nunciation of these profits. It is however our duty to separate the emotional aspects in these matters from justice and national necessity to
secure war results.

1.   At the initiation of these regulations last October, we called
upon the Federal Trade Commission for information and advice,
and members of the Commission participated in the discussions
with the packers which led up to the final regulations. Mr. Davies,
who conducted the investigation of the packers and who participated
in these discussions, has since made the statement:

> "The nine per cent limitation of profit on the most efficient
> meat-packing plants is out of all proportion to the much
> larger profits made by the relatively similarly efficient steel
> and copper-producing agencies."

During the month of March, when it appeared that the profit limitations set out by the Food Administration were proving to be possibly
larger than was anticipated, we requested through you that the
Trade Commission should investigate the working of the regulations and advise as to their fairness and we arranged that they were
to take over the auditing of the accounts to determine the accuracy
of the packers' profit statements.

2.   The initial regulations were formulated on the basis that they
should limit the maximum percentage on turn over to a figure no
greater than the pre-war average, with the further limitation that
the bulk of the business—that is, the meat business—should not earn
over 9% and that the specialty business involving foodstuffs should
not earn more than 15%. Certain classes of business were excluded
altogether,—that is, the businesses in foreign countries and non-food
businesses, such as sporting goods, banks and manufactures into
which foodstuffs did not enter, all these being outside the legal
function of the Food Administration. The application of the 9%
limit fell upon 75% of the regulated business—the meat business
plus transfer value of bye-products [sic], and the 15% limitation
applied to the specialty business and completion of bye-products
[sic]. These percentages were computed upon the total capital used
by the packer in these businesses, including borrowed money.

3.   The Trade Commission report advises that the Food Administration should include all businesses (although this is not legally
feasible) and that a flat maximum of profits should be imposed of
7% plus one per cent additional for each 10% increase in volume

of weight of animals killed up to a maximum of 9%. The prospective business during 1918 would probably allow the packers to realize the full 9%. The Trade Commission basis, however, prescribes that borrowed capital should be excluded from calculations of earnings.

4.   Taking as a basis the tables accompanying the report of the Trade Commission and excluding the non-food and foreign business, and combining all of the five great packers, we find the following essential figures:

Total Investment $853,219,000
"Net Worth" 389,885,000
Consequently Borrowed
    Capital 468,334,000
Total Estimates of Food
    Administration Maximum
    Profit   87,443,000
Less Interest   21,407,000
Net Earning   66,036,000

The profits are gross, without deduction of taxes, which would amount to about $16,000,000, leaving about $50,000,000 net. The Trade Commission's allowance of 9% on "worth" as applied to the above figure of $389,885,000 would give a net earning of $35,089,650. Whether this is before or after taxes, we do not know, but assume from the text that it is net for dividend purposes. We would submit that the estimated interest figure given in the above table is $2,000,-000 less than the actual necessary payment on a five-per cent basis and that therefore the Trade Commission's recommendation would call for a reduction in the maximum earned on this class of business of about $29,000,000 without taxes, or about $13,000,000 if their figures are net. This would imply a reduction of about 40% in one case or 20% in the other, and therefore makes it difficult to understand the statement that the Food Administration regulation allows the earning to be from 2¼ to 3 times as great as normal. This probably arises from the assumption that the Food Administration could control outside profits—which are estimated at $25,000,000 per annum for the five packers.

4. [sic]   The combined five packers will, in 1918, probably kill 12-000,000,000 pounds, live weight, of animals, resulting in 7,000,000,000 pounds of meat products. A profit of one cent a pound would be $70,000,000. Therefore the possible profits under the Food Ad-

ministration regulation are less than one cent a pound and the reduction proposed by the Trade Commission will amount to about
one-third of a cent per pound. It is necessary to emphasize this for
the producing public may be misled into the belief that the bare
volume in these figures—large as they are—will have actual and
tangible results in reducing the cost of living. The fact of the case
is, that one-third of a cent per pound seldom reflects into realiza-
tion in the hands of the subsequent distributing trades after the
meat has left the packer.

5.   The Trade Commission has the feeling that there is little or no
risk attached to these enterprises and that therefore their earnings
should be reduced to practically the terms of a public utility. We
feel that they have overlooked certain great risks. Something like
$250,000,000 invested in food stocks are being carried at high prices
and would depreciate 30% if communications with Europe were cut
off thirty days, or if the production programme in force should out-
run the meat demands and there should be a fall in the animal
market. An increased shipping programme that would open other
food markets to the Allies would have the same effect.

6.   The Food Administration regulations permit earnings upon borrowed as well as packers' own capital; whereas, the Trade Commission proposes that no profits should be allowed on borrowed
capital. This appears to us to strike at the base of most business
enterprise. As we understand it, a large part of the commerce and
trade of the country is founded on the earning of an excess sum on
borrowed capital over the bare interest cost and we feel that if this
principle proposed by the Trade Commission were laid down as a
precedent, it would produce an absolute state of panic in the United
States. This industry must borrow money largely on short-time
paper to carry the large reserve stocks now created for the Army
and the Allies, if they are to be continuously provided for. We are
confident if this question were submitted to any group of competent
advisers they would affirm that businesses in general, and this business in particular, must earn a profit over and above interest charges
on actual capital borrowed.

7.   The food strategy necessary to the handling of war issues has
involved the increase in our exports to the Allies and our Army and
Navy by over 250%. In order that we should be prepared for any
emergency, it has been necessary to call upon the packers to increase
their stocks in storage. Furthermore, the programme of stimulation

of production, particularly the pork so critically needed for war purposes, and the maintenance of a stable minimum price on hogs has involved the packers in much larger stocks than would normally be acquired. All of this has necessitated an increased borrowing on the part of the packers that would not have been called for had they conducted their business in the normal manner. Therefore the compensation of the packers must bear some relation to their borrowed capital.

8.   We must recognize that this great centralized industry is the cheap producer and that an administrative limitation of maximum profits in certain of their specialty businesses that will reduce them to popular ideas of earnings will throw into the hands of these centralized institutions all the business in these specialties by crowding out high-cost producers, and thus will eventually reduce production or aggrandize monopoly. We cannot agree to the answer to this argument in the report as follows:

> "If it appears that the Big Packers can operate these specialty businesses more effectively than the independents, it is sound war-time efficiency to let them do it. The only danger in the situation would be the failure of the Government to continue its regulation of the packers and their affiliated companies after the war."

It is our belief that one of the greatest dangers to the whole of the food trades of the United States is the further expansion of these big packing industries and the elimination of smaller business and individual enterprise. It is not sound war-time efficiency to enable a monstrous growth of this kind to destroy individual enterprise of the United States on the mere hope that regulation of the industry will continue after the war. By that time the competitors will all be dead.

9.   There is one prime difficulty in all regulation of profits in advance. Such advance regulation must provide for stimulation in production, give an incentive to serve war aims, and must provide sufficiently wide margins to cover all possible risk. If the concern regulated is so fortunate as to come through without incurring losses from the risks the profits may be inordinate. Having narrowed the possible profits of the packer to less than one cent a pound in protection to producer and consumer, our point of view was to encourage him to follow the national food strategy at his own risk.

10.   In calling upon the Trade Commission to re-examine this

problem, we had in view some attempt to further regulate down the possible maximum profits of the packers.

Since that time proposals have been formulated in Congress to enact further strong excess profits legislation. Such legislation would be much the most satisfactory remedy. The Food Administration regulations having in some degree accomplished stability in the market, [have stimulated production and][1] served war ends and eliminated vicious speculation, should be broadly supplemented by tax legislation that would restore to the public any inordinate earnings that might be secured by the more fortunate manufacturers. This method also has the great advantage of equalizing situations between different manufacturers, which is one of the objects sought by the Trade Commission plan.

11.   An advance profit regulation operates, if too strictly drawn, to curb incentive, to destroy production and to limit efficiency. The sound method, if possible, is to give a fairly loose profit regulation, sufficiently strict to prevent speculation, stabilize price levels and then, by taxation, to appropriate to the Government any extraordinary profit that may have arisen. There is also a psychological point of great importance.— Any given business enterprise would willingly pay in the shape of a tax whatever may have been its extraordinary profits. But if its profits are limited in advance to the same sum, the same enterprise will feel it is restricted, unable to protect itself against risks of loss and the re-action will damage the efficiency and courage in the conduct of this enterprise.

In conclusion, we are not in disagreement as to the fact that the packers may earn too large profits under the regulations. We are in disagreement as to the method of establishing regulation and perhaps as to the actual percentage. On the other hand, we feel that the whole matter can quite well be deferred until the character of the action now being taken by Congress can be determined. If it should prove ineffective to accomplish these ends, it would be necessary to revise the regulations and I will take it up immediately upon my return from Europe.

I have written a letter to Senator Simmons at his request on the whole relation of a properly founded excess profits tax in its bearing on regulation of industry, which expresses more fully the views which we have formulated in this matter, which I transmit herewith.

Yours faithfully,
HERBERT HOOVER

---

1. Handwritten insertion.

Reply to Simmons on Profiteering

Senator Furnifold M. Simmons was a Democrat from North Carolina who headed the Senate Finance Committee. He had asked Hoover for his views on profiteering in relation to the then pending tax legislation. Hoover obliged with a six-page letter, a copy of which he sent to the President. In this letter he distinguished between the "moral and economic phases." He wrote that "normal profits" even during war were "not immoral." On the other hand, "extra profits out of War are hateful" and "should be appropriated to the public treasury through taxation." The letter to Simmons is not shown.

8 July, 1918

Dear Mr. President:

Please find attached hereto a letter which I have sent to Senator Simmons in reply to a request from him for my opinion on the subject of tax legislation. As this letter contains a summation of my experience in dealing with the question of profiteering versus Government regulation, it may, perhaps, be worth your time to glance over it.

Yours faithfully,
HERBERT HOOVER

Effect of $2.40 Wheat Guarantee

Neither the Wilson nor Hoover papers contain any written request for information on the effect of a bill passed guaranteeing the farmer $2.40 wheat. This could have been made orally, possibly when the two met at 3:45 on Sunday, July 6. In any case, Hoover supplied the information in this July 8 letter.

8 July, 1918

Dear Mr. President:

With respect to your request, for your own information, as to the effect of the $2.40 guarantee on wheat just passed by Congress on prices, I beg to point out the following:

The original figure of the guarantee fixed by Congress was a minimum of $2.00 at the principal, primary markets, for No. 1 Northern wheat. It was practically increased by the price fixed for wheat last August, which took account of the differences in freight rates between terminals and fixed the price at $2.20 at Chicago, thus increasing the price over $2. for a large part of the country. This was confirmed for [the] 1918 crop by your proclamation of February 21st. Since that time, on your authority, I have made further increases at various terminals to cover the increased freight rates and the base price at Chicago is now $2.26. The legislation just passed fixes the price at $2.40 for No. 2 Northern wheat, which is equivalent to $2.43 for No. 1 Northern, and fixes the same minimum price at all of the terminals mentioned in your proclamation of February 21st. This would mean that if we maintain the freight differences in the prices there will be a rise of 43 cents a bushel in the price of wheat, because we must start with the most remote terminal as a base. The most remote terminal today is $2.00, while New York, the highest, is $2.39,—the difference representing freight. Thus the legislation totally neglects the fact that wheat cannot be valued the same at all points because of the difference in freight charges to the common market. Today we simply buy wheat at guaranteed prices that cannot otherwise find a market and the prices maintain the regular flow of grain so we do not need to buy very much.

It would be possible to buy all of the wheat for the Government at $2.43 in terms of No. 1 Northern at each terminal and make a generalized price to the entire Country. This might result in an economy of ten cents or perhaps more a bushel to the public. But it would involve the immediate finding of at least $500,000,000. for which Congress has made no provision, beyond $150,000,000 original appropriation. Such a plan would totally destroy the normal commerce in grain. Therefore under the alternative we would have to increase every terminal by 43 cents and 43 cents a bushel would be approximately $2.00 per barrel on the flour, or a rise from the present price of $10.50 at the mill to $12.50 at the mill door. We are anticipating roughly, 900,000,000 bushels of wheat and a rise of 43 cents a bushel would be equivalent to $387,000,000 increased payment to the farmer.

This rise in price not only affects the United States but will automatically affect the Canadian crop, as their price is based on ours, and as our Government must find the money for Allied purchases, both in the United States and Canada, it means a very considerable increase in advances that must be made to the Allied Governments and this same money must be raised by additional taxation, or loans.

The guarantee on the price of wheat was originally given to ensure to ourselves and the Allied Governments a supply of wheat. As a result of the guarantee given, the wheat acreage increased 28.2% over last year and will produce prospectively a crop sufficient to meet our own and Allied consumption during the coming year. The crop is in course of harvest and therefore the increase in price can in no way affect the quantity available. Therefore the purpose of the guarantee from a National point of view has been accomplished at the lower figure and the increase in price is a gift to the farmer by the nation.

As to whether the farmer deserves this increased price as a gift, is a matter on which there may of course be a difference in opinion. I have not, nor do I believe Mr. Houston has, yet received from any responsible body of farmers a complaint as to the price and we are informed by the most responsible men in the industry and in touch with it, that it is a satisfactory and a profitable price in every quarter of the country, except where there has been some failure in growth. Every statistical calculation on the relative price of the other grains and production costs indicate that the old price is profitable and,—I believe the acreage has demonstrated it to be, a stimulative price to the farmer. Nor do I believe the farmer wishes the outcry of profiteering should be directed toward him.

It can be of no permanent benefit to the farmer to make an extravagant profit on one commodity, for the economic re-action through the country must ultimately reach his door. Further than this, there is great danger of starting a long train of disturbances in labour and damage to our national efficiency over questions of the increased cost of living. If these prices are interpreted in bread amongst the Allies, the same train of difficulties must be established for them.

I believe you will find that the Secretary of Agriculture will fully confirm these views.

Yours faithfully,
HERBERT HOOVER

Glasgow and the War Cabinet

> Before leaving for his long study trip to Europe, Hoover arranged for a committee of top Food Administration officials to carry on his work. However, since Hoover was also a member of the war cabinet, it was necessary to appoint a substitute for this duty. His choice was W. A. Glasgow, chief counsel of the Food Administration. As this letter indicates, Hoover had some difficulty in deciding who should take his place at the Wednesday meetings of the cabinet.

8 July, 1918.

Dear Mr. President:

The nineteen principal departmental heads in the Food Administration are all specialists, none of whom would be able to advise you generally as to food matters outside of their special problems. Moreover, I am completely non-plussed to know which of them to suggest to you to attend the Wednesday conference and, furthermore, I dislike to show a preference between them in this matter. I am therefore returning to the suggestion that Mr. Glasgow, who is the Chief Counsel and has a thoroughly broad knowledge of the whole of the issues involved here, should, if you desire, attend the conferences and on any special food subject he will bring to you either the head of the department concerned or, alternatively, their views and opinions, during my absence.

As you appreciate, Mr. Glasgow is a good deal more than a lawyer and is rapidly becoming a food expert.

Yours faithfully,

HERBERT HOOVER

Committee in Hoover's Absence

The order mentioned in this letter was signed and returned to Hoover on July 9.

8 July, 1918.

Dear Mr. President:

During my absence I have constituted a committee of the heads of departments of the Food Administration as an Executive Board. It comprises the following persons:

Messrs.	Julius H. Barnes	G. H. Denny
	R. W. Boyden	George M. Rolph
	W. A. Glasgow, Jr.,	
	Prentiss N. Gray	
	J. W. Hallowell	
Miss	Gertrude B. Lane	
Messrs.	Charles W. Merrill	
	J. R. Munn	
	G. H. Powell	
	Edgard [sic] Rickard	
	F. S. Snyder	

Miss   Martha Van Rensselaer

Messrs.   C. E. Spens
                Robert A. Taft
                Theodore Whitmarsh
                John Beaver White
                R. L. Wilbur

I have constituted Mr. Edgar Rickard who has been the Office
Director for the past year and in whom I have entire confidence, as the
Executive Secretary of this Board and I am enclosing herewith an
Executive Order which, if you approve, I would be glad if you would
sign, delegating to Mr. Rickard authority to sign on my behalf in my
name any necessary documents for the Food Administration. My instructions have been that Mr. Rickard is to use this authority upon approval of the Executive Board above named.

Yours faithfully,
HERBERT HOOVER

Need for More Office Space

8 July, 1918.

Dear Mr. President:

The expanding activities of the Food Administration by virtue of
the necessity for expansion in grain operations in connection with Allied
shipments and the maintenance of the guarantee over a larger crop,
the expansion in our sugar division, by virtue of the semi-rationing plan
and the creation of the new sugar board all make demands on us for
more office space.

The United States Grain Corporation and the United States Sugar
Equalization Board, Incorporated, require between them approximately
sixty thousand feet and it is my view that it would be perfectly proper
for these two corporations to erect office space for themselves in the city
of Washington without calling upon yourself or the other funds as they
obviously must have office room to conduct their office operations and it
is cheaper to build temporary buildings than to rent in these times.
Furthermore, there is nothing to be rented.

If you approve of this idea and will so inform the Food Administration, they will proceed to find a location and make themselves temporary
quarters.

It is possible that our office will want to make an exchange with Mr. Baruch for some office space but they can work this accomodation [*sic*] out for themselves if you approve of these corporations providing their own office accomodation [*sic*].

Yours faithfully,
HERBERT HOOVER

Sugar Equalization Board

Wilson signed the papers mentioned in this letter and returned them to Hoover on July 10.

July 8, 1918

My dear Mr President:

I beg to submit herewith a proposed certificate of incorporation for the United States Sugar Equalization Board, Incorporated, and a proposed draft of a letter to be signed by you authorizing me to proceed with the incorporation. I also submit an offer to purchase the outstanding capital stock of the corporation in the name of the United States. In case these papers are satisfactory to you, and I am so directed, I am prepared to proceed with the incorporation of the company.

Faithfully yours,
HERBERT HOOVER

Rise in Price of Wheat

Congress had just passed an Agricultural Appropriation Bill which provided for an increase in the price of wheat from $2.20 to $2.40. (See also letter for July 8.) In this letter to the President, written from New York while en route to London, Hoover urged that Wilson veto the bill, which he did on July 12. The House sustained his action. (*Times,* July 13, 1918, p. 8; July 14, p. 16.)

10 July, 1918

Dear Mr. President:

I am informed that the contention has been raised that the $2.40 wheat means a rise of only about twenty cents a bushel to the farmer and a similar cost to the consumer. This argument is based on the contention that our present price basis is, say, $2. Salt Lake, $2.26 Chicago, $2.39½ New York. It neglects the fact that the new Congressional price is based on No. 2 wheat instead of No. 1, in which there is a difference of three cents, but of much more importance than this, it is based on the assumption that it is possible, commercially, to make a universal price for wheat.

I have now consulted the men in the Food Administration Grain Corporation and they have earnestly considered every possible method by which this might be accomplished and the final conclusion is that while it could be accomplished, it would necessitate an immediate working capital of $500,000,000 and would necessitate not only that we buy all the wheat in the country for the Government, instead of 15% or 20%, as under the present scheme, but would necessitate a proportionate expansion in organization. Furthermore, it could not be accomplished unless at the same time we took over the operation, direction and distribution of all the flour mills in the country because the differences in conditions in freight would maintain in flour the same as in wheat. As showing how quickly a rise in wheat may affect other food products with which there is no real relation, many exchanges reported yesterday increased prices of corn on the possibility that the Bill might not be vetoed.

Should you be considering the approval of this legislation I earnestly hope that you would first hear Mr. Barnes, the head of our Cereal Division, on its whole bearings. Any consideration of the problem with all its complexities will come to only one result, that if this legislation is confirmed, it will be necessary to increase the price of wheat at every terminal in the United States by 43 cents a bushel.

Yours faithfully,
HERBERT HOOVER

Food Shipments to Allies

On July 8 Hoover left Washington for New York, where on July 12 he boarded the *Olympic* for London and the Continent on a food investigation trip. The day before embarking he mailed this report to the President. It was actually dispatched with a letter to Tumulty suggesting that it be given wide distribution. Wilson returned it to Tumulty with a note authorizing its publication unless he detected something which suggested that it not be made public. Accordingly, it went to the press within a week. (*Times,* July 19, 1918, p. 9.)

The day after Hoover sailed from New York, Secretary of State Lansing wrote a long letter to the President strongly suggesting that he establish a "Commission for the Relief of Russia" and that Hoover be named its head. He added: "I feel sure that Mr. Hoover's appointment to head such a commission would be widely acclaimed as another evidence of the determination of the United States to assist the Russian people toward the establishment of an orderly government independent of Germany." It would also "for the time being, dispose of the proposal of armed intervention." (*Epic*, vol. 2, pp. 133-34.) But on July 15 Wilson wrote Baruch, who supported Lansing: "I agree with you in your estimate of Hoover, but I cannot without dislocating some of the most important things we are handling spare him from his present functions." (*Life and Letters*, vol. 8, p. 281.)

11 July, 1918

Dear Mr. President:

It is now possible to summarize the shipments of foodstuffs from the United States to the Allied countries during the fiscal Year just closed—practically the last harvest year. These amounts include all shipments to Allied countries for their and our armies, the civilian population, the Belgian Relief and Red Cross. The figures indicate the measure of effort of the American people in support of Allied food supplies.

The total value of these food shipments which were in the main purchased through, or with the collaboration of, the Food Administration, amount to, roundly, $1,400,000,000 during the fiscal year.

The shipments of meats and fats (includes meat products, dairy products, vegetable oils, etc.,) to Allied destinations were as follows:

Fiscal year
1916–17 .... 2,166,500,000 lbs.
Fiscal year
1917–18 .... 3,011,100,000 lbs.
Increase .... 844,600,000 lbs.

Our slaughterable animals at the beginning of the last fiscal year were not appreciably larger than the year before and particularly in hogs; they were probably less. The increase in shipments is due to conservation and the extra weight of animals added by our farmers. The full effect of these efforts began to bear their best results in the last half of the fiscal year when the exports to the Allies were 2,133,100,000 pounds, as against 1,266,500,000 pounds in the same period of the year before. This compares with an average of 801,000,000 pounds of total exports for the same half years in the three-year pre-war period.

In cereals and cereal products reduced to terms of cereal bushels, our shipments to Allied destinations have been.—

Fiscal year
1916–17 .... 259,900,000 bushels
Fiscal year
1917–18 340,800,000   ''
Increase 80,900,000   ''

Of these cereals our shipments of the prime breadstuffs in the fiscal year 1917–18 to Allied destinations were, wheat 131,000,000 bushels, and of rye 13,900,000 bushels, a total of 144,900,000 bushels.

The exports to Allied destinations during the fiscal year 1916–17 were, wheat 135,100,000 bushels and rye 2,300,000 bushels, a total of 137,400,000 bushels. In addition, some 10,000,000 bushels of 1917 wheat are now in port for Allied destinations or en route thereto. The total shipments to Allied countries from our last harvest of wheat will be, therefore, about 141,000,000 bushels, or, a total of 154,900,000 bushels of prime breadstuffs. In addition to this we have shipped some 10,-000,000 bushels to neutrals dependent upon us and we have received some imports from other quarters. A large part of the other cereals exported have also gone into war bread.

It is interesting to note that since the urgent request of the Allied Food Controllers early in the year for a further shipment of 75,000,000 bushels from our 1917 wheat than originally planned, we shall have shipped to Europe or have en route, nearly 85,000,000 bushels. At the time of this request our surplus was already more than exhausted. The accomplishment of our people in this matter stands out even more clearly if we bear in mind that we had available in the fiscal year 1916–17 from net carry-over and as surplus over our normal consumption about 200,000,000 bushels of wheat which we were able to export that year without trenching on our home loaf. This last year, however, owing to the large failure of the 1917 wheat crop, we had available from net carry-over and production and imports, only just about our normal consumption. Therefore our wheat shipments to Allied destinations represent approximately savings from our own wheat bread.

These figures, however, do not fully convey the volume of the effort and sacrifice made during the past year by the whole American people. Despite the magnificent effort of our agricultural population in planting a much increased acreage in 1917, not only was there a very large failure in wheat but also, the corn failed to mature properly and our corn is our dominant crop. We calculate that the total nutritional production of the country for the fiscal year just closed was between 7% and 9% below the average of the three previous years, our nutritional surplus for export in those years being about the same amount as the shrinkage last year. Therefore the consumption and waste in food have been greatly reduced in every direction during the year.

I am sure that all the millions of our people, agricultural as well as urban, who have contributed to these results should feel a very definite satisfaction that in a year of universal food shortages in the northern hemisphere all of those people joined together against Germany have come through into sight of the coming harvest not only with health and strength fully maintained, but with only temporary periods of hardship. The European Allies have been compelled to sacrifice more than our own people but we have not failed to load every steamer since the delays of the storm months last winter. Our contributions to this end could not have been accomplished without effort and sacrifice and it is a matter for further satisfaction that it has been accomplished voluntarily and individually. It is difficult to distinguish between the various sections of our people—the homes, public eating places, food trades, urban or agricultural populations—in assessing credit for these results but no one will deny the dominant part of the American women.

Yours faithfully,
HERBERT HOOVER

Urgent Need to Support the President

It is difficult to discover what might have provoked Hoover to write this hasty letter, revealing as it does distress, annoyance, and discouragement, apparently over some development in Washington just reported in a note from Tumulty. That note must have reached him almost immediately upon his arrival in London from New York on July 19, and he would seem to have answered it at once (on his own stationery, not that of the Food Administration) on a hectic day filled with a multitude of demanding duties. The London *Evening Standard* for July 20 reported that "Mr. Hoover spent a hustling day today," and the *Observer* for July 21 listed the pressing sequence of events thus:

"Mr. Hoover yesterday morning attended a conference at the Savoy Hotel with members of his own Commission. Later he went to Lancaster House for a Conference with some of the officers of the Inter-Allied Maritime Council. A Conference with Ambassador Page followed; and he then lunched with the officers at the headquarters of the Commission of Relief of Belgium, of which he is still chairman. Part of the afternoon was spent in a conference with Sir Guy Granet, Director-General of the British Ministry of Food in the United States, Mr. Charles Dalziel, his deputy, who has just returned from New York, and Sir William Goode, liaison officer between the British and American Food Ministry. A formal conference with the Inter-Allied Maritime Council will take place on Tuesday at 11 a.m., at Lancaster House.

"The first public act of Major Astor, the new Parliamentary Secretary to the Food Ministry, in his new capacity was to welcome Mr. Hoover on behalf of the Food Controller."

Sheer exhaustion may account for the depressing tone of Hoover's letter with its misspelling, non sequiturs, and poor grammar. His statement about "the opportunity to return to my neglected lead mine" may of course refer only to some distant future plan. But inviting more legitimate speculation is his remark about the need "of every man in service to determine the moment he becomes a liability to the President." This of course may be only an oblique hint that some unnamed recalcitrant official in Washington should resign. But Hoover continues to philosophize on the willingness of every such "liability" to "efface himself," and he then reaches the puzzling conclusion that "My anxiety therefore is only to determine this moment." Equally puzzling is Hoover's sudden turning to the subject of conservation propaganda, his "concern" that it be kept in "proper tune," and his search for a "general on the job."

July 20, 1918

My dear Tumulty,

I am indeed grateful for your note. If there was ever a time when decent men should hold up the Presidents [sic] hands it is right now. If I had any ambition other than that our country under the great leadership of the President should carry this war with distinction and thereafter for the opportunity to return to my neglected lead mine, I should get more annoyed. On the other hand this is a time when stock needs to be taken by every man in service to determine the moment when he becomes a liability to the President and not an assett [sic]. The moment this occurs—and it must occur in war conditions to every man in important administrative post—then he should efface himself. My anxiety therefore is only to determine this moment.

The voluminous propaganda we are building up over conservation waste etc [sic] gives me a good deal of concern that it may not only be effective but that it keeps in proper tune. I have been searching the country to secure someone who [sic] I could propose as the general on this job. My eye at the moment is focussed on Larimer of The Saturday Evening Post. Could you find for me what the attitude of the White House would be to him? He has the commendation of such men as Cobb of The World and McAnney of the Times—

Sincerely,
HERBERT HOOVER

A Meeting with the President

Hoover returned to New York from Europe on Friday, August 23, and the next morning was in Washington for a series of appointments starting at 9:30. Wilson had written that he wished to see him, so Hoover sent this memorandum to the President. A telephone call from the White House set the appointment for Monday, August 26, at 4:30.

August 24, 1918.
Memorandum for the President:

Mr. Herbert Hoover is at his office and holds himself at the President's disposal. The President wrote him that he wanted to see him.

[unsigned]

Guaranteed Price for 1919 Wheat

Shortly before his departure for Europe in July, Hoover had convinced the President that he should veto an appropriation bill that would have put a floor of $2.40 under the price of wheat. The bill was vetoed, but upon his return Hoover was confronted with the same general problem of a government guarantee for wheat and he incorporated his views on the matter in a letter sent to Wilson on the morning of August 26. That same afternoon he met with the President at 4:30 and the two reviewed the wheat guarantee once more. (*Life and Letters,* vol. 8, p. 358.)

26 August 1918

Dear Mr. President: Guaranteed Price for the 1919 Wheat Harvest

You are already aware of the recommendation of our Agriculture Advisatory Board to the effect that while they consider the price fixed by you of $2.26 per bushel at Chicago for No. 1 Northern Wheat for the 1918 harvest is a fair price, they now recommend that the increasing costs of production of next year's crop warrant an increase in price by twenty cents a bushel and that a guarantee should be given now upon this basis.

We all desire to secure a | good | [stimulative][1] return to the farmer and at the same time to be just to the consumer and the Government. While the farmers have recommended an increase, the consumers of the country are protesting against such an increase.

In considering whether a guaranteed price should be given for the growing of wheat next year (the only industry guaranteed by the Government), we must realize that it involves considerable national risk. It is impossible to conceive that our wheat production, even without a guarantee, will not equal our own demand, and therefore the object of a guarantee must be solely to secure a surplus for feeding the Allies, and in this sense it must be realized that this surplus will not be needed in Europe until 1920. If there be peace or increased shipping available in the meantime, the Allies will supply themselves from the large stores of much cheaper wheat from the Southern Hemisphere, where between 300,000,000 and 400,000,000 bushels are even now available. Our Government might best quite well be plunged into a loss of anything up to $500,000,000 in giving such a guarantee or [sic] a high level of price maintained to our own people for a long period.

A guaranteed price stabilizes the price and eliminates speculation from our prime food. As you are aware, there has been a great deal of fluctuation in the prices of secondary small grains, ranging from levels above the comparative price of wheat to levels at present lower than the comparative prices, due largely to irregularity in inland and ocean transport. If wheat were unstabilized also, and subjected to these same fluctuations, together with the threat of large supplies from the Southern Hemisphere, confidence of our farmers might quite well be undermined and cause them to relax their efforts in grain production, and speculating on breadstuffs would bring only harm to both producer and consumer.

---

1. "Good" deleted by hand, then handwritten insertion.

In view of all the factors involved, I am of the opinion that we must take the risk of giving a guarantee. But it does seem to me that before increasing this liability above the present level, and thus imposing an additional burden upon our consumers and a greater risk upon the Government, the matter should be subjected to searching inquiry into the true costs of production and therefrom determine such a fair minimum for the farmers as will maintain the present acreage.

It appears to me that such an inquiry by a commission independent of all interests, is not insuperable, despite the complexity of local economic differences, provided this inquiry be directed to determine in a broadminded [sic] way the increased cost of labor and material consumed by the farmer over, say, the average three year pre-war period and to determine a stimulative increase in profits over that represented | by | [in]² the average pre-war price of wheat. It would not only be a sound guide to yourself in determining the basis of the guarantee, but also an assurance to the consumers of the country.

Many of the factors cannot be determined until the volume of the next harvest can be well approximated, and pending this time and such inquiry, I would suggest that the guarantee be given upon the present price basis, with the additional assurance from you that if the results of the above inquiry warrant, it will be increased.

If an increase should result from such inquiry, it will be necessary to evolve the Administrative machinery by which the increase would apply only to those farmers who had disposed of their 1918 wheat; otherwise we will be faced with considerable and possibly embarrassing hoarding by some minority.

I have the feeling that with the above assurances of a preliminary guarantee, and the possibility of an entirely fair readjustment of prices upward, our farmers will feel warranted in continuing their fine endeavor to meet the demand.

Yours faithfully,
HERBERT HOOVER

---

2. "By" deleted by hand, then handwritten insertion.

Expansion of Views on Wheat Supports

26 August 1918

Dear Mr. President:

In further amplication [sic] of the memorandum which I sent you

this morning, on the wheat guarantee, I send herewith a letter addressed
to Judge Glasgow in my absence by Mr. Barnes, the head of our Cereal
Division, which elaborates other arguments than those I have brought
to bear on the situation.

Faithfully yours,
HERBERT HOOVER

Approval of Hoover's Wheat Views

27 August, 1918.

My dear Hoover:

Our conversation of yesterday and your memoranda of the 26th
have been entirely convincing to me in the matter of a guaranteed price
for wheat, and I would be very much obliged if you would have a public
statement prepared, continuing the present guarantee and stating, as
you suggested yesterday, the circumstances under which it may be recon-
sidered. I shall be very glad to make any suggestions concerning it, if
you will be kind enough to let me see it when it is prepared.

In haste, Faithfully yours,
WOODROW WILSON

Coordinating the Economic War Effort

> In their meeting of August 26 Wilson and Hoover discussed, among
> other things, the subject of the coordination of economic effort among
> the four principal Allied nations. The next day Hoover wrote this
> letter containing some of his reflections on that meeting. On August 28
> Wilson sent a copy of the letter to Secretary of War Newton Baker
> with his own letter in which he said, "I am particularly interested in
> the suggestion about timber which Hoover makes in his letter."

27 August 1918

Dear Mr. President:

In thinking over our discussion yesterday with regard to the coordination of economic effort in Europe among the four nations, with a
view to the provision of sufficient tonnage to fill the American Army
program, I feel that I perhaps neglected to emphasize one point that

dominates my own conclusions on the subject. That is that I believe that whoever is sent to deal with this matter should not only have your complete confidence, and as your personal representative be able to coordinate directly with the Prime Ministers of Europe, and at the same time to head up all of the American economic representatives in Europe, but that above all things, he should be able to remain there constantly during the next twelve months. In my view the problem cannot be solved by a temporary negotiation or declaration of principles. New phases of the matter will arise daily and new adjustments will be required constantly, for such a program will tax the whole economic capacity of the four nations to the utmost limit, and we can only expect to get that maximum output from an industrial point of view, the maximum curtailment of consumption on all sides by a continuous effort and adjustment. I could recite a score of adjustments that are needed at the present moment referring to combined activities of the Food Administration, War Trade Board, Treasury, War Industries Board, Shipping Board, etc.

A typical such question lies in the provision of timber for the American Army from Spain and Switzerland. This would mean a great saving in tonnage and would need to be accomplished by a negotiation in which we undertook to supply and even transport larger amounts of other commodities to these nations than programs hitherto, but it would represent a very much less tonnage than the transportation of timber from this country to our own Army. Such a transaction involves the American Army, War Trade Board, Treasury, Food Administration, etc.

As I stated above, these problems will arise every day and every week, and it appears to me that a solution can best be accomplished by some individual who can formulate and coordinate the views of all three of the European governments, together with ourselves, and present a consolidated front of economic action as we have now on the military side.

I write this in view of the fact that I feel that Mr. Baker's large responsibilities must mean that his visit to Europe could only be temporary in any event, and that if he could be accompanied by such a representative of yours as above mentioned, it would go far to produce the situation that I feel is necessary.

Yours faithfully,
HERBERT HOOVER

Appreciation for August 27 Letter

28 August, 1918
My dear Mr. Hoover:
    I appreciate the considerations urged in your letter of yesterday, and you may be sure will have them in mind in the arrangements I shall attempt to make.

In haste, Cordially and sincerely yours,
WOODROW WILSON

Book Sent by A. G. Patterson

29 August, 1918.
My dear Hoover:
    Mr. A. G. Patterson, Secretary of the Intermountain Association of Sugar Beet Growers, has sent me the enclosed volume. I am taking the liberty of sending it to you to look over, for such grains of helpful information as you may be able to get out of it about our difficult sugar situation.

Cordially and faithfully yours,
WOODROW WILSON

Cuban Sugar and Price Controls

On August 28 Carlos Manuel de Céspedes, the Cuban minister in Washington, saw Hoover about his proposal for selling Cuban sugar to the Food Administration for ninety cents above the price of the previous year. Hoover immediately communicated this information to President Wilson in a letter of August 29 and then made use of the occasion to discuss generally the sugar situation in America. On September 2 the President penned a short note giving his approval.

29 August 1918
Dear Mr. President:
    The Cuban Minister, representing the members of the Cuban Sugar Mission, has today offered to sell us the Cuban sugar crop for 90 cents per hundred pounds above the price of last year, being about $5.50, f.o.b. Cuba. I am in favor of accepting the Cuban proposal, which is an even

compromise between the extreme figures on both sides. In order to make sure that there is no misunderstanding in Cuba as to the operations which we are about to undertake and which I describe lower down, I have taken the attached letter from the Cuban Minister.

After duty, freight, refining, etc., this will result in a price of this sugar seaboard, ex-refinery, of 8.66 cents per pound.

I am and I think the country is generally convinced that unless the price of sugar is controlled it will in the face of the present shortage go up to 25 or 30 cents per pound from the 9 cents seaboard for refined that it can be held. As every cent is $80,000,000 to our consumers, and confers extortionate profits on the producers and trade, I am sure we are right in rigid control. We have proved by a year's experience that the price can be controlled by a mixture of commercial operations and voluntary agreements.

As I explained to you in a previous communication, our problem is extremely complex this year because of the greatly increased cost of production of our domestic sugar. The careful investigation of the beet industry by the Tariff Commission on our behalf shows roughly:

11½ cents per pound seaboard refined will be required to cover 100% producers with a profit of 1 cent per pound to the high-cost producer.

9 cents per pound will cover about 85% of producers with a minimum profit of 1 cent per pound.

8.66 cents per pound (the Cuban price) will cover about 72% of the producers with a minimum of 1 cent profit.

7.45 cents per pound (last year's price) will cover about 30% of the producers with a minimum profit of 1 cent per pound.

Much the same economic situation applies to Louisiana sugar. If we make a price of 11.5 cents per pound, seaboard, for domestic sugars to cover all producers, we will have raised the price to the consumer by nearly 3 cents per pound. Also we will have given the low-cost producers a profit of several hundred per cent.

A further complexity arises from the fact that sugar is sold retail at the nearest one-half cent per pound; i.e., 10, 10½ or 11 cents per pound. The wholesaler and retailer take 1½ cents per pound, and if the price, for instance, to the retailer is 9 cents, he takes 10 cents from the customer; if it is 9.15, he take 10½. Therefore, it is little use to reduce the price so as to come out below certain even figures or one-half figures.

We consider it fundamental in these times of short shipping to maintain domestic production. Our plan is therefore a compromise on the whole situation as follows:

First, we propose to make the price of refined, seaboard basis, 9 cents per pound. The Sugar Equalization Board will buy the Cuban crop and resell it to the refiners at a profit of about 36 cents per hundred, after equalizing sea freights to different ports, thus leveling the Cuban price up to 9 cents, and we will make this 9 cents seaboard the basis of [voluntary agreement with][1] domestic sugars as well.

This will result in: (a) An increase to the consumer of about 1 cent per pound instead of 3 cents; (b) a loss to some 15 to 20% of the beet and Louisiana producers.

Out of the profits on Cuban sugar we propose to compensate losses to these particular producers. It will eventuate that at even 9 cents some domestic producers will make extortionate profits, but they will be fairly well taken care of by the excess profits tax.

There is one feature of these operations by the Equalization Board that I am anxious shall be clearly understood by you, and that is the large sums that will accrue to it by our present programme. We shall probably make $15,000,000 on the 36 cents from the Cuban crop. In addition to this, the Sugar Equalization Board, as I mentioned to you, is now in effect taking over the present stocks of sugar in refiners' hands, in order that when we increase the price of sugar by 1 cent per pound in the course of the next few days, there shall not rest in the hands of the American refiners the large sums of money to be earned from stocks purchased at lower levels, and the Equalization Board may have an income from this source of as much as $10,000,000.

Furthermore, in line with the policy that we should sell export commodities at prices to neutrals somewhat commensurate with the prices they are charging us for shipping and other commodities, and to cover their depreciation of our money, the Equalization Board will earn considerable profit from such exports of sugar to neutrals as we make during the next year. It is possible that the net profits of this Board may during the next twelve months accumulate to as high as twenty-five millions of

---

1. Handwritten insertion.

dollars above the compensation given to domestic producers, and I mention this for your approval against any criticism that might arise from it. This money will, of course, ultimately need be either distributed to consumers by some device or converted into the Treasury by some arrangement.

During the past year we have had a great deal of difficulty in sugar distribution for the lack of adequate stocks in the United States. Owing to financial and other conditions, the refiners have not been disposed of their own interests to carry such stocks and every fluctuation in the shipping condition jeopardizes our distribution. I am anxious to build up at least a sixty-day stock in the country, and our first use of the profits of the Equalization Board would be to secure such a stock. It may be that later in the year when we know our profit position with accuracy we can work out some device for a redistribution of these profits to the consumer.

I have had the advantage of the advice of Messers. [sic] Taussig, Rolph, Whitmarsh, Zabriskie, Glasgow and Wooley, [sic] all of whom I esteem as men of the first quality of commercial experience and ability.

I would be glad to know if the above plan meets with your approval. It may be necessary for us to vary it in detail as is essential.

Yours faithfully,
HERBERT HOOVER

Order and Statement on Wheat

> In his letter of August 26, Wilson asked Hoover to prepare a statement on the wheat guarantee which he could give to the public. On August 30 Hoover sent him such a statement and in addition an executive order which when issued would make the guarantee official. That statement, dated August 29, is given below. (The memo as printed here includes Wilson's handwritten changes.) It was given to the press on September 3. (*Times,* Sept. 3, 1918, p. 11.)

30 August 1918

Dear Mr. President:

You will please find enclosed herewith the executive order making the guarantee on next year's wheat, for your signature. Also a draft of a statement that I have prepared to go with the guarantee.

I would suggest that when complete they should be issued through the Committee on Public Information.

Yours faithfully,

HERBERT HOOVER

MEMORANDUM:

29 August 1918

In issuing today the Government's guarantee of the same price for 1919 wheat crop that was guaranteed for the 1918 crop, I wish it to be understood that in the spring of 1919 I will appoint a disinterested commission who will secure for me the facts by that time disclosed as to the increased cost of farm labor and supplies, using the three-year pre-war average prices of wheat, of labor, and of supply costs as a basis, and that from this information I shall determine whether there should be an increase in price above the present level, and, if so, what advance, in order to maintain for the farmer a good return. Should it then appear that an increase is deserved over the present guarantee, however, it will be applied only to those who have by next harvest already marketed their 1918 wheat.

It is the desire and intention of all Departments of the Administration to give to the wheat-grower a fair and stimulative return in order that the present acreage in wheat may be maintained.

I find a great conflict of opinion among various sections of the country as to the price that should be named as a minimum guarantee. It must be obvious to all, however, that the factors which will make for increased or decreased cost of production of next year's harvest cannot be determined until the near approach to the harvest.

In giving a guaranteed price for wheat one year in advance (the only industry guaranteed by the Government), there is involved a considerable national risk. If there should be peace or increased shipping available before the middle of 1920, Europe will naturally supply itself from the large stores of much cheaper wheat now in the Southern Hemisphere; and therefore the Government is undertaking a risk which might in such an event result in a national loss of as much as $500,000,000 through an unsalable surplus; or, in any event, in maintaining a high level of price to our own people for a long period subsequent to freedom in the world's markets.

Despite this, the desirability of assuring a supply to the world of prime breadstuffs by insuring the farmer against the fluctuations in prices that would result from the uncertainties of the present situation and from the speculation these uncertainties, entail, seems to me to make the continuation of the guarantee for another year desirable. On the other hand, it is clear that before increasing this liability by large sums with the risks set forth above, and before increasing the burden of the consumer, the matter should be subjected to searching inquiry at the appropriate time,—the time when the pertinent facts will be known.

I feel confident that with this preliminary fixed guarantee and with the assurance that justice will in any event be done to the grower, he will continue the fine patriotic effort by which has served the country hitherto; that the Government will have acted prudently; and that the consumer will be satisfied that his interests are not unduly sacrificed, but just an exhaustive consideration given to every element of the matter at the proper time.

W. W.

Thanks for Patterson Book

August 31, 1918

Dear Mr. President:
Very many thanks for your letter of the 29th, and the book which you enclosed. I shall look through it at the first opportunity.

Faithfully yours,
HERBERT HOOVER

Approval of Hoover's Sugar Views

This note was written by hand in answer to Hoover's letter of August 29 containing his plans for the purchase of Cuban sugar. Wilson's phrase "the enclosed" probably indicates the President returned the letter with his own for September 3. (See facsimile section.)

2 Sept. 1918

My dear Hoover,
The conclusions and plans stated in the enclosed have my entire approval.

WOODROW WILSON

Commandeering and the War Industries Board

Here President Wilson asks that, to avoid conflicts, the chairman of the War Industries Board be consulted by the various agencies before using their commandeering powers over any industry. The same directive was sent to Daniels, Hurley, and Garfield. It is perhaps significant that Hoover met with the chairman of the War Industries Board on August 31 and again on September 4, the day he probably received Wilson's letter.

3 September, 1918.

My dear Mr. Hoover:

As was to have been expected and indeed could hardly have been avoided, the exercise by several different agencies of the Government of the power to commandeer has resulted in some cases in conflict, not alone with one another but with the rulings of the Priorities Committee, as to the distribution of material among the various interested departments and industries. The instances of this sort have been numerous and serious enough, I believe, to justify me in making this request: that the commandeering power should not hereafter be exercised over any of the material industries or industrial agencies of the country without first consulting the Chairman of the War Industries Board.

I think that this is one of the most important and urgent coordinations remaining to be effected. I am confident that the consultation that I request will lead to the fullest cooperation and not to embarrassment, and I hope that it will be possible by this method to effect better results than could be effected by concentrating the commandeering power in one agency.

Cordially and sincerely yours,
WOODROW WILSON

Power of the Grain Corporation

On the morning of September 4 Hoover had a meeting in Glasgow's office and may well have discussed the matter of this letter. In the afternoon he was at the White House for the weekly session of the war cabinet.

September 4th—1918

Dear Mr. President:

A few days ago I applied to you for an appropriation from the Presidential Fund of $5,000,000. with which to extend the character of commodities purchased by the Food Administration chiefly for export purposes.

Since I made that application, I have asked our Legal Division to reconsider the question as to whether or not the Food Administration could not make these purchases under the appropriation [in][1] [the] Food Act itself, based on the theory that in giving to the Administration the right of requisition of all food commodities, Congress must be [have?] intended that the Administration could purchase without the necessity of requisition, if it agreed upon a price with the seller.

Mr. Glasgow has now laid this matter before the Attorney General who has replied affirmatively and it is, therefore, not necessary for me to ask financial assistance from your fund. I, therefore, propose to extend the purchases of the Grain Corporation at the present to barley, rice, oats, and possible [sic] corn for export purposes, as you have already approved. This should facilitate the flow of these grains to the seaboard and secure the most advantageous handling by the railways and ports and secure a better control of distribution amongst the different countries in Europe. Furthermore, it places us in a position to make a special price on these commodities where sold to neutrals. I can see no possibility of loss of these transactions as they would be entered upon only against known demands from abroad.

Yours faithfully,
HERBERT HOOVER

---

1. Handwritten insertion.

Reply on the Grain Corporation

5 September, 1918

My dear Hoover:

Thank you for your letter of yesterday about the purchase of barley, rice, oats, and possibly corn for export purposes by the Grain Corporation. I am very glad that the matter has been simplified for you.

Cordially and sincerely yours,
WOODROW WILSON

Interpreting the Commandeering Rule

6 September 1918

Dear Mr. President:

With respect to coordinating the power of commandeering with the War Industries Board, I am, of course, very glad to place myself in line.

There is one phase of this matter that I think requires a little consideration and that is, that a large part of our voluntary agreements are based on a background of possible commandeering and further the whole problem of the Food Administration involves this power. I assume, however, that the consultation with the Chairman of the War Industries Board only evenuates [sic] in cases where we are going to perform the actual operation of commandeering.

Yours faithfully,
HERBERT HOOVER

Approval of Interpretation

6 September, 1918.

My dear Hoover:

Thank you for your letter about the commandeering business. You are quite right in your interpretation of my request, namely that the consultation with the Chairman of the War Industries Board will be necessary only in cases where you are contemplating the actual exercise of the power to commandeer.

In haste, Faithfully yours,
WOODROW WILSON

Cotton Telegram on U.S. Imports

Joseph P. Cotton, a member of the meat division of the Food Administration with headquarters in London, had telegraphed from England on August 27 to inform Hoover of criticism abroad that the United States was not sufficiently curtailing its imports and thus was failing to make the sacrifices needed to supply the tonnage necessary to bring its army to France. Hoover assured him on this point in his telegram of September 7.

6 September 1918

Dear Mr. President:

You will please find enclosed herewith a copy of the telegram that I have received from Mr. Cotton in London, and my reply thereto. This correspondence is apropos of the difficulties in securing an adjustment among the Allies on the Food Programme for next year to meet the tonnage necessites [sic] of our Army.

There is only one food import over which criticism can be directed and that is bananas, and so far as the food problem of the United States is concerned, I have taken the attitude for the last eight months that we do not require the import of bananas, and that the many vessels now employed in the banana trade, capable of trans-Atlantic use, could and should be taken out of that service. I, therefore, do not include bananas in the import commodities for which the Food Administration considers itself responsible.

Yours faithfully,
HERBERT HOOVER

Cable Message from American Ambassador at London, August 27. 1 p.m. 1405.

PARAPHRASE:

Confidential. Cotton sends the following telegram to Hoover, No. 292. There is a painfully slow advance in business here. According to Beale's expectation, within a few days the situation will be cleared up by Reading, all tonnage control being transferred to representatives and Beale becoming the representative of Great Britain in place of the present representative. The food program will be taken up at the end of this week by the Maritime Council. The program will in all probability not be completely approved by the council but a commencement will be made, 85 percent of the priority figures being lifted. It will be 30 days before the munitions programs appear but a substantial increase in these will be shown and America's need will be included in them. Bliss has forwarded the demands of the United States Army for tonnage and these are now under consideration. The people here show much disquiet over the presentation of these demands for the reason that tonnage estimates will not be given in detail and because it seems that the United States indicates no readiness to cut down the imports into that country. The French Government is in the consultation and the position will probably be assumed by France that her demands for tonnage for the United States Army may be accepted no matter what sacrifice is caused thereby, but the result of that position means that imports of food and materials for industries by the Allies must meet the severe reductions. It is their view that the United States must accept for her imports the same basis of necessity which the Allies have accepted and which they do not believe the United States has yet done. Such being the situation the official question has been put to me whether the United States Government will present its program of imports of food to the representatives of the Allies for their criticism and at what date. I hope that you will give to this question an early reply. Outside Allied programs having been criticised by us, the present requirements of tonnage by the United States for imports of food is liable to be criticized except in so far [sic] as the essential necessities of oils, tea, coffee, and sugar are concerned. Sacrifice by Great Britain of imports would be made more promptly and easily by reduction of the matter to the above basis and by a conservation campaign on the part of the United States to save tonnage. The securing of sacrifice is now terribly slow and difficult. The statement recently made by Hurley and published in the London Times is deemed very important, but the British show apprehension concerning it because they consider that the statement lacks definiteness and because they are persuaded he is endeavoring now to build up connections. A direct message sent to some person here to the effect that the sacrifice of the Allies for the common cause is recognized by the United States which intends to cut its own trade to the bone would have a decided effect in obtaining, with regard to the Army program, prompt action.

CABLEGRAM:

September 7, 1918.

Cotton
AmEmbassy
London

Your telegram two ninety two ten days in transmission we have arranged use no transatlantic tonnage for food imports except some minor liner space and two tankers for oil therefore our food import programme cannot interest allies and should be sufficient evidence of our stripping to the bone Stop Assurances on the lines you request are being given through war trade board and partially by shipping Stop In result we should find more tonnage than Shermans estimate Stop Wish you would consult Baker Stop It is extremely dangerous to cut into priority food tonnage I fear it works proportionate injustice to France Italy and even endangers Englands food supplies Stop I don't believe it is necessary but Baker can inform you fully

                                                              HOOVER

Consulting Independent Packers

> Hoover's difficulties with the packers dated back several months. (See letters of February 19 and 20.) Other government agencies were equally dissatisfied with their performance and in early August the Federal Trade Commission had urged the President to commandeer the Armour, Morris, Wilson, and Swift packing companies. (*Times*, Aug. 9, 1918, p. 1.) In his letter of July 8, Hoover had already expressed his opposition to any such action, although he still strongly disapproved of the profiteering activities of many of the packers. His opposition to government ownership of the packing industry persisted through the war as proven by his September 11 report to the President and its release to the press on February 19, 1919.
>
> At 2:45 on September 6 he met with Louis F. Swift, president of Swift and Co. from Chicago; the following Monday, September 9, he held the Washington conference with the independent packers mentioned in this letter to Wilson.
>
> Actually Wilson apparently had already accepted Hoover's opinion on takeover by the government of the packing industry. On September 6 he wrote to William B. Colver of the Federal Trade Commission about the commission's proposed bill to this effect, saying in part: "Mr. Hoover tells me that . . . it would be of no real service to the public for the government to take them over and attempt to operate them. . . . [I] am convinced after my conference with him that no real material advantage would result from the action proposed by your bill, at any rate at this time." (*Life and Letters*, vol. 8, pp. 387–88.)
>
> Hoover met with the President on Monday, August 26, at 4:30, and it is possible that this is the "conference" to which Wilson referred in his letter of September 6 to Colver. The two were also together on August 28 and on September 4 for meetings of the war cabinet.

                                                6 September 1918

Dear Mr. President:

In order that I may get before you as constructively as possible the problem of handling the Chicago Packers, as we view it, I have asked a number of the independent packers to come to Washington to consult with me early next week.

While the theoretical views of the Trade Commission are in my mind the ultimate desiderata, I feel there are some practical difficulties that might subject the program to a great deal of criticism.

The men I have chosen are men who have hewn their way up by sheer ability against a good deal of tyranny, and I believe their views will be of value. I am, therefore, delaying forwarding to you our recommendation until I have had the opportunity to discuss the matter with them.

Yours faithfully,
HERBERT HOOVER

Taft's Food Administration Report

The "Mr. Taft" who compiled the report mentioned in this letter was Robert A. Taft of Ohio who was a member of the legal staff of the Food Administration. In November Hoover took him to Paris as his legal adviser. Many years later he was elected Republican senator from Ohio.

7 September 1918

Dear Mr. President:

I send herewith a report compiled by Mr. Taft upon the Food Administration operations for the period January 1 to July 1, 1918. I assume that it is not for publication;—it is, in fact, too dull.

Faithfully yours,
HERBERT HOOVER

Armour Company and Profits

The Armour letter referred to by Hoover here undoubtedly made a stout defense for the packers in an attempt to prove that their profits were not excessive.

9th September 1918

My dear Mr. President:

So far from the regulations of the Food Administration having accrued in large profits to the packers, I would be glad if you would read this letter which I just received from the Vice-President of Armour and Company.

Faithfully yours,
HERBERT HOOVER

Draft Exemptions for Food Administration Men

> A new draft bill was enacted on August 31, 1918, and signed into law on September 1. It provided for drafting men between the ages of eighteen and forty-five into military service and thus made it more possible that Food Administration personnel and men from other important war-related agencies might be taken. This possibility disquieted Hoover and prompted him to take an anticipated problem directly to the President. On September 10 Wilson answered with a letter that gave a reassuring interpretation of the new law as he had heard it from Provost Marshal General Enoch H. Crowder. Crowder had an appointment with the President on September 3, and it was probably on this occasion that the discussion mentioned by Wilson took place. (*Life and Letters*, vol. 8, p. 377.)

9 September 1918

My dear Mr. President:

There are something between 3500 and 4000 volunteers in the Food Administration giving practically their whole time, and approximately another 1500 paid staff. Of the large number that are subject to the new draft some three or four hundred are absolutely indispensable, if we are to carry on the Department. The work has developed in complexity and difficulty, and to take away our principal men at the present time would practically crush the Department's effectiveness for months to come, even if we were able to secure men of equal ability outside of the draft area. Moreover, the men of devotion, character, independence of interest and ability are becoming scarcer every day with the constant drafts of other necessary service. I feel, therefore, there will need to be wholesale deferred classifications. On the other hand, these men are men of a type who will not themselves appeal for deferred classification in any case. They say resolutely that they will not be accused of dodging more dangerous occupations. I understand that, under General Crowder's new rule, that [*sic*] such men would have to apply for their own deferred classification, and I would say at once that the Food Administration would collapse under this rule. I, myself, do not ever intend to apply for exemption from this draft. I can see but one solution, and that is, that when the appropriate moment arrived, I could apply for deferred classification for the Staff in the Food Administration, and that you, in turn, could see your way to give a positive direction to this list of men to remain in this Department during the war, as being the most effective service that they can do to the Nation.

It does appear to me that the Government has got to go on behind the lines just as much as in the trenches, and the whole sense of selective draft is lost unless some sort of arrangement of this character can be arrived at.

Faithfully yours,
HERBERT HOOVER

Interpreting Draft Exemptions

10 September, 1918.

My dear Hoover:

I think you are mistaken in the impression you have received about the way the new draft is to be managed, or rather, exemptions from it. The purpose of the new regulations, as I discussed them with General Crowder, was to take the burden of claiming exemption off of the individual and put it upon his employer or superior, and that is certainly the way in which I expect the matter to be administered.

At any time that the matter matures with regard to the men connected with the Food Administration, I should be glad to have a suggestion from you as to any action on my part that you think may be necessary, for I entirely agree with the conclusions stated in your letter of September 9th.

Cordially and sincerely yours,
WOODROW WILSON

Distrust of Packers

This letter of Wilson's was in answer to Hoover's note of September 9 which contained a letter from the vice-president of Armour Packing Company. This official undoubtedly presented facts and figures meant to prove that the packers were by no means making excessive profits. Hoover had great difficulty in his previous dealings with these people; therefore it was not likely that he was favorably disposed toward them. However, personal meetings on a few occasions during this period may have softened his attitude somewhat, and he may have felt justified in accepting the facts in the Armour letter. Wilson, however, manifests skepticism in his response.

10 September, 1918.

My dear Hoover:

Thank you for having let me see the enclosed, which I return. My fundamental trouble about all of this matter is that I do not trust the information which these men give us. I say this with hesitation and regret, but must say that the remark is justified by many circumstances and dealings of which I have knowledge.

Cordially and faithfully yours,
WOODROW WILSON

Daniels's Letter on the Beef Trade

No written communique appears to exist in which Hoover gave Wilson his "angle and comment on the matter" discussed in the Daniels letter. However on September 16 Hoover and Daniels met at 2:30 and it is not unlikely that there was an exchange of views on the subject matter of the relevant letter. Moreover, on September 11 Wilson saw Hoover at the regular meeting of the war cabinet and on Saturday September 14 at 2:15 Hoover was once more at the White House. On either occasion he might have given the President his comments on the beef trade, as Wilson requests in this letter.

10 September, 1918.

My dear Hoover:

I wish you would "read, ponder, and inwardly digest" the enclosed letter from Daniels. It has made a very great impression on me, because of the intrinsic credibility of what the Navy is afraid is taking place in the beef trade. Will you not let me have your angle and comment on the matter?

Cordially and sincerely yours,
WOODROW WILSON

Report on the Packers

In September 1918 Hoover answered President Wilson's request for advice on the Federal Trade Commission's recommendation relative to the Chicago packing industry. He reaffirmed his views, expressed to Wilson a year earlier, that "a growing and dangerous domination of the handling of the nation's foodstuffs" existed. But he accepted only part of the suggestions of the FTC for meeting the problem. In particular he opposed government ownership of the packing companies, for he did "not consider that the prime object of maintaining the initiative of our citizens and of our local communities is to be secured by this vast expansion of federal activities."

On September 16 Hoover wrote to Wilson about the desirability of releasing the report to the press but Wilson replied on September 20 and suggested that "perhaps it would not be wise to publish" the information contained in Hoover's letter as he wished "to avoid even the appearance of a controversy between two agencies which really trust one another." The report was finally released to the press on February 19, 1919, after Hoover had endured a monthlong attack in Congress on charges that he had been favoring the packers' interests. On September 24, 1919 Wilson explained that fear of creating a panic was his reason for holding up release of the report. (*Times*, Sept. 25, 1919, p. 7.)

REPORT TO THE PRESIDENT ON THE CHICAGO
PACKING INDUSTRY.
Washington, September 11, 1918.
Released to the Press February 19, 1919.

In response to your request I beg to set out my observations on the recommendations of the Federal Trade Commission with regard to the five large packing firms.

I scarcely need to repeat the views that I expressed to you nearly a year ago that there is here a growing and dangerous domination of the handling of the nation's foodstuffs. I do not feel that appreciation of this domination of necessity implies wrong doing on the part of the proprietors, but is the natural outgrowth of various factors which need correction. In an objective understanding of this situation, it is necessary to review the underlying economics of its growth.

At one time our food animals were wholly slaughtered and distributed locally. The ingenious turning to account of the by-products from slaughtering when dealt with on a large scale gave the foundation for consolidation of slaughtering in the larger centers. From this grew the necessity for special care for live stock transport and the largest stockyards at terminals. The creation of those facilities were largely stimulated and to a considerable extent owned by the packers. Added to this was the application of refrigeration processes for the preservation of meat which at once extended the period of preservation and the radius of distribution from the slaughter centers, enabled larger slaughtering nearer the great western producing area, and further contributed to the centralization of the industry. This enlarged scope, particularly to refrigeration operations, requires not only the expensive primary equipment, but a network of refrigerator care, icing stations and cold storage at distribution points. This special car service in products is of the nature of the Pullman service; it must traverse railroad lines independent of ownership, and moreover it is seasonal and varies regionally in different seasons. For each railway to have foreseen and to have provided sufficient of this highly specialized equipment is asking the impossible, and in any event no particular railway could be expected to provide sufficient of these cars to answer the shifting of seasonal and regional demands outside its own lines.

Thus the provision of a large part of the stockyards and our services has naturally fallen in considerable degree to the larger and more wealthy packers who have used their advantages, in effect as a special and largely exclusive railway privilege with which to build up their own business. From the stage of establishment of a multiplicity of marketing facilities, such as cold storage warehouses, branch offices, etc., grew direct dealing with retail dealers, and finally resulted in a large elimination of the wholesale traders.

Through this practical railway privilege, the numerous branch establishments and elimination of wholesale intermediaries, and with large banking alliance, this group have found themselves in position not only to dominate the distribution of interstate animal products, but to successfully invade many other lines of food and other commodity preparation and distribution. Their excellence of organization, the standing of their brands and control of facilities now threaten even further inroads against independent manufacturers and wholesalers of other food products. They now vend scores of different articles, and this constantly increasing demand approaches a dominating proportion of the interestate [sic] business of the different food lines.

It is a matter of great contention as to whether these five firms compete amongst themselves, and the records of our courts and public bodies

are monuments to this contention. Entirely aside from any question of
conspiracy to eliminate competition amongst themselves and against out-
siders, it appears to me that these five firms, closely paralleling each
other's business, as they do with their side knowledge of business conditions in every section, must at least follow confident lines of action and
must naturally refrain from persistent sharp competitive action towards
each other. They certainly avoid such competition to considerable extent. Their hold on the meat and slaughter houses, cars and distributing
branches and banking alliances which each of the five controls, are such
that it is practically inconceivable that any new firms can rise to their
class, and in any event even sharp competition between the few can only
tend to reduce the number of five and not increase it. Of equal public
importance is the fact that their strategic advantage in marketing, equipment, capital and organization must tend to further increase the area of
their invasion into trade outside of animal products. Furthermore, as
these few firms are the final reservoir for all classes of animals, when the
few yards where they buy become over-supplied with more animals than
their absolute requirements, it remains in their hands to frustrate any
reduction in prices by mere refusal to buy, and not necessarily by any
conspiracy. In other words, the narrow number of buyers undoubtedly
produces an unstable market which reacts to discourage production. It
can be contended, I believe, that those concerns have so developed economic efficiency that their costs of manufacture and profits are made from
the wastes of forty years ago.

The problem we have to consider, however, is the ultimate social
result of this expending [sic] domination, and whether it can be replaced
by a system of better social character and of equal economic efficiency
for the present and of greater promise for the future. It is certain to my
mind that these businesses have been economically efficient in their
period of competitive upgrowth, but as time goes on this efficiency cannot
fail to diminish, and, like all monopolies, begin to defend themselves
by repression rather than efficiency.

The worst social result of this whole growth in domination of trade
is the undermining of the initiative and the equal opportunity of our
people and the tyranny which necessarily follows in the commercial
world.

The Federal Trade Commission's recommendations fall into three
parts: (a) that the Railroad Administration take over all animal and
refrigerator car services; (b) that they take over the stockyard terminals;
(c) that the Federal Government itself take over the packers' branch

house, cold storage warehouse, etc., with a view, I assume, to establishing of equal opportunity of entrance into distribution among all manufacturers and traders.

As to the first part of this recommendation on car service, I am in full agreement, and may recall to you that soon after its installation we recommended that the Railway Administration should take over and operate all private carlines in food products. This has to some degree been accomplished through their car service divisions.

These arrangements are purely under war powers, and if the reforms proposed are to be of any value, they must be placed upon a permanent basis and not merely for the war.

There can be no doubt that the car services in order to obtain the results desired must be considered from the greatest national point of view, rather than from that of each individual railway. Moreover, they are highly technical services beyond the ordinary range of railway management and need to embrace all cooled cars as well as meat cars. Whether this service on a national scale should be conducted by the Government or by private enterprise under control as a public utility seems to me to require further thought, and in any event to depend upon the ultimate disposal of the railway question.

As to the stockyards, I am in agreement that they should be entirely disassociated from the control of the packers. A distinction must be drawn between the stockyards as a physical market place and the buying and selling conducted therein. In the first sense the complaints largely center around the exclusion, not of buyers and sellers, but the prevention of competitors from establishing packing plants either upon land of the stockyards or of obtaining track and other connections therewith. The solution of the railway problem [sic]. If the Government should acquire the yards [sic]. If the Government returns the railway to their owners, it would appear to me that these ends could be accomplished by the appropriate regulation under the Interstate Commerce Commission, and this should be done ad. interim. As to the wrong practices between buyers and sellers these would not be corrected by the Government owning or controlling the physical yards. They are in fact now under war regulations by the Department of Agriculture.

As to the recommendation that the Federal Government should at once take over the packers' branch houses, cold storage and warehouse facilities, I find much difficulty. I do not assume that the Trade Commission contemplates the Government entering upon the purchase and sale of meat and groceries at these establishments, nor does it appear to me that the individual separate and scattered branch houses of the packers furnish any proper physical basis for free terminal wholesale markets. In discussion with the independent packers, I find no belief that the packers' branch houses would serve as a basis of universal market service, and I find much difference of opinion as to public markets as a solution. Any of the great packers' equipment in this particular would in any event require a great deal of extension to effect such objectives, and we are in no position to find the material and labor during the war.

We do need an absolute assurance to the food trades of such terminal facilities as will allow any manufacturer or dealer in any food product equal opportunity to handle and store his goods pending their final distribution. The usefulness of either public wholesale or retail markets in the promotion of these ends is a matter of great division of opinion. The most predominant feeling in the independent trades is that if sites can be made available adjacent to railway facilities the trades themselves would solve the matter. In any event the whole public market question is peculiar to each city and town and my own inquiries find little belief that the present branch houses of the packers would serve this purpose. Furthermore my own instinct in any event is against Federal ownership of such facilities and our own inquiries indicate that if transportation questions together with factors mentioned later on are put right, this probably will solve itself. Altogether I do not consider that the prime object of maintaining the initiative of our citizens and of our local communities is to be secured by this vast expansion of federal activities. These are certain matters relating to the development and control of the packing industry which are not referred to in the report of the Trade Commission, which appear to be of first importance. One effect of the great centralization of this industry has been the stultification of decline in slaughter near many large cities and towns. I believe this has been initially due to the inability to recover by-products to such advantage as under the centralization advisability that does not generally exist for most of those plants now have an outlet. It has also been partially due to the cheaper animals from the cheaper lands of the west and this disparity in costs of animal production has greatly diminished with settlement of the country. It is also partially due to at least the fear that the great packers would direct their power of underselling any such enterprise. If proper abattoire could be extended near the larger towns, possibly with municipal help and the operations therein protected from illegitimate competition, I believe they would not only succeed, but would greatly stimulate the local production of meat animals. One effect would be a great stabilization of prices by a wider based market than that now so largely depended upon on [by?] a small group of buyers.

Another phase of the question lies around the fact that I feel the solutions proposed by the Trade Commission will not entirely solve the problem of the invasion of many other lines of food handling besides animal products. This portion of their business is more largely supported by their larger credits and their elimination of the wholesaler, rather than upon railway privileges. As to whether such goods can be vended more economically direct than through the wholesaler is a matter of such [much?] contention. It seems to me, however, that this whole phase of absorption of other food industries requires consideration.

It appears to me at least worth thought as to whether these aggregations should not be confined to more narrow and limited activities, say those involved in the slaughter of animals, the preparation and marketing of the products therefrom alone. Such a course might solve the branch house problem and it is not an unknown legislative control as witness our banks, railways and insurance companies.

One other cause also chokes the free marketing of food in the United States which will not be reached by the ultimate action on the above lines and that is the present insufficient standardization of our food products and this would contribute to strengthen the independent manufacturer.

In summary, I believe that the ultimate solution of this problem is to be obtained by assuring equal opportunity in transportation, equal opportunity in the location of manufacturing sites and the limitation of the activities of these businesses. In this situation, I believe that the fifty minor meat packing establishments and the hundreds of other food producers could successfully expand their interstate activities and the local slaughter would increase with economic gain to the community and all through continued competition constantly improve our manufacturing and distribution processes to the advantage of both producer and consumer. The detailed method except in the manifest case of car and stockyards control require [sic] much more thought.

Proclamation on Beer and Malt

> Wilson accepted Hoover's advice given in this letter and on September 16 he issued a proclamation forbidding the use of foodstuffs in the production of malt liquids. (*Times*, Sept. 2, 1918, p. 9.)

On September 12 Hoover had asked for an appointment with the President and it may have been related to the subject of the proclamation. He actually saw Wilson on Saturday, September 14, at 2:15.

13 September 1918

Dear Mr. President:

You will please find attached hereto a Proclamation for signature with regard to the Brewing Industry.

At a conference yesterday morning with Messrs. McCormick, Garfield and Baruch, it was decided to recommend to you the present form. The effect of this is to limit the making of beer to the use of malt alone from the first of October to the first of December, and at the latter date a complete cessation of the use of foodstuffs including malt. I would like to mention that on December 1st, there will be a good deal of beer in the vats all over the country and we shall have, no doubt, a great deal of pressure from these industries to allow them to use some fuel to revive these beers so that they can be marketed, and they will represent an alternative that there will be enormous losses for them to suffer by the throwing into the sewers of material which otherwise would otherwise have food values.

Faithfully yours,
HERBERT HOOVER

Release of Report on Packers

16 September 1918

Dear Mr. President:

If your overcrowded time has permitted you to look over my memorandum upon the Trade Commission's report on the Packers, I would be glad if you could give me your view as to whether it would be desirable to issue it to the press. It not only supports the critical recommendations of the Commission, but approaches the subject from other angles and would possibly stimulate discussion and lend support to such action as you might desire to take.

Faithfully yours,
HERBERT HOOVER

Kellogg and "Rampant Business"

On Saturday, September 14, Hoover met with Wilson at the White House at 2:15 and discussed with him a federal licensing act. On Tuesday, September 17, at 4:00 Hoover reviewed the same matter with Senator Frank B. Kellogg, Republican from Minnesota, 1917–23. The following day Kellogg incorporated his ideas into a letter to Hoover who forthwith sent it on to Wilson. Several years earlier Kellogg had been special government counsel in the prosecution of antitrust suits and in 1912–13 he was president of the American Bar Association. Between 1925 and 1929 he was Secretary of State under Coolidge.

In this letter of September 18, Hoover enclosed the letter he had received from Kellogg together with a draft of a proposal to curtail "rampant business." These enclosures are not to be found in the Hoover or the Wilson papers. Wilson returned the proposed bill to Hoover on September 20, but Hoover probably sent it back to Kellogg with his and the President's comments.

18 September 1918

Dear Mr. President:

Following up our conversation of last Saturday, I have had a discussion with Senator Kellogg as to the Act that he some years ago proposed for the curtailment of rampant business. I have today the enclosed letter from him, together with a copy of the original draft. It appears to me there are some ideas in it that are extremely well worth while, more especially the difficulty of dealing with the whole problem of aggregate business instead of narrowing it to one individual class of business.

Yours faithfully,
HERBERT HOOVER

Appointment of Cotton to the Inter-Allied Council

18 September 1918.

Dear Mr. President:

Mr. J. H. Skinner, who has since Spring represented the Food Administration in London on the Inter-Ally Council on War Purchases and Finance, has resigned and is returning to the United States.

You will recall that I left Mr. J. P. Cotton as our chief representative in Europe. I feel that for the sake of representation on the Council,

and in furtherance of closer coordination, that it would be very desirable
to have Mr. Cotton succeed to the post left vacant by Mr. Skinner, and
I should so like to appoint him, subject to your approval.

Faithfully yours,
HERBERT HOOVER

Nominees for European Food Administration Staff

18 September 1918

Dear Mr. President:

We have need of three or four more men on our European staff to
represent us on commodity Committees in London, Paris and Rome.
Subject to your approval, I have chosen Mr. Edwin G. Merril, Mr. Charles
A. Platt and Mr. Frederick C. Walcott. Mr. Merril was for eight years
President of the Union Trust Company of New York until its merger
with the Central, and he is now Vice President and Vice Chairman of
the Central Union Trust Company. Mr. Platt is well known and a successful architect of New York, and a student of French and Italian affairs.
Mr. F. C. Walcott is a partner in Bonbright and Company, and has been
connected with the Food Administration almost since its inception.
These men are all under the direction of Mr. Cotton and act as his
assistants.

Yours faithfully,
HERBERT HOOVER

Approval of Cotton's Appointment

19 September, 1918.

My dear Hoover:

I must admit I know very little about Mr. J. P. Cotton, but I am
quite ready to accept your judgment with regard to the advisability of
substituting him for Mr. J. H. Skinner who is returning from London,
and hope that you will feel free to make the substitution.

Cordially and sincerely yours,
WOODROW WILSON

Approval of Men for Europe

In this letter Wilson sounds a cautionary note in expressing a hope
that the men nominated for the European posts "will attend strictly

to their business." Perhaps he had in mind such men as Oscar T. Crosby, Assistant Secretary of the Treasury with headquarters in London, who frequently upset the President by his activities and public statements about international affairs. On January 9, 1918, Wilson wrote to Secretary of the Treasury McAdoo that "I am very much afraid of Mr. Crosby's inclination to go very much outside his baliwick, an inclination of which I have many evidences." On February 20 he complained that "just the other day he joined his colleagues of the Inter-Allied Board in advising us not to recognize the Bolshevik Government" which was "a serious departure from his instructions." Neither "the Supreme War Council" nor the board, he wrote, "has any business to formulate political opinions." (*Life and Letters*, vol. 7, pp. 459–60, 559.)

20 September, 1918

My dear Hoover:

I have your letter about sending Mr. Merril, Mr. Platt, and Mr. Walcott over to assist Mr. Cotton on the other side. Unfortunately, I know nothing about any one of the three, but I am willing to accept your judgment about them, provided you are quite sure that they are in no sense politicians and will attend strictly to their business.

Cordially and faithfully yours,
WOODROW WILSON

Reply to Kellogg's Proposal

20 September, 1918

My dear Hoover:

I have been as much interested as you evidently are in the enclosed bill and Senator Kellogg's discussion of it. I think with you that there are ideas in it which are thoroughly worth considering, and I would be very glad if Senator Kellogg or someone whom he could employ would redraft the bill in conformity with recent legislation, so that we might have a measure to which we could apply particular scrutiny.

Cordially and sincerely yours,
WOODROW WILSON

Publication of Report on Packers

20 September, 1918.

My dear Hoover:

I have read the enclosed with close attention and take the liberty of suggesting that perhaps it would not be wise to publish it. I particularly want to avoid even the appearance of a controversy between two agencies which really trust one another, and while I think the considerations you urge are of great weight, it seems to me best that we should thresh the matter out with as little appearance of public discussion as possible.

Cordially and faithfully yours,
WOODROW WILSON

Food Exports for 1919

21-September-1918

Dear Mr. President:—

We have now completed a preliminary programme of exports of food needed during the coming twelve months to support the Allies, the Belgian Relief, the American Expeditionary Forces and the minimum shipments of necessities to the Neutrals, which I attach hereto.

You will see the progression—

Average 3-year pre-war exports—	5,533,000 Tons,
Last year,	11,820,000 "
Next year,	17,550,000 "

While our wheat situation is better this year than last, the draught [*sic*] has affected our grasses and corn to an extent that gives us on balance about the same food values as last year. It will, therefore, be a year of strenuous conservation.

The enlarged programme is due in part to increased Army shipments, but in the main to diversion of Allied tonnage to us instead of the Argentine, Australia and the East. The Allied countries will receive less total food from all sources than last year by some 3,000,000 tons, this reduction having been made largely in animal feeds in order to release tonnage for the American Army. This arrangement necessitates larger meat and fat exports from us and the killing of further capital in animals by them.

Yours faithfully,
HERBERT HOOVER

	Average 3-year Pre-war Shipments Tons	Shipped Year ending July 1, 1918 Tons	Must ship Year ending July 1, 1919 Tons	Increase This year over Last year Tons
Meats and Fats (Beef, Pork, Dairy, Poultry and Vegetable Oil Products)	645,000	1,550,000	2,600,000	1,050,000
Bread Stuffs (Wheat and substitutes in terms of grain)	3,320,000	6,800,000	10,400,000	3,600,000
Sugar (From United States and West Indies)	618,000	1,520,000	1,850,000	330,000
Feed Grains (Mostly Army Oats)	950,000	1,950,000	2,700,000	750,000
Totals,	5,533,000	11,820,000	17,550,000	5,730,000

Farmers' Complaint of Markets

A Ralph Carr had written to Wilson on September 23 complaining about the difficulty farmers experienced in finding markets for their wheat. Hoover answered the letter September 25 and on the same day gave the President a resumé of his reply.

23 September, 1918

My dear Hoover:

I would be very much obliged if you would suggest a reply to the enclosed communication from Mr. Carr, or still better, if you will be generous enough to do so, I would be obliged if you would reply to it as at my request.

Cordially and faithfully yours,
WOODROW WILSON

Reply to Carr Letter

Hoover attended the weekly meeting of the war cabinet at 2:30 on the day he wrote this letter. In answering Carr's letter for the President, Hoover explained that the basic problem was that the American army was at that time demanding more shipping. This resulted in "a temporary stop in marketing" of wheat because of the consequent "embargo by the railways on wheat movement." He assured Carr (and the President) that it would be perhaps only a matter of weeks before "the Government will have bought all the wheat offered."

25-September-1918

Dear Mr. President:—

In respect to a letter sent over today, from the County Agricultural Agent of Monroe County, Michigan, on the subject of the failure of the farmers to find market for their wheat at the Government price, I beg to say that this is due to the temporary filling of elevators and the consequent embargo by the railways on wheat movement.

We are searching for some method of penalizing flour mills for failure to pay the Government price, but in fact the whole matter will solve itself if we could get a freer movement from seaboard and restart the internal movement of wheat in the country. I am replying to this gentleman directly as per copy enclosed.

Yours faithfully,
HERBERT HOOVER

Stabilizing Price of Hogs

In this letter Hoover suggests that the government extend to hog producers a carefully limited assurance of a minimum price so as to guarantee a sufficient supply of pork for the coming year.

26-September-1918

Dear Mr. President:—

During this week I have sat for 17½ hours in consultation with a group of 18 to 25 leading hog producers from various parts of the country, over the problem of stabilization of the price of hogs. The Committee has made the attached recommendations.

These recommendations, coming from the agricultural community, enable us, by giving directions to the 55 packing firms who participate in export and Navy and Army orders, to curb the high and low price in the movement of pork products. There are some particulars as to the method of arriving at a formula of stabilization, which I propose to amend, that I will not trouble you with. The main issue on which I wish to consult you is that they wish, in order to maintain the stimulated production of pork, that we should give an "assurance" of a minimum of $15.50 per hundred pounds for hogs during the period of the war. The price recently has been as high as $21.00.

While I have little doubt of our ability, by the regulation of the large controlled purchases, to affect this, I do not wish to take any unnecessary responsibility in giving "assurances", even though they are carefully stated not to be guarantees. My suggestion is that we should extend the present minimum, which applies to hogs farrowed in the spring of 1918, also to hogs farrowed in the autumn of 1918. This will maintain the production for the present and we can before next spring consider whether we want to extend assurance again. I am confident that the assurances that we gave last fall have been the mainspring of the great increase in production, which production is of vital importance to us during the coming winter.

I have also had extensive conferences over the question of cattle, but we have been able to come to no particularly constructive suggestions, as the cattle business is infinitely more complicated than the production of pork.

If you approve, I will give the limited assurance as mentioned above. You will understand that this is a carefully guarded statement of assurance; that it is not a guarantee; that it is merely a statement of our intention within our abilities arising from purchases under government control, and the agricultural community well understands that physical situations may develop under which we could not make good.

Yours faithfully,
HERBERT HOOVER

Approved
WOODROW WILSON [handwritten by Wilson]
1 October, 1918.

Regulations on Malt

A secretary or clerk in the White House typed the following on this letter of Hoover's: "Regulations approved Sept. 30th and sent to Mr. Hoover, October 1, 1918."

September 30, 1918.

Dear Mr. President:

I beg to submit herewith for your approval regulations to be issued under your proclamation of September 16, 1918, regarding the manufacture of malt liquor. These regulations cover a number of secondary matters which have arisen since September 16 with regard to the effect of that proclamation. They do not alter the principle of closing December 1st.

Faithfully yours,
HERBERT HOOVER

Loss of Administrator to the Army

> This letter to President Wilson reveals Hoover's anxiety over the lively possibility of losing a valuable administrator whose sense of duty had urged him to volunteer for the armed services. The written message (mentioned below) which Hoover asked Wilson to send to the person concerned does not appear to be extant. Nor does there seem to be any available evidence one way or the other as to whether the President dispatched the letter in accordance with Hoover's request. On October 14 Gutterson, the person concerned, had an appointment with Hoover at 3:45 but there is no indication of the purpose of their meeting.

4 October 1918

Dear Mr. President:

In the matter of our conversation at one of the Wednesday meetings, to the intent that you would be prepared to request certain men to continue in their occupation of Government service rather than enter the Army, I have this morning an acute case of great importance. Mr. Herbert L. Gutterson, who is the head of our Division of Co-ordination of Purchase and in this position coordinates Army, Navy, Allied, Belgian Relief and other large purchases of foodstuffs, will be subject to the new draft. He has just had an offer of admission to the Artillery Officers Training Camp.

The position he holds here is not only one that requires a great deal of ability, in which he has been signally successful, but is one which requires a degree of integrity and single-mindedness as high as any official in the Government, as these co-ordinations amount to the direction of expenditure of anything up to $400,000,000 per month. There has never been a suspicion as to the conduct of his division and but one small attempt to undermine his rigid control, which failed owing to his vigorous action.

On the other hand, he feels that as the only male member of a family which has been represented in every great war of the United States he cannot remain in civil life. I shall probably have several of these cases and the men involved are the absolute pillars of the whole Administration and for whose positions it is almost hopeless to break in men with anything like equivalent experience,- experience that they have now gained in building up a work over fifteen months, to say nothing of the extreme care required to select men of integrity and known abilities. I should therefore appreciate it very greatly indeed if you could see your way to direct the enclosed letter to Mr. Gutterson.

Yours faithfully,
HERBERT HOOVER

Maltbie for Food Administrator

The following deals with the rather routine affair of a Hoover nominee for a post as a state food administrator.

October 7, 1918.

Dear Mr. President:

For several months Mr. E. G. Baetjer, the Federal Food Administrator for Maryland, has been ill. During this time Mr. W. H. Maltbie, of Baltimore, has been Acting Federal Food Administrator.

Mr. Baetjer has tendered his resignation as Food Administrator for Maryland and I now wish to suggest Mr. Maltbie as his successor.

As Mr. Maltbie is thoroughly conversant with the details of [the][1] Food Administration in Maryland, and as he has been recognized by the people of the State for several months as the Representative of the United States Food Administration, the work under him would proceed without interruption.

Faithfully yours,
HERBERT HOOVER

Approved
WOODROW WILSON [handwritten by Wilson]
10 October, 1918.

---

1. Handwritten insertion.

Appointment with President

> This memorandum was dated Thursday, October 17. A secretary, or possibly Wilson himself, wrote, "Thursday—24th—4.45 OK." The meeting took place at that time and the subject discussed, according to Hoover's letter to Wilson of October 26, was Belgian relief. Hoover was concerned, among other things, that unfair advantage would be taken of Belgium's distress by those forming new trade relations when occupation had come completely to an end. They may also have discussed the matter contained in Hoover's October 24 letter to the President. (*Life and Letters,* vol. 8, p. 509.)

October 17, 1918

Memorandum for the President:

Mr. Herbert Hoover asks if he may have a fifteen-minute appointment with the President some time this week. Mr. Hoover hopes the President can make appointment for Monday.

[unsigned]

Food Price Indices 1917–18

> In this letter Hoover mentions "attached compilations of . . . indices." These cover four pages and are omitted here. Hoover summarizes them in his letter.

17-October-1918

Dear Mr. President:

I think it will be of interest to you to glance over the attached compilations of several independent price indices in foodstuffs. The summation of these tables shows that in the first year of the Food Administration, according to the Department of Labor index, the wholesale prices have fallen 8%; according to the Times Annalist [*sic*] index, they have risen 8%; according to the Food Administration index, they have fallen 3.6%—a fall, averaging the three independent indices, of about 1.17%.

During the same period, according to the Department of Agriculture index, there has been a rise of 15.1% in farm produce; according to the Department of Labor index, an increase of 23%, according to the

Food Administration index, an increase of 3.9%, or an average of all of about 14%. During the same period there has, on various indices, been a rise in the cost of clothing, house furnishings, etc. of from 45% to 65%. The differences of indices arise out of the different bases of calculation, but this difference of calculation adds emphasis to the fact that the currents are properly interpreted. These indices would seem to substantiate:

(a) That there has been an appreciable stabilization in the price of food and a reduction of wholesale prices.
(b) That as farmers' prices have risen and wholesale prices fallen, there has been a great reduction—about 16%—in the profits of middlemen.

There has been a coincident reduction in consumption of some 7% and there is this season apparently a 4% to 6% nutritional increase in production. There have been rises in retail prices in congested areas which give rise to much complaint, but Congress gave us no control in this matter.

I mention this as a number of theoretical economists have lately been loud in the old outcry that our interference with the sacred law of supply and demand endangers our production and that reduction of consumption can only be obtained by higher prices.

Yours faithfully,
HERBERT HOOVER

Disapproval of Washington, D.C., Conventions

19 October 1918

Dear Mr. President:

I believe it would be a great help to the conditions in the city if we could get out an expression indicating your disapproval of the holding of any more conventions in Washington until the present pressure on housing is over. This will probably not be until after the war. I have notice of several such conventions and they particularly choose Washington as a setting because of their very natural desire to obtain speakers from the national bureaux on war questions.

Yours faithfully,
HERBERT HOOVER

Restoring Belgium after the War

Hoover's appointment calendar was invariably full. The entries for
October 23 reveal a fairly typical day and include the 2:30 war cabinet
meeting mentioned in the letter below.

Washington   Mr. Hoover's Appointments—Wednesday October 23rd
                 9:00 . . . . Sherman-Gutterson-Snyder-Munn-
                                          Whitmarsh
                 9:45 . . . . T. E. Wilson
                 10:00 . . . . Gov. Stuart and Swine Producers
                                          Committee
                 10:15 . . . . Packers
                 11:00 . . . . Salmon Canners
                 11:30 . . . . Yancey-Hagenbarth
                 12:00 . . . . Col. McIntosh
                 12:30 . . . . Everett Brown (Chicago Live
                                          Stock Exchange)
                 12:45 . . . . Swifts
                 1:00 . . . . De Cartier (Lunch)
                 2:30 . . . . White House
                 4:45 . . . . Pearson (Apec)
                 6:00 . . . . Lincoln-Funk-Brown-Evvard-
                                          Gentry-et al
                 7:30 . . . . Snyder-Pearson-Powell-Roy etc.

The German government had sent Wilson a note in which it accepted
his proposal for evacuation of occupied territory. Although not delivered formally until October 23, its general contents undoubtedly were
known in Washington on October 20. (*Life and Letters,* vol. 8, p.
492.) At 2:30 on Wednesday, October 23, Hoover attended the regular
meeting of the war cabinet with four other members. It has been described as "a most solemn occasion." In the course of this meeting,
President Wilson asked each man present to give his opinion on the
acceptance of the German proposal for an armistice. Hoover and most
of the others present agreed on accepting such armistice as the military would regard as safe. He was most anxious to see a quick end to
the fighting and stated that "he took no stock in a triumphal march
down the Unter den Linden." Moreover he wanted a note of encouragement sent to the German people who were trying to establish self-
government for their country. He also asked Wilson to say that the
German upper house should be changed and made popular, that is,
more democratic. (*Ordeal,* pp. 37–38; *Life and Letters,* vol. 8, pp. 492,
505–6; *Daniels Diaries,* pp. 343–44.)

By contrast, the meeting of the official cabinet on October 23 prompted Lane to write thus: "For some weeks we have spent our time at Cabinet meetings largely in telling stories." As for the previous meeting, Lane observed that "for three-quarters of an hour told stories on the war, and took up small departmental affairs." (*Letters of Lane,* p. 293.)

The subject matter of this October 21 letter was also that of a discussion Hoover had with Wilson on October 24 at 4:45 at the White House.

In this letter Hoover enclosed a "short memorandum" on Belgian relief that covered seven pages. It is omitted here since Hoover presents its major points in the letter itself.

21 October 1918

Dear Mr. President:

The task of the Belgian Relief Commission,—the preservation of the life of 10,000,000 occupied Belgians and French over these four years—is now rapidly drawing to conclusion and questions as to what further assistance should be extended to these people and as to what organization should be set up are pressing as the Governments in Europe are taking steps on the matter.

I enclose herewith a short memorandum on—

(a) The relief during occupation.

(b) The relief required for rehabilitation.

The released French population can be best cared for by their own government through France and I do not therefore consider that we need concern ourselves therewith.

The Belgian people, while more fortunate than the Serbians and Poles in that they are all alive, come out of occupation under-nourished, under-housed, under-clothed, industrial plants ruined, without raw material and without resources in shipping and money to find a remedy.

There is immediate need for 550,000 tons of shipping of which 350,000 are now in use by the Relief Commission. The Allied governmental aid needs be at once increased from about $15,000,000 per month at present being given (of which our government furnishes $9,000,000) to about $30,000,000 per month. With these resources over twelve to eighteen months I believe the people could be made self-supporting.

Assuming this must be accomplished, the problem of organization at once arises. Certain Belgians are anxious that the Relief Commission should liquidate and be handed over to the restored Belgian government—who should undertake all further relief with loans from the Allied governments; others wish the Commission to continue to perform such functions as may be assigned by the Belgian government; others are anxious that the Commission should undertake the great problem of economic restoration, acting as hitherto, in co-operation with Belgian unofficial organizations, and drawing its support from our own and Allied governments and public charity. The British government is opening discussion with our government on the question.

From a purely Belgian point of view the direct operation by their government is a mixed argument of sturdy independence and of natural amour propre and, to some extent, of individual political ambitions; the second proposition of a continuance controlled by the Belgian government is an argument of utilization of the organization until it can be dispensed with at will; the third is an argument which I believe should be further discussed, as it has both moral and economic bearings for the American people. I need hardly mention that the selfish view of myself and my colleagues would be entirely with the first proposition. We would like to have relief from this especially poignant anxiety that has now extended over four years.

With the present misery and economic difficulties facing Europe there can be little hope of Belgian recuperation without the major help coming from the United States. The American people, under your guidance, through its citizens and with the help of its officials, took the lead in internal protection and sustenance of this population four years ago. This imposes no obligation but offers an opportunity for further service—the completion of which would confer moral values to our country not to be under-estimated.

Intangible as these values are, they cannot be gained by our people unless they are won through some bond of definite American organization participating in the labour and its consummation.

While it can be said that the Belgians are an efficient administrative people, it is my impression that security and effectiveness in the application of these funds, without religious, political or racial bias, could be much more effectively secured by American participation in organization and administration.

There will be a large outpouring of charity towards the Belgian people which could be stimulated, but in the expenditure of which, unless there is some single channel, there will be enormous waste and corruption, and re-actions will set in to the disadvantage of both Belgian and American people.

If the matter were undertaken by the Belgian government alone, they would naturally have to take their position with the other needy

Allied governments under the various Allied controls; whereas, if a distinctly American organization, maintained by the American government, were to be installed for this service, such an organization could easily secure the same tenderness in obtaining priorities and supplies, and complete independence of action from other Allied control that it now possesses.

As these controls are dominated by the other needy governments I feel that the Belgians will get off much worse in shipping and in supplies than if they are particularly under our wing. If American participation in organization of rehabilitation is to be maintained it would seem logical to continue it through the Relief Commission whose organization is in action and simply requires larger resources and the use of this media would avoid discussion of any new instrumentality with the Allied governments. It would represent the rounding out of an enterprise of our people toward another in which we could have lasting pride.

One of the objectives in peace conferences must be the re-payment, in addition to other damages, to Belgium of the whole of the sums that have been spent by the Relief Commission, together with such further moneys as are spent on rehabilitation. It would appear to me that it would be a pointed and positive lesson to the world for all future time if it could be made a peace condition that the expenditures of the Relief Commission both in the past and in the future are made re-payable by the Germans, directly to the Relief Commission, and that this Commission should refund the sums advanced by the various governments.

I should be glad to have your views in the matter and if you consider the Commission should be continued to this new purpose and that it will have the support of the government, it is desirable that its relations to Belgian and other governments should be properly defined.

Yours faithfully,
HERBERT HOOVER

The United States and the Food Pool

In October 1918 the European Allies created an organization whereby for some years after the war the Allied and associated powers were to pool all their credit, food, raw materials, ships, and coal. The organization was to be operated by a board on which the United States would have but one vote although it would be the major contributor. The unveiling of this plan provoked Hoover into writing a letter to the

President protesting the forfeiture of American independence that would inevitably result from its implementation. This independence he deemed essential if the United States were to have an effective voice in the reconstruction of Europe.

Although Hoover had seen Wilson on Wednesday, October 23, he returned to the White House for another consultation with the President at 4:45 on October 24. He again expressed his concern that Belgium would become the victim of trade exploiters. In addition he most likely discussed the question of the food pool. Also on October 24 Wilson composed and sent out his appeal for a return of a Democratic Congress in November. Whether or not he mentioned this matter to Hoover is mere conjecture. (*Life and Letters*, vol. 8, pp. 509–10.)

24 October 1918

Dear Mr. President:

I feel that despite the great burden of anxiety which you must entertain, it is necessary for me to present for your consideration one or two phases of the after-war situation in food, for peace-making might catch us suddenly. Until peace, even though it be deferred until next harvest, the Western Allies and neutrals can get along without drawing appreciably on supplies otherwise than North America. You are of course aware that considerable accumulations have taken place in the Far East and the Southern Hemisphere as the result of short shipping. These accumulations are of course available as additional support to the German occupied area after peace. If peace should come before Christmas, even with these accumulations referred to, there will be an international shortage in several vital commodities if consumption is to be restored to normal pending next harvest. If peace did not come until, say, April, then these accumulations would carry the burden.

The principal reason why this problem arises at the moment is that some members of the Allied Food Council are putting forward suggestions for international control of world distribution of food after peace. My own instinct is entirely against any such agreements or entanglements for, at least morally, any international body on this subject in which we participated would involve us in acceptance of their views and, practically, in acceptance of their distribution of our supplies.

If peace arrives at any time during the next few months, we will have the dominant supplies and my own view is that we should maintain a complete independence and, upon information that we are to obtain, distribute our resources so as to fill in the gaps in supplies that are not secured by the various nations from other countries. In other words, we could use our food supplies to level up, in a rough manner, the deficiencies that will ultimately arise from the general grab for the balances of the world's food. If we maintain our independence we can confer favours instead of complying with agreements and we can use our resources to make economic exchanges which will maintain justice all round. For instance, our best implement to restore government and order in Russia is through food and raw material relief. Another instance lies in that our Army would need rapid transport home and if we maintain control of our own foodstuffs and other materials we could make it a requirement that for every ton of these materials, England, France, Germany, Austria and the neutrals should furnish us a certain amount of transportation for this purpose.

I think it would be desirable if you could consider whether such a policy should not be extended to the raw materials. There will be a shortage of many of these materials for European manufacturing purposes and the control of them could be used to maintain some sort of justice. For instance, Germany has wantonly destroyed the entire spinning industry in Belgium, Northern France and Poland, with a view to acquiring the markets in these industries subsequent to the war. If we took in hand the control of our distribution of cotton, we could no doubt ration Germany in such manner as to allow the other localities to again get on their industrial feet.

Another phase of the matter lies in the fact that we will require some imports of raw material and if we maintain control of our own supplies of food and raw material we will be in position to make such arrangements as will insure our own interests.

I should be glad indeed if I could have your views in this matter, for if you hold the view that we shall enter no entanglements whatever I shall take steps at once to maintain such a stand.

Yours faithfully,
HERBERT HOOVER

Control of Belgian Restoration

Hoover met with Wilson on Thursday, October 24, at 4:45 and they discussed the question of the restoration of Belgium after the end of occupation. But on Saturday, October 26, the question appeared even more pressing, so Hoover addressed a letter to the President enclosing "two memoranda." One of these was a draft of a letter which Hoover had written as a message for Wilson to send to "various departments." The draft is not now among the Hoover or the Wilson papers. However, its substance was probably contained in letters Wilson sent out on November 6, the day of his weekly meeting with Hoover and the war cabinet. The letters were identical and addressed to the concerned individuals after "verbal discussions." The recipients were Secretary of State Lansing, Secretary of War Baker, Secretary of the Treasury McAdoo, E. N. Hurley of the Shipping Division, Bernard Baruch of the War Industries Board, and H. P. Davison of the Red Cross. In this letter, Wilson wrote thus: "In view of the approaching evacuation of Belgium and the new problems that confront this unfortunate people, I have asked Mr. Hoover to expand the activities of the Commission for Relief in Belgium to cover the entire relationship of this government, and possibly that of other governments, together with all American public charity, to the whole business not only of food but also clothing, raw material, tools, machinery, exchange and other economic relief involved in the reconstruction of Belgium.

"I would be obliged if your Department would give him all support and cooperation in this matter and refer to him for guidance in all questions of an economic order that arise in any connection between Belgium and this country." (*Life and Letters*, vol. 8, p. 558; *Epic*, vol. 1, pp. 389–90.)

The second "memorandum" mentioned in Hoover's letter of October 26 is given as a November 7 Wilson letter. (See p. 285.)

26 October 1918

Dear Mr. President:

I enclose herewith two memoranda about which I spoke to you on Thursday. The first of these I would be glad if you could see your way to address to me so as to give me a measure of authority and standing in undertaking this problem. I find that the matter is even more necessary than I contemplated on Thursday as already there have sprung up various attempts in this country to formulate important trade relations with the Belgians, some of which, at least, I feel could not but have a bad reflection on the whole situation. Doubtless it is desirable to secure the rehabilitation of trade with the United States, but if we are to prevent advantage being taken of the distress of this people, it must be under firm control.

I have formulated this memorandum so that I can use it as a basis for approach to the state departments of the other governments, indicating the future attitude so far as this government is concerned and, therefore, a basis for them to agree to.

The second memorandum I would like, if you approve, to have addressed to the various departments which are indicated in the heading, for it will be necessary to have the co-operation of these departments and that they should act from a common center in all matters of trade and shipping, if we are to direct our energies to the great objective, that is, economic rehabilitation rather than trade.

Yours faithfully,
HERBERT HOOVER

Reported Destruction in Belgium

In October 1918, as the Germans were retreating through northern France, they destroyed the French coal mines. On November 2 Hoover received word that they had ordered the same treatment for the mines in occupied Belgium. Forthwith he dispatched a letter of protest to Wilson, who in turn addressed himself to Secretary of State Lansing in these terms: "I entirely agree with Mr. Hoover in what he says in the enclosed letter, and if you think it not too irregular a course of action, I beg that you will request the Chargé of the Swiss Legation to convey through his government in the form you deem best, our very earnest protest against any such action as is here forecast." The following day at 9:45 in the morning Hoover saw Lansing himself and may well have personally expressed his deep concern about the impending disaster. The next day, November 6, he met with Wilson at the 2:30 session of the war cabinet. On November 7 the Secretary of State wrote to the Swiss minister in Washington requesting that he approach the German government on the matter. Early the following morning, November 8, Hoover hurried from a 9:15 dentist appointment to confer with Lansing at 9:45 in the latter's office. At 2:15 that same afternoon he was back again at the State Department. Three days later, November 11, the Swiss minister transmitted to Lansing a message from the German government avowing that no such destruction of Belgian mines had been undertaken. (*Foreign Relations*, 1918, Supp. 2, p. 790.)

2 November 1918

Dear Mr. President:

I am informed through our correspondents this morning that the Germans in Belgium have given notice to the coal mines to the effect that all men and animals should be brought out of the pits, all raw materials in possession of companies to be delivered to the Germans and that the mines will be destroyed at once. They have already started in two places in Belgium.

I can scarcely express the concern that I feel over this matter. It means the loss of an absolutely vital necessity to these people over the coming winter. It will result in enormous loss of human life. It seems to me hardly in accord with the professions recently made by the German government in their communications to you.

I have not a great deal of faith in protests but it does seem to me that if you could see your way to point out in a note to the Germans that this does not accord with their professions; that it means the most terrible of human hardships; that it is absolutely wanton and that the continuation of this policy will necessitate the imposition of a greater burden upon the German people at the hands of the Allies. It might be that it would cause them to hesitate and at least appears to me could do no harm.

Yours faithfully,
HERBERT HOOVER

Available Food Supplies

4-November-1918

Dear Mr. President:

We have now completed a broad survey of the food supplies available in the world in case of an early peace, together with the world's necessities. We have calculated the supplies as being the surplus in any given commodity exportable from any country and have assumed the total export of such a surplus. In the matter of necessities we have formulated our estimates on the basis of the preservation of public health and tranquility, not upon the restoration of conditions to normal; that is, there would be an increase of food supply to the area at present controlled by the Central Empires but no very consequential increase to the Allies. The period covered by these calculations is that until the next harvest. I will not trouble you with the elaborate details referring to each country.

The following table shows the results in tons and the amounts of such exports as the United States would have to contribute under these conditions—

	Total export supplies	Total import necessities	Deficiency or surplus	From United States
Breadstuffs	19,000,000	16,000,000	+3,000,000	9,000,000
Pulses and				
rice	1,400,000	1,400,000	....	300,000
Feeds	8,000,000	11,000,000	−3,000,000	5,000,000
Beef	1,600,000	1,600,000*1	....	300,000
Pork Products ...	1,700,000	2,400,000	−700,000	1,300,000
Oils	800,000	1,200,000	−400,000	200,000
Dairy Products ...	500,000	800,000	−300,000	300,000
Sugar	5,000,000	6,700,000	−1,700,000	1,500,000*2
Coffee	1,400,000	1,000,000	+400,000	

*1 This being the limit of refrigerating ship capacity.
*2 Assuming Cuba as part of U.S. supplies as we own their crop.

The following general points stand out on this survey:

1. The amounts given as "total import necessities" are probably 10,000,000 tons short of enough to provide normal pre-war consumption.
2. The total export supplies are insufficient to provide even the "total import necessities" as based on this table. In other words, there is a deficiency below what we consider is desirable to preserve health and tranquility.
3. This situation will be politically somewhat ameliorated by the fact that there is a sufficiency of breadstuffs which indeed comprise fifty per cent. of the food intake of European people and therefore largely dominate [the] public mind.
4. The critical shortage is in the fats where the deficiency amounts, in our view, to about 35%.
5. The only deficiency in which the United States participates is that of sugar, and this will indeed present a serious problem.
6. Of the above quantities of exportable food, United States and Cuba will be furnishing about 50% of the total calculated world's import necessities.
7. With the inability to even complete this programme of necessities, which is itself below the amount that would be consumed if available, it is positively necessary that we have a continuance of the embargo so that we may regulate the outlet, or every one of our foodstuffs will be overdrawn and our own people faced with shortages next spring.
8. Another and very pertinent reason for continuance of the embargo

lies in the fact that with the whole world bidding in our market without restraint, we shall have an era of high prices, of profiteering and speculation, such as we have never yet experienced.

9. Some systematic arrangement will be necessary for the determination as to how our available surpluses are to be divided amongst the various nations and to see to it that these divisions are carried out without disturbing our markets.

10. Our surpluses might be somewhat increased by a continuation of conservation.

Faithfully yours,
HERBERT HOOVER

Thanks for Election Support

In early October 1918 it was clear that the defeat of Germany was inevitable and imminent. It was then that President Wilson definitely decided to attend the peace conference that would ensue upon cessation of hostilities. But the President feared for his party in the November midterm congressional elections; should the Democrats lose seats, not to mention control of the House, Wilson would indeed be a lesser figure among his European counterparts. To forestall such a possibility, he resolved in late October to issue an appeal to the electorate, warning that a Republican victory would be interpreted abroad as a repudiation of his leadership. In this appeal of October 24 he asked voters for an election of Democratic congressmen if "you have approved of my leadership and wish me to continue to be your unembarrassed spokesman at home and abroad. . . ."

On November 2 Frederic R. Coudert, a New York attorney, invited the Food Administrator to express himself on the need of "unity in achieving . . . a just and enduring peace." Hoover obliged and wrote a letter to Coudert that conveyed the desired message. Immediately Coudert arranged to have his letter published in the *New York Times* on November 4, 1918, the day before the congressional elections. Hoover himself had been a registered Republican since his twenty-first birthday and had supported Theodore Roosevelt in the 1912 campaign against Wilson. Moreover, he had looked upon Wilson's October 24 appeal as "a shock" and "a mystery." (*Ordeal*, pp. 14–15.) However, he now considered that the problems of war and peace transcended all others and that consequently there should be "no party politics" but rather "united support" for the incumbent commander-in-chief. Hoover was at the White House in private conference with Wilson on the afternoon of October 24 shortly before the President wrote out his appeal for a Democratic Congress. However, the purpose of this visit was to resolve a pressing Belgian problem and there is no indication that words were exchanged on domestic politics. (*Life and Letters,* vol. 8, p. 509.)

Hoover's November statement brought him a warm letter of appreciation from the President, but it also brought him unpleasant heat from Republican sources. As he wrote in his 1951 *Memoirs*: "My only participation in politics during the war got me in some hot water." (Vol. 1, p. 266.)

Wilson was unsuccessful in the November elections, his party losing both houses of Congress. Many analysts conclude that the President's intervention was largely responsible for this defeat. Others assert that the loss would have been of even greater measure but for his own appeal and the public endorsement of his loyal Food Administrator.

President Wilson wrote his letter of appreciation on the very day that Hoover's letter appeared in the *Times.* On the sentiments the President expressed and on the whole episode in general, Lewis Strauss, a secretary for Hoover at that time, revealed the following information to this writer in a September 1972 private interview: Wilson did not ask for the public manifestation of support from Hoover, though quite probably he did expect it. The letter in the *New York Times* was prepared by Strauss, who had a free hand with Hoover's correspondence, and was signed by Hoover under pressure of immediate departure for Europe. Soon thereafter when the letter drew editorial criticism, Strauss realized that he had erred in not guarding Hoover against an act which might have future political liabilities for him. Strauss was eager to assume responsibility but Hoover would not permit him to do so.

4-November, 1918.

My dear Hoover:

Your letter to Mr. Coudert has touched me very deeply, and I want you to know not only how proud I am to have your endorsement and your backing given in such generous fashion, but also what serious importance I attach to it, for I have learned to value your judgment and have the greatest trust in all your moral reactions. I thank you from the bottom of my heart.

Cordially and sincerely yours,
WOODROW WILSON

International Control of Supplies

In his October 24 letter to President Wilson, Hoover had expressed his opposition to any plan for pooling resources after the war. In his short message of November 4, the wary Hoover reveals the directions on the matter that he had just dispatched to Joseph P. Cotton, the Food Administration's representative in Europe. Hoover's firm note to Cotton was really his response to an October 30 cable from William Graves Sharp, United States ambassador and plenipotentiary in France. This cable discussed the contemplated pool of raw material, food, and ships. The message cabled by Cotton from London on November 1 dealt with a wartime complaint, then current in England and France, that arose from an allegation that the United States was using ships to import nonessentials while the European allies themselves were making heroic sacrifices to allow a sufficient supply of vessels to bring American troops to France. In the following brief note to Wilson, Hoover makes no mention of this allegation.

4 November 1918

Dear Mr. President:

I have received the two attached cables from our representatives in Europe. The one on the subject of international control of distribution of food, raw materials and ships does seem to me to require urgent consideration. In the meantime I have directed Mr. Cotton, my representative, that he should in no form take any part in pledges that would even appear to commit our government.

Yours faithfully,
HERBERT HOOVER

Authority for Belgian Work

In his October 26 letter to Wilson Hoover included a draft of a "Dear Mr. Hoover" letter. This was one of the "two memoranda" he sent to Wilson at that time. His purpose was to have the President sign and return it and thus provide him with an authoritative document for his use when dealing with foreign governments on the subject of the restoration of Belgium. On this original draft Wilson wrote several alterations in wording and sentence structure. Then on November 6 the President himself, or a secretary, retyped the modified letter, making a few additional verbal changes in the process. Soon thereafter, Wilson in his own hand made eight more unsubstantial improvements—a "which" for a "that," a "would" for a "should," etc. Finally, the polished product was again freshly typed and sent back to Hoover as a November 7 letter, the authorization that Hoover had requested on October 26. Hoover's original draft, or "memorandum," with Wilson's first handwritten emendations is shown in the facsimile section. Following that are additional changes made by the President on November 6. The letter below is Wilson's final product. The facsimiles of the early drafts illustrate how carefully Wilson worked over documents that were needed for important work by men in his administration.

7 November, 1918

Dear Mr. Hoover:

The probable early evacuation of Belgium brings us face to face with the problem of this distressed people, not only in regard to continued food relief, but also with regard to the many questions of economic rehabilitation. The initial task of preserving the bare lives of the people during German occupation, undertaken four years ago under your direction, is now nearing completion. I believe that the American people will willingly accept a large share of the burden of assisting in the now all important work of reconstruction and rehabilitation, pending re-payment by Germany for the injury done.

In order that such assistance should be exerted in the most liberal, efficient and comprehensive manner, I feel that it should be organized under a single agency, which may co-ordinate the whole effort of the American people and government, in the furnishing of supplies, machinery, finance, exchange, shipping, trade relations and philanthropic aid. I also feel that such an agency, in addition to being the sole vehicle of supplies, should also have some proper participation in the expenditure and distribution of assistance. Such unity of administration would give much greater assurance of proper assistance and should be effective in preventing profiteering.

The large experience of the Belgian Relief Commission, the character of its organization without profit, its established use of shipping, and the sympathetic bond which it now forms with the Belgian people point to its continuation and enlargement as the natural agency for this purpose. I should therefore be glad if you and your colleagues of the Commission would undertake this extended work.

I understand that it is also the wish and purpose of the English and French people to participate in carrying this burden. It would seem to me desirable to inquire if these governments would not therefore continue and enlarge their present support to the Commission to these ends, so that we may have a comprehensive and efficient agency for dealing with the entire problem on behalf of all.

It is of course of primary importance that our assistance in this expenditure and organization shall be built upon co-operation with the Belgian government and the use of such internal agencies and methods as may be agreed upon with them, to whom our whole solicitude is directed.

It is also of first importance that the expenditure of all the philanthropic aid of the American people toward Belgium, of whatever character, should be conducted by or under the control of the Commission, if duplication and waste are to be avoided.

With a view to the advancement of these ideas, I have addressed a note to the various departments of our government, indicating my wish that all matters relating to these problems should be undertaken under your guidance and that they should give to you every co-operation.

I wish you to proceed at once with the undertaking so far as it relates to the United States and I should be glad if you would, through proper agencies, take up a discussion of these matters with the Belgian government and with the English and French governments as to their relationship and participation.

Cordially and sincerely yours,
WOODROW WILSON

Reply to October 30 Cables

On November 6 at the weekly war cabinet meeting, Hoover and Wilson discussed the October 30 cable that had been dispatched to Secretary of War Baker from representatives in London and forthwith sent on to Hoover. (See November 4 letter above on international control of supplies.) Hoover then composed an answer to the cable's report that the Allies intended the establishment of a postwar pool of food and raw materials and sent a copy to the President. Hoover wrote thus: "For your general advice, this Government will not agree to any programme that even looks like Inter-Allied control of our economic resources after peace." The same cabled response was sent by Secretary of State Lansing to Colonel House, then in London, with the notation that "The Department of State approves entirely the policy above set forth." (*Memoirs*, vol. 2, pp. 91–93.)

7 November, 1918

Dear Mr. President:

Please find enclosed herewith a telegram which I am despatching to Mr. Cotton in respect to the proposals for the world's food and shipping supplies to be vested in the Inter-Allied Food Council and the Inter-Allied Maritime Council.

I believe this cable is in accord with the conclusions of our conference yesterday and I am wondering if you could see your way to despatch this same telegram to Colonel House, informing him that it has been sent to Mr. Cotton by myself and that it is with your authorization and, furthermore, if you could state to Colonel House that I will be leaving within the next few days for Paris and that no arrangements looking forward to the handling of food for liberated populations should be undertaken until after my arrival and consultation with him.

Yours faithfully,

HERBERT HOOVER

Strengthening the Committee for Relief in Belgium

> Hoover wrote this letter to Wilson on Saturday, November 9, a day filled with appointments from 9:00 to 4:00. On Tuesday, November 12, he went to the White House with the food administrators from the states for an introduction to the President. The following day he attended a meeting with Wilson and the war cabinet at 2:30, and there the President gave his approval to the proposals contained in this November 9 letter. (*Epic,* vol. 1, p. 392.)

9-November-1918

Dear Mr. President:

In enlarging the functions of the Belgian Relief Commission to cover the entire reconstruction and relief programme for Belgium, I would like to suggest for your approval the following matters:

1. To strengthen the C.R.B. organization I propose to set up a new executive committee, under my chairmanship, comprising representatives of the Food Administration, the Belgian Relief Commission, the War Industries Board, the Shipping Board, the War Trade Board and the Treasury; during my absence Mr. Edgar Rickard, who has been

associated with the Relief Commission from the beginning, to act for me as chairman of this executive committee.

2. Any programme will require an assurance of at least $200,000,000 to pay for the food and reconstruction materials necessary to be shipped from the United States, pending the restoration of trade conditions and of possible legislation providing money for definite reconstruction and credit relations to Europe. It is necessary that we should have at once an assurance of at least this sum of money under the present legislation and resources of the government. It would probably only be required over a period of from 8 to 10 months. In addition to this I have hopes of establishing some commercial credits for Belgian Banks with our banks, to take care of any programme over and above the amount outlined. In other words, to press the Belgians to use all the self help that they can find.

3. Under the present powers of the government, the Treasury is able to make advances to the Allied governments for purposes of the war, and it has, as you know, made very considerable advances to the Belgian government for the purposes of the relief and direct war expenditure. It would seem to me a right interpretation of the law for the Treasury to undertake to furnish $200,000,000 to the Belgian government and stipulate that the money is to be used for expenditures in the United States through the Relief Commission. It appears to me that the prevention of starvation and disturbances in this population is vital to the making of the status quo during armistice, and is therefore a perfectly legitimate advance under the present law. In case peace should come suddenly, in order to avoid a debacle in the relief, it seems to me necessary that the Treasury should take a commitment to furnish this sum of money at once; otherwise, we shall have a lot of liabilities out in the United States and be entirely unable to fulfill them. I would propose that these advances should be subject to the Belgian Government finding from other governments all monies necessary to pay transportation charges on any materials shipped from here and to find monies from other quarters for all purchases made outside the United States.

4. Another feature of this matter which appeals greatly to Mr. Baruch and myself is the fact that with the armistice we will at once be closing a large number of factories on war work and if we can at once place in their hands orders for material from such sources as this, we will have contributed in a very large measure to prevent industrial difficulties in the United States, and that an assurance of such orders will be of profound value just at the present juncture.

I would be very glad indeed to have your views in the matter.

Faithfully yours,
HERBERT HOOVER

Feeding the Liberated People

At the weekly session of the war cabinet on November 6 the subject of major concern, according to the *Daniels Diaries* (p. 347), was the starving people of liberated Europe, especially the Austrians, and methods for relieving their desperate situation. It was revealed that Hoover would soon depart for Europe to address himself to the general problem of food. Daniels records that Hoover expressed the opinion that since "this country would have to furnish money direct or lend it to England and France, we ought to undertake it and let it have our brand." This latter probably refers to the marking of the food with a U.S.A. stamp to indicate its source.

The war cabinet also pondered the question of financing the food program for liberated Europe, finally deciding to ask Secretary of State Lansing for a statement on the legalities involved. Significantly, Hoover himself consulted Lansing the next morning at 9:45. Moreover, he returned to the State Department again at 2:15 in the afternoon. Saturday, November 8, he saw Secretary of War Baker as well as Hurley of the Shipping Division, who had just recently been appointed to accompany Hoover to Europe. He also consulted with many of his own staff, including William A. Glasgow, chief legal counsel. At 8:00 that evening, a Sunday morning appointment was finalized with Dr. Thomas Masaryk, Czechoslovakian patriot, soon to become president of that republic.

Sometime during the day of November 9, after the above round of conferences, Hoover composed the following letter to President Wilson on the feeding of the people in the liberated countries.

9 November 1918

Dear Mr. President:

In the matter of feeding the liberated peoples of Austria, Serbia, Bulgaria, Turkey, et cetera, I have had conferences with Messrs. Hurley and Baker and our own staff and, as a result, I have to propose to you the following measures, which meet with approval on all sides:

1. That the Army should hand to us certain cargo boats at once which we will load with foods at their expense. This food will be of a char-

acter than [that?] can be used by the American Army or the Allies in any event, and will be despatched in the first instance to Bordeaux for orders.

2. In order to secure an organization to carry on the work during my own and Mr. Hurley's absence, and to co-ordinate the various branches of the government concerned, I would like your authority to set up a committee under my chairmanship and to comprise Mr. Theodore Whitmarsh of the Food Administration, who would act as my alternate when away; Mr. Julius H. Barnes of the Food Administration Cereal Division and Mr. F. S. Snyder of the Food Administration Meats Division; Mr. John Beaver White of the War Trade Board; Mr. Prentiss N. Gray representing the Shipping Board and someone to be selected by Mr. Baker representing the War Department; Mr. William A. Glasgow of this department to act as counsel.

3. It appears to me that it will be absolutely necessary to secure an appropriation for the handling of this enterprise. It is entirely probable that I can make such arrangements in Europe that will permit of the sale of the food, but, in the present disorganized conditions, it will be almost hopeless to secure rapid enough implementing of credits to solve the situation and that, for some preliminary stages at least, this relief enterprise would have to revolve on advances from our government. I should also, when I arrive in Europe, ask all the Allied governments if they wish to participate in the enterprise. It appears to me with the state of mind of the well-thinking people of this country that the government could agree to appropriate $200,000,000 for the feeding of the liberated populations in Europe,—such a sum to be placed at your disposal. In the ordinary course of events, I would not think that much of this money would be lost, for, at least, obligations could be obtained from municipalities and governments for its ultimate re-payment.

It is my view that the critical moment is right now to carry over the period pending the rehabilitation of trade and that if we can worry through the next four or five months we will have solved the problem. It is not necessary for me to mention how fundamental it appears to me that this is, if we are to preserve these countries from Bolshevism and rank anarchy.

Yours faithfully,
HERBERT HOOVER

Cotton's Cables on the Food Pool

Joseph Cotton dispatched two cables in response to Hoover's cabled message of November 7. In one cable, Cotton expressed himself in favor of American participation in the Inter-Allied food pool. In another he urged that Hoover promptly communicate his ideas on the postwar feeding of the Continent and not wait until his arrival in Europe before revealing his plans. Hoover met with the President at 2:30 on Wednesday, November 13. Possibly they discussed the contents of these cables on that occasion. In any event, on November 14 Hoover sent the President a short note in which he wrote, "I enclose herewith copy of the cablegram which I have dispatched to Mr. Cotton in accordance with your suggestion." In this cable of November 13, Hoover reaffirmed his opposition to the pool plan and restated his position that any decision involving American food or credit must wait upon his arrival in Europe. Two days later he departed for Europe accompanied by Robert Taft, Lewis Strauss, Alonzo Taylor, and Julius Barnes. (*Organization,* p. 41.) He arrived in London on November 24 and left for Paris on November 25. (For further information on problems that were soon to face Hoover see *Hoover and Germany.*)

As for the final point in this letter of November 11, Hoover had already advised Secretary of State Lansing in an earlier letter that no arrangements for handling food for liberated people should be made until he had arrived in Europe. On November 7 Wilson wrote to Lansing thus: "I think the suggestions of Mr. Hoover . . . should be complied with, and I would be glad if you would convey our attitude in this matter to House. . . ." (*Life and Letters,* vol. 8, p. 572.)

11 November, 1918

Dear Mr. President:

I enclose herewith two cables which I would be grateful if you could find time to peruse.

The first, with regard to our entering into a joint inter-Allied pool for the purpose of distributing all of the world's wheat until the middle of 1920, fills me with complete horror. Of all of the import wheat in the world, seventy per cent must come from the Western Hemisphere and I assume that we would be called upon to finance it and to place the distribution of it in the hands of a body that we could not control.

I can see no objective in such a plan as I believe there is sufficient wheat for the world to get through with, unless it is the intention to use this control of the prime necessity of life to dominate other measures in the world.

As to the second telegram on the subject of arrangements which the English may set up in London for provisioning the world with our foodstuffs and on our credit, I have a similar reaction.

Both of these telegrams bring me to express to you the urgency of a definition of our principles in these matters, to be conveyed to the Allied governments in order that I and the other agents of the government in Europe may be able to act in entire unison with your own views.

If I might make a suggestion in this direction, it would be on the line that we consider ourselves as trustees of our surplus production of all kinds for the benefit of the most necessitous and the most deserving. We feel that we must ourselves execute this trusteeship; that we are not unmindful of the obligation which we have to the sustenance of those who have fought with us against Germany and that, together with the necessities of those populations released from the German yoke, we feel that they may well deserve a priority in our distribution. On the other hand, we cannot undertake any co-operative arrangements that look to the control of our exports after peace and furthermore—and equally important—that the inter-Allied councils hitherto set up in Europe were entirely for the purpose of guiding inter-Allied relations during the period of the war and that any extension of their functions either by way of their control of our relations to other nations or the extension of their present functions beyond peace, cannot be entertained by us; that all relationship involving the use of American food or credit for the people of other nations than the Allies themselves, must await Mr. Hoover's arrival in Europe, so far as any such supplies or interest of the United States is concerned.

I believe that the settlement of this question requires some specific statement from you.

Yours faithfully
HERBERT HOOVER

E P I L O G U E

THE EXCELLENT RELATIONSHIP that existed between Hoover and Wilson during the war continued for the most part throughout the eight months the Peace Treaty was being drafted in France. From December 15, 1918, to July 1919 Hoover showered the President with letters and memoranda on the blockade, the feeding of Germany, and the rise of Bolshevism.[1]

Although Hoover was not on the American five-member delegation at the treaty negotiations, he was director general of European relief with headquarters in Paris. In this capacity, he was mightily concerned with every action of the treaty craftsmen. Moreover, he had an intimate knowledge of Europe that far surpassed that of the official American delegation. He had lived abroad for 18 years—much of the time in Russia, Germany, France, England, and Belgium. Moreover, his knowledge of these countries and their peoples was intensely practical. Wilson's knowledge, on the other hand, was that of a scholar and had been gained almost exclusively by study of European cultural institutions from a distance. Prior to December 1918 his only physical contact with the Continent had come during a three-week tour in the summer of 1903.

Wilson seemed to recognize Hoover's deep knowledge of Europe, and he placed a high premium on the many pieces of advice that the relief director sent him during those eight months when the two lived in Paris. Even Hoover's lengthy letters of June 4 and 5 sharply criticizing the treaty did not cause a break in his relations with the President. Indeed, Wilson was so impressed that he requested a personal conference with Hoover. It was then, however, that the first fissures in their close association appeared. Several months later, on November 19, 1919,

---

1. These letters are the subject of a second book in preparation by the author (1974) entitled *Two Peacemakers in Paris: The Hoover-Wilson Letters, November 1918 to November 1919.*

Hoover wrote one of his last letters to the stricken President. In it he urged Wilson to accept a compromise with the moderate reservationists in the Senate and thus assure America's acceptance of the League of Nations. There was no reply. Perhaps the fallen chief was too ill even to read Hoover's letter.

But never, neither before nor after, did they write a sharp word to one another in spite of their evident differences of view on the treaty and the League of Nations. Wilson died on February 3, 1924. Four months later, on June 13, Hoover sent a confidential letter to William Allen White. It seems fitting to conclude this account of the six-year association of two great men by quoting a portion of this letter:

> I do not want to be put in the position of criticizing Woodrow Wilson. I believe men should be judged for the good they do. The whole tendency of modern public criticism is to damn men for their very minor mistakes and to take no proportional vision of their accomplishments. That immortal son of Holland who saved his native land by keeping his fist in a leaky dike no doubt sassed his mother. My personal view has always been that the failure of Mr. Wilson was pathological and began with his first physical shock in April or May, 1919. . . . Therefore, his real history ought to end right there. . . . The petty incidents of his personal relations with myself or Colonel House or any other of the men with whom he got out of patience and refused to cooperate are in my mind not worth consideration. . . .

INDEX

Adamson, W. C., Congressman
  profit-limiting views, 43
  proposes food bill, 46–47

Baker, Newton, Secretary of War, 236,
  237, 249, 286, 289, 290
Barnes, Julius, 225, 228, 236, 290
  to Paris with Hoover, 291
  supports Hoover, McAdoo controversy,
    142
  supports Hoover, wheat prices, 176
Baruch, Bernard, Chairman of War In-
  dustries Board, 215, 216, 227, 229, 260,
  278
  praised by Hoover, 160–61
Belgium
  Commission for Relief in, 5
  German destruction, 279–80
  Hoover-Wilson discussions, 270, 276
  King Albert, 92
  restoration, 272–79
  work threatened, 183–85, 191–94
Bolshevism
  Hoover's fear, 290, 293
  and Russia, 132
Brandeis, Louis D., Supreme Court Justice
  Hoover consultation, 127–28
  supports Hoover for president, 127
  Wilson consultation, 127
Bryan, William Jennings, 3

Cabinet, subordinated to war council,
  164–65, 272–73. See also War cabinet.
Chamberlain, G. E., Senator, favors Hoo-
  ver's food views, 35, 37, 54–55
Cotton, Joseph P., 37, 260–62
  Allied food pool, 284, 286–287, 291–92
  reports on Allies' U.S. criticism, 242–49
Creel, George, 121, 123
Crosby, Oscar T., criticized by Wilson,
  177, 262–63

Daniels, Josephus, Secretary of Navy, 244,
  254, 289
  on beef trade, 253
  on Hoover, 22–23, 104
  on Hoover-McAdoo controversy, 145
  on liberated people, 289
  prohibition views, 35, 104
Draft exemptions, Hoover's views, 56, 251–
  52, 268–69

Embargo
  neutral nations, 42, 50–51
  postwar, 293

Food Administration
  auditing method, 75–76
  and civil service, 96–97
  money for building, 83–84
Food Control Bill. See Lever Bill
Food pool with Allies, Hoover's views,
  203–4, 275–77, 284, 291–92
Forster, Rudolph, Wilson's executive
  clerk, 26, 27, 59, 60, 62

Garfield, Harry, Fuel Administrator, 75,
  85, 165, 244, 260
  Wilson recommendation, 30
George, Lloyd, British Prime Minister,
  ships for Belgian Relief, 183, 191,
  193–94
Germans
  peace overtures, 272
  sink Belgian Relief ships, 17
  submarine warfare, 13, 20
  warned on arming merchant marine, 19
Glasgow, William A., 224, 225, 236, 241,
  244, 245, 289, 290
Gore, T. P., Senator
  and changes in Lever Bill, 49–50

Gore, T. P., Senator *(continued)*
  critical of Hoover, 166–67
  and increased wheat price, 150
Gronna, A. J., Senator, misquotes Hoover,
  53–54

Hallowell, John, 62–63, 225
Hollis, Henry F., Senator, proposes own
  food bill, 51–52
Hoover, Herbert
  and Belgian king, 92
  congratulates Wilson on war message,
    20
  congressional elections 1918, 282–83
  criticizes Versailles treaty, 293
  defers food-conservation pledge week,
    87–90
  dines with Franklin Roosevelts, 105
  disagreement with Wilson, 293–94
  disagreements with McAdoo, 138–41,
    145, 147, 153–54
  and draft exemptions, 56
  education and family background, ix–x
  embargo, 41, 42
  food pool with Allies, opposition, 286,
    287, 291–92
  inflation, 40
  intoxicants, views, 22–23, 119
  knowledge of Europe, 293
  opposition to Food Administration
    Board, 49–50, 51–52, 53
  press conferences, 143
  problems with meat packers, 116–17,
    153, 156–57, 170–72, 180, 189–91,
    195–98, 208–9, 249–50, 252–53, 254–
    59, 260
  profits in wartime, views, 42–43, 215–22
  and summer 1918 European trip, 231–33
  trouble with Pinchot, 103–4
  and voluntarism, 28–29
  wartime prices, 49, 270–71
House, Edward M., 286
  channel for Hoover-Wilson exchanges,
    5, 6, 7
  correspondence with Hoover, 127, 132
  mission to Europe, 131
  praises Hoover, 23
  war information from Hoover, 6
Houston, David, Secretary of Agriculture,
    105, 145, 151, 224
  food control views, 23
  food embargo on neutral nations, 41–42,
    50
  meets with Hoover, 80, 179
  supports Hoover on wheat price, 151
  views on meat packers, 156, 195–96, 209
Hurley, Edward N., Chairman of Ship-

ping Board, 184, 192, 194, 244, 278,
  289
member of war cabinet, 164–65

Kenyon, William, Senator, aids passage of
  food bill, 31–32

Lane, Franklin K., Secretary of the Interior
  endorses Hoover, 3
  Hoover and Food Administration post,
    21
  on Hoover-McAdoo dispute, 154
  "taffyless" day, 97
Lansing, Robert, Secretary of State, 13,
    132, 278, 279, 286, 291
  meets with Hoover, 289
  seeks views on Pope's peace plan, 66
  suggests Hoover for Russian mission,
    229
Lawrence, David, 58
Lever, A. A., Congressman, 54, 55
  and higher prices for wheat, 152
  proposes food bill, 23
  talks with Hoover, 167
Lever Bill
  enacted by both houses, 23
  features, 24–25, 47
  Gore amendments, 49–50
  passed in House, 33
  proposed, 23
  Senator Gronna's opposition, 54
  Senator Hollis's substitute, 51–52
  struggle in Senate, 35–37, 48–50, 53, 55
  Wilson signs, 56–58
Lodge, Henry Cabot, Senator, claims
  Hoover violates Logan Act, 122
Lusitania
  Hoover books passage, 3
  Hoover criticizes Wilson's speech on
    sinking, 7–12

McAdoo, William G., Secretary of Treasury, 58–59, 177, 278
  blamed by Julius Barnes, 142
  complains to Wilson about Hoover,
    136, 153
  criticized by Hoover, 138–41, 145–49
  letter from Wilson, 153
  sees Hoover, 157
  unable to provide auditing for Food
    Administration, 76
McCormick, Vance, Chairman of War
  Trade Board, 35, 63, 84, 91, 161, 165,
    166, 260
Masaryk, Thomas, meets with Hoover, 289
Meat packers. *See also* Hoover, problems
  with meat packers

commandeering, 249, 254–59, 260
profits, 250–51

New York Times, supports Hoover against
    Reed, 124

Paige, Walter Hines, U.S. Ambassador to
    England, 4, 7, 21
Pershing, John, General, 210
Pinchot, Gifford, Hoover's trouble with,
    103–4
Pope Benedict XV, peace proposals and
    Hoover, 65–66
Price Fixing Board, 201
Profits in wartime
    government control of packers' profits.
        255–56
    Hoover on limitation, 42–43, 112–13,
        116–19, 134, 215–21, 222
Prohibition
    connection with food conservation, 22,
        35–36, 71–72, 104–5, 199–203, 207–9,
        213, 214, 260–61,
    Hoover's views, 22, 104, 199–201, 203,
        260
    Wilson's views, 104, 201, 203

Reading, Lord, British Ambassador to
    U.S.
    demands answered by Hoover, 168–70
    urges more wheat for Allies, 157, 162–63
Reed, Thomas, Senator
    opposes Hoover, 57, 68–69, 122, 125–26,
        128–29
    rebuke by *New York Times*, 129
Rickard, Edgar, 226, 227
Russia
    Bolsheviks, 132
    collapses, 183, 193
    Hoover food mission, 229
    1917 revolution, 20

Sherman, Lawrence Y., Senator, critic of
    Hoover, 33
Sherman Anti-Trust Act, applicability to
    food controls, 67, 86–87, 109, 129
Simmons, F. M., Senator
    Hoover on wartime profits, 215, 221,
        222
    suggests new food bill, 48–50
Strauss, Lewis L., Hoover's secretary, 83
    on Hoover and 1918 congressional elec-
        tions, 283
    to Paris with Hoover, 291
Swem, Charles L., Wilson's confidential
    stenographer, 26, 87, 112

Taft, Robert A., 226
    legal aid to Hoover, 250
    to Paris with Hoover, 291
Taussig, F. W.
    Food Administration investigator, 154–
        55, 179–80, 241
    supports Hoover for president, 129
Todd, Helen, embarrasses Hoover in food
    controversy, 57, 68
Tumulty, Joseph P., Wilson's personal
    secretary channels Hoover-Wilson let-
        ters, 6, 7, 18–19, 22, 31, 32, 33, 52, 56,
        57, 59, 80, 81, 82, 88, 93, 96, 126, 128,
        138, 201, 228
    Hoover reveals discouragement, 231–33

Untermyer, Samuel, controversy, 125–28

War cabinet
    established, 164
    meetings, 164, 166, 176, 179, 202, 203,
        213, 244, 249, 253, 265, 272, 276,
        279, 286, 287, 289, 291
    quality of work, 165, 272
War council. *See* War cabinet
Wilson, Woodrow
    accepts Hoover's view on brewers, 259–
        60, 267–68
    approves Hoover's sugar views, 243
    arming of merchant fleet, 19
    asks Hoover's suggestion on message to
        Congress, 115, 117–18
    consults Baker on a Hoover plan, 236
    education, x
        31–32, 35, 37–38
    follows Hoover's advice on wheat price,
        227, 233, 236, 242–43
    food board, accepts Hoover's opposition,
        53, 106
    food pool, supports Hoover's opposi-
        tion, 286–87, 291–92
    Fourteen Points, 132, 133
    German peace plan received, 272
    influence for passage of food bill, 24–25
    intervenes in congressional elections,
        276, 282–83, 284
    makes Hoover head of Belgian restora-
        tion, 277–78, 284–86
    meat packers, views on, 153, 263–64
    praises Hoover's Belgian work, 14
    prohibition views, 35–36, 199, 202
    publicity stunts, 57–58
    supports Hoover against Spreckels, 161
    supports Hoover in McAdoo contro-
        versy, 153–54
    supports Hoover in Reed controversy,
        69
    war message, 19–21